NATURE and HEAVEN in the Xunzi

SUNY Series in Chinese Philosophy and Culture
David L. Hall and Roger T. Ames, editors

NATURE and HEAVEN in the Xunzi

A Study of the *Tian Lun*

by
Edward J. Machle

State University of New York Press

Published by
State University of New York Press, Albany

Printed in the United States of America

For information, address State University of New York Press,
State University Plaza, Albany, N.Y., 12246

Production by Marilyn P. Semerad
Marketing by Bernadette LaManna

Library of Congress Cataloging-in-Publication Data

Machle, Edward J., 1918–
Nature and heaven in the Xunzi : a study of the Tian Lun / Edward J. Machle.
p. cm. — (SUNY series in Chinese philosophy and culture)
Includes bibliographical references and index.
ISBN 0-7914-1553-8. — ISBN 0-7914-1554-6 (pbk.)
1. Hsü-tzu, 340-245 B.C. — Hsün-tzu. 2. Philosophy of nature. I. Hsün-tzu, 340-245 B.C. Hsün-tzu English 1993. II. Title. III. Series.
B128.H74M33 1993
181′.112—dc20

92-31573
CIP

10 9 8 7 6 5 4 3 2 1

Contents

Preface

This book first germinated a number of years ago, as a response to the labelling of Xunzi (Hsün tzŭ), in the valuable W-T. Chan *Sourcebook in Chinese philosophy*, as representing "naturalistic Confucianism." In view of the widely different meanings of "nature" and "naturalism" in the West, and because I entertained a large measure of doubt that any of these meanings could be appropriately applied to a Chinese thinker of 2200 years ago, Chan's label posed a problem—not merely one of nomenclature, but of philosophy: just how should Xun's beliefs about nature be reconstructed? This puzzlement was increased by the widespread attribution to him of ideas it did not seem to me possible to derive from his writings with such confidence as writer after writer seemed to assume[1]—a confidence that should belong only to views made unquestionable by an overwhelming weight of evidence.

Search for such a preponderance of evidence seemed instead to show that what existed was but a somewhat tenuous tradition of interpretation, going back, apparently, for 1100 years, and drawing on opinions still older—but not in any traceable, direct line back to Xun Qing or his students. Indeed, the first thousand years of interpretation (if interpretation there was), are represented only scantily in extant sources, and these quote him largely for their own purposes, rather than to inquire carefully into his thinking. It is only recently that serious attempts to depart from the received tradition of interpretation have appeared.[2] This book aims to join them.

The core of the work is a translation of the *Tian lun pian* which is different in a number of places from the previous English translations of Dubs, Chan, Watson, Chai and Eno[3] and the partial translation by Hughes, and from those of Köster (German) and Belpaire (French),[4] with extensive commentary. This is preceded by chapters dealing with some problems of interpreting the *Xunzi* and problems specific to the *Tian lun*, and followed by chapters sketching out aspects of Xun's views of nature and their relation to other elements in his thought. Finally, there is a summary, plus some final ruminations.

Holmes Welch, in his *Taoism, the Parting of the Way*, speaks, in regard to the *Laozi*, of

> two classes of problems under one cover. The first class is philological; the second is philosophical. To solve the first requires a thorough grounding in Chinese studies, which make the most crushing demands on memory and patience. If there is any *metier* designed to smother the imagination, it is Sinology. Yet imagination above all else is what is required to solve the second class of problems, the philosophical.[5]

Though the *Xunzi* is not the *Laozi*, the saying is still apt. As a philosopher of religion who is only an amateur sinologist, I tremble both that my 'memory and patience' may not have been up to the task, and that my philosophical imagination may have been too active. In either case, however, interaction with my interpretation may contribute to advancement of the study of a most interesting philosopher.

Over the years that I have wrestled with the *Xunzi*, I have received help from far too many people for all to be acknowledged here. Particular thanks are due, however, to Wing-Tsit Chan and Yi-pao Mei, who helped me more than they knew; to colleagues Walter Veazie and William Doub; to my son Douglas, to whom I owe a number of ideas; to my not always patient but always encouraging wife, Mary Lou; and to Director William D. Eastman and Marilyn Semerad of SUNY Press, without whose skills this book would not have come to be. All these individuals share in whatever virtues the work has; none is responsible for any of its faults.

Special thanks are due to my father, who introduced me as a child to the thought of Confucius and "Laozi" and to many other things Chinese; and to Homer Dubs, who, nearly half a century ago, first introduced me to Xun Qing, and who encouraged a young graduate philosophy student not to neglect his Chinese studies.

Acknowledgments

Gratitude is expressed to the following publishers for permission to quote from their copyrighted materials, more complete identification of which may be found in the notes and bibliography: to Cambridge University Press, for material from R. J. Ray, "Crossed fingers and praying hands: remarks on religious belief and superstition," *Religious Studies* (1990); to Columbia University Press, for that from Wing-Tsit Chan, *Religious trends in modern China* (1953), Tu Wei-ming, "Yen yüan: from inner experience to lived concreteness" in *The unfolding of neo-Confucianism*, ed. deBary (1975), Thomas A. Metzger, *Escape from predicament* (1977), and Burton Watson, *Hsün tzŭ, basic works* (1963); to *The Journal of the American Oriental Society*, for that from Herrlee G. Creel, "Confucius and Hsun tzu" (1931), and "*I* as equivalent to *Tao*" (1932); to *The Journal of Chinese Philosophy*, for Chung-ying Cheng, "On implication (*tse*) and inference (*ku*) in Chinese grammar and Chinese logic" (1975), and Benjamin Schwartz, "On the absence of reductionism in Chinese thought" (1973); to Penguin Books Ltd., for D. C. Lau, *Mencius* (1970); to Arthur Probsthain, for Homer H. Dubs, *Hsüntse, works from the Chinese* (1928); to Scholars' Press, for David N. Keightly, "Late Shang divination: the magico-religious legacy," in *Explorations in early Chinese cosmology*, ed. Rosemont (1984); to Stanford University Press, for John Knoblock, *Xunzi, a translation and study of the complete works* (1988–); to the State University of New York Press, for Sarah Allen, *The shape of the turtle: myth, art and cosmos in early China* (1991), Roger T. Ames and David L. Hall, *Thinking through Confucius* (1987), A. C. Graham, *Studies in Chinese philosophy and philosophical literature* (1986), Rodney Taylor, *The religious dimensions of Confucianism* (1990), and Tu Weiming, "The continuity of being: Chinese visions of Nature," in *Nature in Asian traditions of thought*, ed. Callicott and Ames (1989); to *The Tsing-*

hua journal of Chinese studies, for Chen Ta-tsi, "Kaotse's view of righteousness being external and the spirit of the natural sciences" (1957) and Chung-ying Cheng, "A generative unity: Chinese language and Chinese philosophy" (1973); to University of California Press (Regents of the University of California), for C. K. Yang, *Religion in Chinese Society* (1961); to University of Chicago Press, for David N. Keightley, "The religious commitment: Shang theology and the genesis of Chinese political culture", in *History of Religions* (1978); to University of Hawaii Press, for Chung-ying Cheng, "Model of causality in Chinese philosophy: a comparative study" in *Philosophy East and West* (1976) and Thomas Berry, review of *The religious life of man* series, ed. F. J. Streng, in *Philosophy East and West* (1974), and to Westminster Press, for a quotation from George A. Lindbeck, *The nature of doctrine: religion and theology in a Postliberal age* (1984).

Introduction

This is not primarily a book for sinologists, although we hope sinologists will read and respond to it. It is a book for comparative philosophers, philosophers of religion, historians of religion, and, possibly, philosophers and theologians of ecology. What sinological hurdles it may present for these latter are only what seemed necessary properly to unfold or justify what it has to say, to whatever degree that has been in fact accomplished.

Anyone dealing with ancient Chinese philosophy or religion has to pay attention to the *Xunzi* (or *Hsün tzŭ*); one can hardly deal with Xunzi without studying the tractate *Tian lun*, called *The essay on Nature* or *Discussion of Heaven*. Though there are a number of translations of it into English, and a number of short expositions as well as numerous commentaries and explanations of it in Chinese, there seems to be nothing that could be called a "close reading" of it in either language—a reading that continuously asks, "Does it *really* say what it traditionally has been taken to say?" (Eno's book, discussed in Chapter 2, contains what might be considered only a partial such reading; volume 3 of Knoblock's massive work, which is to contain the *Tian lun*, is not yet available, but volume 1 has already shown that we can expect an interpretation close to what Eno calls "the consensus view"—the view we have been driven to call into question at some important points.) This work is an attempt to give such a close reading, one that is intended to be helpful and stimulating both to those with knowledge of Chinese and to those without.

Since how the *Tian lun* is interpreted affects the way the whole of the *Xunzi* is understood, and one's understanding of Xunzi and his place in it may affect understanding of Confucian philosophy as a whole, a new reading of the tractate may have considerably wider impact than might at first be thought. Our discussion will at least show its effects on our own understanding of the rest of the *Xunzi*, and of the issues between Xun and Mencius.

Since throughout the text certain words are used in transliterated rather than translated form, some explanation is in order. Our reasons for never (or rarely) translating *Tian*, except as its common surrogate "Heaven" in the title, are discussed extensively and need not be given here. Unless the Chinese word itself is being referred to, *Tian* will be frequently anglicized to "Tian." Because the idea it bears is a main focus of the book, its nuances will reveal themselves as the book unfolds.

Among the other important words involved is *li*, often translated "ritual," "rites," "ceremony," "propriety," or "rules of proper conduct," but in the *Xunzi* often including "proper assignment of roles," and bearing such distinctive relationships to humane culture, government, music, and dance that it is only in a rare context that any English word is a satisfactory translation. It is an important word in the book because it is so important an idea in the Xunzi. It will be represented in the text as *LI*, fully capitalized, to distinguish it from another important word, *li*, often translated (though questionably) as "principle," though its other overtones could yield "reason," "internal order," perhaps even *logos*.[1]

Another term we shall not translate is *junzi*, though it is familiar as "the superior man," "the gentleman," "the princely man." Its variety of uses in the *Xunzi* would be a study in itself. Though Xun uses it at times as if it meant "advanced scholar," at times as if equivalent to "you, my students," and at still other times as "one fit to govern" or "one who is governing," or, at other times, almost as an equivalent for "the sage," we stress its connotations of "one who does nothing contrary to LI," and take it to indicate, descriptively, a sage-presumptive, one who has achieved perfect Confucian discipline but has not yet received (or achieved) the "divine manifestation," *shenming*,[2] that would complete his transformation into a sage. Taken thus, it indicates the goal of the Confucian scholar's study and discipline (since *shenming* "comes of itself," sagehood is not an automatic product of effort but rather a hope, however confident). Being a goal, Xun sometimes uses *junzi* proleptically to apply to students who are still "on the way." We simply transliterate and anglicize *junzi* as "*Junzi*." Ouside of one passage where it occurs a number of times (but which is possibly an interpolation), it appears only once in the *Tian lun*; but it is so important all through the rest of the *Xunzi* that it cannot be treated lightly.

It may already be apparent to the reader that we refer to the author we are discussing, Xun Qing, as Xunzi, or just Xun (though once or twice, in a context referring to later times, we use his "style" or appellation "Kuang"). In quotations, however, the spelling of the author quoted is kept, so the name may appear therein as "Hsuntze" or as "Hsün tzŭ." The book he wrote is referred to as the *Xunzi*; it has no other name. It contains, in the standard editions, 32 sections or *pian*, each an essay, a group of essays or poems, or a collection of miscellaneous material. These are referred to as *pian* I to XXXII, treating "*pian*" as either singular or plural.

The essay we are specially treating, the *Tian lun*, is usually referred to in English as the *Essay on Nature* or the *Discussion of Heaven*, or by some similar title. Since part of our thesis is the inappropriateness of both such appellations, we refer to it only as the *Tian lun* or as "the essay."

Other well-known philosophers are referred to by their familiar names, italicized when it is the writings attributed to them that are meant, in Roman type when it is the (presumed) author. Names of modern Chinese scholars who have published in English are spelled as they themselves, or occasionally their translators, have transliterated them. We shall refer simply to the *Analects* and the *Mencius*. Other Chinese classics are referred to by their Chinese titles. Exceptions to this practice are abbreviations for works whose titles run to more than two words: *DDJ* for *Daodejing*, *HSWC* for *Hanshi Waichuan*, *LSCQ* for *Lüshi Chunqiu*, *QSZY* for *Qunshu Zhiyao*, and so forth. Reference works of interest mainly to sinologists may be indicated by their normal abbreviations, as the HY concordances, KX dictionary, PWYF, etc., with no further bibliographical information.

Quotations from other translations of the *Xunzi* will be indicated by an initial and a page number: (W 91) for Watson, page 91; D for Dubs, K with Roman numeral I or II for Knoblock, volume 1 or 2, and so on.

As has been obvious from the first, we use the pinyin transliteration rather than the more traditional Wade-Giles. We suggest to those who find this confusing simply to replace *x* with *hs*, *q* with *ch'*, *z* with *ts*, *c* with *ts'*, and *r* with *j* (not vice versa), to remember that *i* may represent *ih* as well as *i*, and to read aloud; the other differences should take care of themselves.

1. "Nature" and "Heaven"

Xun Qing (305?–225? B.C.), also called Kuang but most often Xunzi, an avowed follower of Confucius, was without doubt one of the greatest of early Chinese philosophers. Whether he was "the moulder of ancient Confucianism"[1] or worthy to be called "the Chinese Aristotle" has been disputed, but his stature is unquestioned even by those who consider him a maverick among Confucians. Liu Wu-chi calls him "a prose master, a profound thinker,"[2] and one of my former colleagues, a classmate of Hu Shih and a longtime teacher of Chinese philosophy, was fond of saying, "Xunzi is the only classical Chinese philosopher who consistently talks sense."[3] Though Xunzi suffered a long, though only partial, eclipse, the twentieth century has seen increasing interest in his work, with detailed and acute analysis being given to his ethical argumentation, his theories of language, his treatment of ritual, and other topics.[4]

Despite this interest, there has been little challenge to the traditional interpretation of one of his most interesting and oft-quoted essays, *Tian lun*, appearing in Watson's translation as *A discussion of Heaven* but titled by Knoblock *Discourse on Nature*.[5] The word *Tian* has been long translated in the West as "Heaven," a translation requiring qualification and interpretation, but one that has proved useful—perhaps because few in the West would confuse what the Chinese were talking about with some popular uses of "heaven." "Heaven" has become useful primarily because no more suitable alternative word has been found.

"Nature," however, is a word with a long history of uses and a wide range of meanings in the West (Baldwin's *Dictionary of Philosophy* gives 37 meanings for the word[6]), and one may well doubt that it corresponds closely enough to any Chinese word to be a really useful translation. For instance, in the West "nature," the realm of "the natural," has been defined over against "the supernatural," "the unnatural," "the artificial," and it is doubtful that Chinese ideas of any of these opposites to "nature" are congruent to ours. Nature is spoken of as including humans and as excluding them; as being their enemy and as being their friend, even their "Mother." Above all, "nature" has become, over the last three centuries, something mechanical, value-free, and exploitable for any ends we wish to bend it to—while still being seen as spontaneous, creative, beautiful, dangerous, and sometimes healing.

These lexicographic inconveniences of the translator are not, however, the root of the problem, for translators draw on a tradition of understanding *Tian*, especially in uses of the kind found in Xun's *Tian lun*, in a way that invited the translation "Nature." This tradition goes back at least to the Daoism of Guo Xiang in the fourth century A.D., which had roots in the rejection of Confucianism of the late Han and its view of Tian. This Daoism penetrated Confucianism over the centuries, and was drawn upon by the Sung neo-Confucian efforts of 900 years ago to set Confucianism firmly over against Buddhism and Daoist religion, and in so doing to provide a solid foundation for moral and political life. Their view of Tian was as indebted to Guo Xiang as it was to Han Confucianism. Its function as the complement of humanity, in a polarity that was not a duality, gave Tian a character for which we, perhaps, have no better word than "Nature," although even in that case it needs careful explanation. There is much room for doubt, however, that Xun Qing held a neo-Confucian, a post-Han, or even a late-Han idea of Tian.

The central problem of this book has been pointed out in the Foreword: Just how should Xun Qing's understanding of *Tian*, particularly as presented in the *Tian lun*, be reconstructed and articulated? Is there indeed the preponderance of evidence for the generally received view that its widespread acceptance would suggest? Does the essay, and the corpus as a whole, allow some alternative construction?

In the Preface we said:

> Search for such a preponderance of evidence seemed instead to show that what existed was but a somewhat tenuous tradition of interpretation, going back in some respects at least 1100 years and drawing on opinions still older, but not in any traceable, direct line back to Xun Qing or his students.

This tenuous tradition of interpretation, as far as the *Tian lun* is concerned, became notably robust with the impact of interest in science in the twentieth century.

Although Chinese philosophizing is traced back to Confucius, one can say that the "history of Chinese philosophy" is a twentieth-century development, just as the West's parochial "history of philosophy" was a nineteenth-century one. The Chinese knew their philosophizing went back to Confucius or "Laozi," but although their textual studies were well aware of the passage of the centuries, their method of commentary was not conducive to historical study in the Western sense. Past Chinese thinkers, in general, tended to be evaluated, even interpreted, in terms of the authorities accepted at the time, whether scholarly or political. (There is some ground for saying that the same pattern has continued under the Marxist regimes of mainland China, although Marxist authorities are always, in their own quasi-Westernized terms, "historical.")

The development of the history of Chinese philosophy coincided rather closely with the modernization of China, and some of the emphases that emerged were seriously affected by the enthusiasms and conflicts of ideas that accompanied the downfall of the old regime and the struggles entailed by attempts to discern what the new institutions and standards would be. Those, like Kang You-wei, who would retain the old philosophical heroes, sought new interpretations that would enable old customs to be revised. Some who would reject the old guides outright turned to the West, to Haeckel and Russell, or to Bergson, Eucken, or Dewey, and many eventually to Marx. Others, more interested in maintaining confidence in their own ancient culture, manifested a burgeoning interest in such figures as Modi, Xunzi, and even the Logicians and Legalists.

From this last trend resulted interest not only in these figures, but in seeing what they might contribute to the modernization of Chinese thinking. The nineteenth-century project of borrowing from the West the "function" of Western science and technology without importing its "substance" had failed. Was there something substantially scientific in the long tradition of Chinese philosophic thought? Any materials that could be used in this quest were welcome.

Modi's "universal love" sounded like a Chinese version of the substance of Christianity (always identified with the West in China) and his "benefiting all" like a version of utilitarianism. His epistemology, suitably reinterpreted, could be quoted to indigenize scientific method ideologically. But one other ancient figure was enthusiastically embraced as a Western-style philosopher of Nature: Xunzi (much as some enthusiasts in the West's recently emerging ecology movement once embraced Laozi). Tu Wei-ming writes,

> Scholars since Liang Ch'i-ch'ao have been impelled by a sense of cultural urgency to look for Western-like values in the body of traditional ideas. Their search was concentrated mostly in the ancient period. The technological ingenuity of Mo Ti, the art of logic of Kung-sun Lung, the spirit of science in Hsün tzŭ and Wang Ch'ung, all these and others supported their image of what the new China should be.[7]

Xunzi was not at all unknown to Chinese scholars, or even to the West, but hardly as a philosopher of Nature. Of human nature, certainly, as questions regarding "Kuang's doctrine," that human nature is evil, occurred in Chinese civil-service examinations, as foils for the approved contrary doctrine of Mencius. Except for his deviation from Mencius and some of his ideas on language and ritual, he was held to be of little importance. In the West, in what is perhaps the first history of Chinese philosophy in English, Suzuki's *Brief History of Early Chinese Philosophy*, first published in article form in *The Monist* in 1907–1908 and in book form in 1914, Xun is expounded as a ceremonialist, a pessimist regarding human nature, an ethicist stressing the need for external discipline, and a stylist, with no mention in the text of any idea of Nature. In the notes, Xun is quoted on Heaven and omens, and rather than relating these in any way to natural sciences, Suzuki calls his view of Heaven "prosaic."[8]

As a somewhat Westernized Japanese, Suzuki was not involved in the ideological struggles of early Republican China. The next influential author was deeply so involved. Following Suzuki's book came Hu Shih's *The Development of the Logical Method in Ancient China*, his doctoral dissertation written for Columbia University in 1915–1917. This was written under John Dewey, who was then moving from his instrumentalist stage to his last, more naturalistic one. In his chapters on Xunzi, Hu translates *Tian* sometimes as "Heaven," but also directly as "nature," and the phrase *zhi Tian ming* (which we discuss at length later) as "control her [that is, Nature's] course."[9] He speaks of Xun's "exaltation of man over nature," but later calls it "exaggerated" to the extent that it "excluded natural science from the realm of philosophy," and criticizes Xun's comment (as he translates it) that, "To neglect man and speculate about Nature/ Is to misunderstand the facts of the universe."

This work was not published in English until a Shanghai issuance in 1928,[10] but in the meantime Hu had published his influential history of Chinese philosophy in Chinese, which he said was "essentially a Chinese version and expansion" of the earlier work.[11]

Hu was willing to identify Tian ("Heaven") with Nature in the *Xun-*

zi, at least in some important passages, and anyone who has studied John Dewey, or known his pupils closely,[12] knows that "Nature" cannot be separated from investigation by scientific method in his thought. Yet Hu was not willing to attribute to Xun a sufficiently "scientific" view of nature. Despite this, the intellectual momentum of the times tended in the direction of such an identification, sometimes manifested tentatively, sometimes with enthusiasm, until it was widely taken for granted that Xun held a view of nature akin to that which lies behind the sciences as they have developed in the West. In fact, as the earliest translator of much of the *Xunzi* into English, H. H. Dubs, put it, "Heaven, according to Hsuntze, is unvarying Law . . . Thus Heaven comes to mean very nearly the same as our popular concept of Nature."[13] Since Dubs was for many years the only extensive translation of the *Xunzi* into any Western language, his usage became customary, no matter how many explanatory qualifications one might put upon it.

"Nature" and its modern Chinese equivalent, the ancient phrase *ziran*,[14] thus became the standard readings for *Tian* in a number of passages of the *Tian lun*, (though rarely elsewhere[15]), and it often carried the overtones of nature as the object of scientific investigation. Thus W-T. Chan, in his valuable *Sourcebook*, comments at the close of the poem in the *Tian lun*, "Nowhere else in the history of Chinese thought is the idea of controlling nature so definite and so strong. It is a pity that this did not lead to a development of natural science."[16] Chan here (and elsewhere in the translation) equates Tian, "Sky," formerly the name of the sky god, with Nature, just as Hu had done, and many after him.

There is some apparent justification for such a translation. When Knoblock, in his valuable set of volumes on the *Xunzi*, says flatly, "The term that the Chinese use to refer to Nature is *tian*,"[17] he is guilty of serious overstatement, but is not entirely wrong—particularly as far as neo-Confucianism was concerned. Some (though not all) Chinese-English dictionaries do indeed give "nature" as a translation of *Tian*,[18] and some Chinese dictionaries (though not all) give *ziran*, an ancient Daoist and general modern term for "nature" (in the sense of "all that happens naturally") as one of many quasi synonyms for *Tian*.[19] My student English-Chinese dictionary does not mention *Tian* in its entry for "Nature," though it does appear under "God," "Heaven," and "Sky."[20] And a patently Marxist (and hence "scientific") Chinese-English phrase book, with 29 entries for *Tian*, has not one wherein it means "nature," though in five it does mean "natural."[21] Knoblock's claim would seem to be tendentious, at the least.

That *Tian* is used much as we use "natural" is patent, but may mislead. When we say, "He isn't using what God gave him" instead of, "He's not using his natural gifts," we are hardly saying 'God' is a synonym for 'nature,' though we are relying on a tradition of God's priority to nature. We may even be referring to something we might call someone's individual nature, or, in a more Aristotelian vein, his human nature (which, tradition might say, God gave him). If one looks, for instance, at the 118 examples given under *Tian* in Mathews' dictionary, as "nature. Providence. The Supreme Ruler." only seven using "Heaven and Earth" as an encompassing reality might with some reason be translated as "nature"; whereas of the 45 examples given under *Tian* as "natural" (as opposed to artificial), every one bears the same ambiguity as our "God-given" example.[22]

That *Tian*, in other places translated as "sky," "Heaven," even by some as "God," should in this essay often be translated "Nature," may not seem at first too strange to us in the West who recall the Stoics, the *Deus sive natura* of Spinoza, and even Descartes, or the ambivalence of Jefferson's "Nature and Nature's God" in the Declaration of Independence. A little study, however, leads to the conclusion that "God" is not a fit translation of *Tian*, and hence "Heaven" is not, either, since it still either carries echoes of St. Matthew's "Heaven" as a euphemism for "God" (as it did for the early European sinologists who popularized that translation), or it is so bland as to need much further explanation. "The heavens" is, of course, an appropriate near-synonym for "sky," but it is just those occurrences of *Tian* where "sky" is not very useful that raise the problem. That "Nature," too, might be a misleading translation, in the particular passages where its use became widespread, has not been much discussed. We contend it should be.

Therefore, when referring to *Tian* as a Chinese word, we shall use *Tian*; when to its original, physical referent, we shall use "sky" or "the heavens"; otherwise "Tian" will be used, without italics and usually without quotation marks. We hold the word to be vague, rather than ambiguous. That is, its various uses, sometimes quite distinct in our eyes, tend to shade into each other in Archaic Chinese use, rather than clearly excluding one another.[23] This does not mean they are indistinguishable, but that their identification is highly contextual, and one can never assert that any overtone is completely excluded. One cannot assume without careful hermeneutic attention just how narrowly or broadly the term is focused.

Serious work has been done on clarifying the earliest history, various uses and connotations of *Tian*, some of its ritual and religious involvements, and its political significance.[24] Typical of the twentieth century, however, is the selection of some occurrences of the term, especially in the *Tian lun*, as ones that should be unquestionably translated simply as "Nature."

Several paragraphs ago we quoted W-T. Chan's comment equating Tian with nature. Some have gone farther that Chan did. Thus, Chen Ta-tsi writes,

> The philosophical thought of the pre-Ch'in period as embodied in Hsüntze's argument concerning the controllability of Heaven . . . was much pregnant with the spirit of the natural sciences. The special treatise in which Hsüntze propounded that man may control Heaven—by Heaven is meant Nature—has come down to us through the centuries; unfortunately, however, this theory of his was not sufficiently emphasized and elaborated by later generations . . . it may be said that back of the fact that natural sciences were not developed in China, the overlooking and neglect by succeeding generations of Hsüntze's argument concerning the controllability of Heaven . . . had an immense, far-reaching effect.[25]

Here Chen sounds a note typical of much twentieth-century Chinese comment on the history of scientific thought in China and on Xun Qing in particular, a note possibly derivative from Hu Shih, but one whose popularity undoubtedly rested on the interest in Western science that characterized modern China's attempt to gain some appropriate freedom from its past.

This motif has been particularly attractive to scholars in mainland China, who found in Xun's writings an evident reflection of the presumed incipient scientific materialism of proletarian culture. Thus Li De-yong, in an article in *Wen Shi Che*, makes the phrase Hu translated as "control her (Nature's) course" his entrance key to Xun's whole metaphysics, and, in his later book on Xun, explains that the latter's

> 'Tao' also manifests a sort of scientific approach. So far as reliable knowledge of objective laws is concerned, and the putting of them to use, his philosophical theory of "controlling Nature's course" is in complete accord with science . . . He raised the battle cry, "Control Nature's ways and use them!" . . . He is the only one of the pre-Qin philosophers to have the scientific spirit and to fight actively for a materialistic philosophy. First of all, he presented the ideal of transforming nature. His idea of "controlling Nature's course" not only differed from the Taoists' passive "wu-wei-ism" but also departed from the subjective idealists' blind path of adventurism.[26]

Since Marxism takes as humans' defining characteristic their 'transformation of the environment,' and since the social history of materialism is a central theme of Marxist scholarship, it is easy to see the grounds for Li's enthusiasm.

The phrase Hu translated as "control Nature's course" has certainly fascinated non-Marxist students of the Xunzi also, whether by itself or by setting the tone for the interpretation of the poem in which it occurs. Chen Yuan-te quotes the poem, in his history of ancient Chinese philosophy, under the heading "Man acts to control nature" (*ren wei zhi tian*). Jiang Shang-xian, in his *Xunzi sixiang tixi*, makes out the thrust of the poem to be "Control nature and use it" (*zhi tian yung tian*). In Wei Richun, *Xunzi xueshu*, we find two pages of expansion on the same phrase, which seems to have become more of a slogan than a text to be interpreted.[27]

Although some of the recent work on the *Xunzi* has been more restrained, the tradition still is dominant. Thus, the latest critical text of the Xunzi, that of Li Di-sheng,[28] shows many examples of the use of modern Chinese scientific terminology to explicate old terms that are far from synonymous with them, and of a leaning toward interpretations close to modern scientific naturalism. Some of these we shall treat in the commentary.

One cannot take exception to modern China's quest to anchor its modernization somewhere in its own past, and not just in intellectual importations. Every people must reexamine its heritage in each new cultural situation to gain the freedom from the past that the new situation requires; anything else results in ideology and stagnation. When we in the West study China's past, we may not have the same pressure to interpret it in the context of our own cultural needs—or we may. In any case, we are tempted to apply Western labels such as "naturalism" to ancient Chinese thinkers, and in doing so we try to draw them into the ambit of our own past struggles to free ourselves from cultural inheritances we felt to be confining. While our battles are still in progress, we seemingly use such labels in an attempt to make allies out of ancient intellectual warriors, whose own engagements, in their own time, were skirmishes in a quite different war.[29] Later, when our particular struggle has subsided, the labels still function as museum cards telling us in which glass case we may find the mummy of so-and-so. In the one case, the label helps us very little to understand the thinker himself. In the other, it prevents him from contributing anything to our understanding of ourselves.

Quotations such as those we have given could be multiplied indefinitely. Mainland Chinese writers have consistently praised Xunzi for his incipient "scientific outlook," regardless of the wide variety of other judgments they have uttered concerning his contribution to social change at the end of the Zhou period.[30] In the West, there seems to have emerged in the movement of "comparative philosophy" dating from World War II an orthodoxy that includes and repeats the view that Xun secularized Heaven and naturalized ethics, enabling him to stand for "controlling Nature" in a way suggestive of modern technology. There have been, as one would expect, some important dissenting voices, particularly among Japanese scholars (whose work, unfortunately, I cannot read[31]), and those who would identify Tian (in appropriate contexts) with Nature without going on to claim the parallel to technological thinking.[32] Despite this, the general tenor of interpretation seems to accept the nature identification readily, with only slight variation regarding the technological aspect. It is this, apparently, that Eno calls "the consensus view."

It is revealing to consider that this widespread attribution to Xun Qing of a naturalistic theory of nature and a technological inclination, though supported in part by some general beliefs about cultural currents in his time, is based to a large extent on disputable readings of a very few loci, and particularly of one unclear passage in one poem—a poem set in a context emphasizing quite other interests. It is one aim of this study to deal with the fact that the passages need not be interpreted as they have been; that neither Xun's thinking as a whole, the essay most commonly quoted as embodying such a naturalistic vision, nor the poem it contains, clearly support that interpretation; and that a coherent interpretation of Xunzi's philosophy implies that the so-called "technological interest" or "naturalistic view of nature" is somewhat of an intellectual will-o'-the-wisp. Indeed, our intention is to show that his idea of nature and his attitudes toward it are quite different from anything parallel to modern Western culture. Along with this, though logically separable from it, goes an intention to question whether even the sort of attitude toward deity and holy things that characterizes much that calls itself "naturalism" in the West is present in the *Xunzi*.

One may well ask, "If this is typically a twentieth-century view, isn't the corrective already at hand in the earlier Chinese understanding of Xunzi?" The point is well taken. Creel, in his article, "Was Confucius agnostic?" studied commentaries on the *Analects* written from recent times back to the Han dynasty. The first attribution of agnosticism to Confucius he found was dated 1915! (Interestingly enough, one can still find treatments of Confucius as "agnostic.") And though he later remarked, "My more general conclusions in that article require considerable modification," his evidence stands, and he did not abandon his specific conclusion.[33] Why should not a similar study of Xun yield a satisfactory resolution?

One answer to this question is that although Creel's study did a great deal to show what the Chinese commentatorial tradition had said about Confucius, it did nothing positive toward giving an understanding of how Confucius' religious position should be understood by Westerners—if it can be.

Another answer lies in the apparent attitude of the Chinese scholarly tradition toward Xun Qing. It is a surprising fact about the *Xunzi* that it was, for most of Chinese history, largely bypassed by Chinese thinkers. Until the nineteenth century, few studied him intensively,[34] and that century was immersed in text-critical and philological work, rather than philosophic interpretation.[35] Creel remarks,

> The number of commentaries is significant. Before the Sung dynasty (and probably until the nineteenth century) only one complete commentary on the book of Hsün-tzŭ had been written, and this not until the T'ang dynasty, so little, apparently, was the scholarly interest which it attracted. On *Mencius*, on the other hand, the Yu Han collection alone lists and quotes from nine pre-Sung commentaries, five from the Later Han dynasty, one from the Chin dynasty, and three from the T'ang dynasty.[36]

Since commentary was the usual pattern of study, this is significant.

This neglect may have appeared very early. One of his early disciples has left us a plaint in a later addition to Xun's writings:

> His virtue was like that of Yao and Yu, but his generation knew it but little. . . . The world did not recognize him . . . Today the critics likewise do not investigate the facts, but credit only his reputation. The times had changed; what means had his fame of being born?[37]

Xun was for a time quoted as a stylist, and was drawn upon as an authority on the *Odes*; some of his ideas on language, ritual, and music became so generally accepted that they were held without reference to the distinctive characteristics of his overall thought. In this way his thoughts did have their own sort of lasting influence, which some have overstressed,[38] but that influence was so general, and not always distinguishable from that of other schools of Confucianism, that it did not generate much in the way of direct interest in his writings.

This lack of interest in the *Xunzi* appears to continue throughout the Han and beyond. Thus Wang Chong, a bibliophile, scholar, and skeptic, clearly of a critical mind, does not appear even to mention Xun in his best-known work, the *Lun Heng*.[39] When he refers to an example of the belief that men are evil, he mentions Sun Wu's *Art of War*; when he speaks against rain sacrifices, he makes no mention of Xunzi.[40] As already pointed out, though all the recognized classics had commentaries written before the end of the Han, or soon after, there was none, so far as we know, written for the *Xunzi*; Yang Liang, writing in the ninth century A.D., gives no indication of any predecessors—for more than ten centuries!

Material from the times between the Han and the Tang are unfortunately limited, but that was a time when lively minds were fascinated first by Daoism and then Buddhism. Confucian scholarship was moribund. During the Tang revival Xun was quoted, but there is no evidence he was seriously interpreted. We have, for instance, Wei Zheng, who in A.D. 631 quotes some 29 extracts from the *Xunzi*, about one-ninth of the whole, in his extensive *Qunshu zhiyao* (hereafter *QSZY*), a collection of extracts from various works, commissioned by the throne and aimed at the instruction of political officeholders. Devoid of interpretation or comment, its main value for *Xunzi* scholarship today is its confirmation or occasional correction of the text that later appeared in the first known commentary on the *Xunzi*, that of Yang Liang in 818, more than a thousand years after Xun Qing's death.

Since the *Xunzi* was only one of many works, and the early Tang manifested a restrictive government orthodoxy, it seems to have received little study until the more liberal, later Tang times, when Yang Liang complains that the copies of the *Xunzi* were "torn, tattered, with parts missing, and showed mistakes from inaccurate copying"[41]—so that "even those who wished to study Hsuntse found him unattractive and difficult and desisted from their study."

He was occasionally referred to, even praised, but was not studied for his own sake. Yang Liang's contemporary, Han Yu, seems typical. He was willing to rate Xun as the second greatest Confucian after Mencius, but considered him to be important because he "selected elements [from Mencius], but without reaching its essential portion," and "discussed it, but without sufficient clarity,"[42] not because Xun had anything new of value to offer. In that case, one could pass over Xun and simply study Mencius, as scholars apparently largely did. In fact, it would appear that the compliments Han Yu paid to the *Xunzi* were directed at least as much to its style as to its content.

This history of neglect underlines the fact that *there was no reliable tradition of interpretation of Xunzi before the time of Yang Liang, and little creative analysis of his thought subsequently*. It is evident in Yang's commentary that he had no real predecessors; he quotes the *Liji, Shiji, Hanshi Waichuan, Shu, Shi*, etc., but no later authorities. This means that, careful and competent as his textual and lexical work was, when interpreting Xun's ideas, he was working out of his own Tang situation, and, to the extent that subsequent interpreters have based their understanding on his work, they have started with essentially a Tang (or later) understanding of it, not a Zhou one. Since every subsequent commentary has been based on that of Yang (which was, indeed, a very good and helpful commentary), his work has been occasionally corrected in detail and amplified in thought, but not seriously departed from. Not long after his time, a dominant neo-Confucianism determined the way early Chinese philosophers were understood—something that has continued into this century. There was finally a significant collation of the various texts of the *Xunzi* by Xie Yong (1719–1795), and the first attempt at careful explication since Yang Liang by Wang Zhong (1745–1794), early in the remarkable outburst of Ching textual studies. It is only recently that alternative interpretations of the *Xunzi* have appeared, and it is clear that further explorations are needed, even though, with the Zhou data so limited, we are not likely ever to attain an understanding of early Chinese philosophy that is not seriously tainted one way or another.

That the Tang period was not Zhou may be of little importance as far as his political ideas are concerned—and such do make up a large part of the *Xunzi*. But in the areas of cosmology and religion, areas relevant to this essay, it may be crucial. In the late Han and for some time after, Daoism was the intellectual stimulant, rather than Confucianism, and there were important differences between its understanding of what might be called nature and that of Xun. Then, for several centuries before the Tang, the best minds in China had been attracted to Buddhism. This last changed the Chinese mind significantly: it expanded the cosmological imagination tremendously through its Indic mythology of infinite Buddha-fields; it introduced a distinctively new analysis of cause and effect; it taught an entirely different idea of the relation of the individual to his or her own thoughts and emotions; and it presented a transcendence of Nature by identifying it with illusion.[43] These last two were somewhat qualified by the early use of Daoist terms, and the last, in particular, largely modified by the emergence of the distinctively Chinese quasi-Daoist forms of Mahayana, but Chinese philosophy could never go back to the compact nature-myth[44] that underlay Zhou philosophizing (including that of Xun Qing).

What our historical survey indicates, then, is that there was very little attempt to question the traditional interpretation of Xun Qing as primarily a foil for Mencius' view of human nature, although the neo-Confucians' effort (itself probably religious) to rid Confucianism of any shreds of what they recognized as religion undoubtedly moved their reading of him somewhat closer to the modern interpretation.[45] I know of no attempt on their part to make the sorts of criticisms of his view of Tian that they would undoubtedly have made of what Dubs called "our popular concept of Nature" (and did make of its forerunner in the teachings of Matteo Ricci and later Jesuits).[46] All this changed with Hu's study of logical method, and subsequently the attractiveness of taking Xun to be a precursor of science steered thinking into treating him as primarily a naturalistic thinker, even a promising anticipator of modern views. It also gave the *Tian lun* a kind of importance it had not had before.

This book is focused on two words, one English, one Chinese, and on one Chinese document, which we will translate and comment on. As is obvious to the reader by now, the two words are "Tian" and "nature," and the document is the *Tian lun* of the *Xunzi*. Our basic thesis is straightforward: that in the *Tian lun* and the *Xunzi* generally, translating *Tian* as "Nature" introduces such serious systematic distortions that some alternative should be found, and appropriate changes in the understanding of the *Tian lun* should follow.

That this may be true not merely of that document, but of other pre-Qin literature is not denied, but left aside. To what extent Xun Qing's thought agrees with, overlaps, or was influenced by Daoism is a problem we do not essay to answer, despite the acknowledgment that some possible answers to it might suggest modifications in our conclusions.

A lesser ground for our thesis is that both *Tian* in Archaic Chinese and "nature" in English are vague, and, at least in the case of "nature," ambiguous. This would not be, in itself, sufficient reason for writing this book, since, no matter how vague or ambiguous the words may be, they could have sufficient overlap to make the translation of one by the other quite understandable to any reader of normal intelligence.

More important is the contention that the two words are vague or ambiguous in different ways, and carry opposed connotations and overtones, so that whatever conceptual overlap they may have cannot overcome the misleading character of such a translation. Most important, however, is our belief that the practice of translating *tian* by "nature," and the Chinese practice of explaining *Tian* (in the essay) by a Chinese equivalent of "nature," *ziran*, in the modern sense in which the latter has come to have close affinities with the sciences, involve a misreading of the *Tian lun*, and, no doubt, other texts.

The issues we are particularly concerned with may be stated in a few theses, which the various interpreters affirm in different degrees and understand with differing nuances. These are as follows:

1. Xun represents a naturalistic or thoroughly skeptical stance toward what was basic in the supernaturalism of his times.
Interpreters vary in the degree they press this point. Dubs writes in 1927, "Having disposed of any personal God, the way was clear to dispose of all other spiritual forces and superstitions. . . . Hsüntze categorically denied the existence of spirits and made fun of their worship," conceding only that Xun held "the conviction that virtue is rewarded and vice punished."[47] Six decades later, Knoblock writes, "Xunzi discounted the magical qualities of ritual and disbelieved entirely in the spiritual realm. He rejected any notion of a sentient Heaven . . . He endorsed ritual only as an embellishment to life that gave form and expression to our emotions."[48] Graham, however, moderates the received interpretation somewhat by admitting, "There is also in Hsün-tzŭ a certain residual awe of the sacred in nature."[49] And 60 years ago Shryock, in his review of Dubs, writes, "It is very misleading to say that Hsüntze 'eliminated God.'"[50]

2. Xun takes Tian or "nature" to be an impersonal system, devoid of intention, consciousness, or moral significance.
Thus Li Disheng: "Xunzi's Tian is nature; not at all honored nor revered."[51] Or Li Du, "Tian is nature, devoid of will."[52] Or compare Fung Yu-lan: "Hsün tzŭ's Heaven, however, is a naturalistic one . . . inasmuch as it contains no ethical principle."[53]

3. Xun sees the events of nature (=Tian) to be regular, law-abiding, and predictable.
Li Du, continuing the above, "This nature has necessary, objective laws." Again Li Disheng: "That Tian's way has constancy means there are necessary physical laws."[54] Or Dubs: "Heaven, according to Hsüntze, is unvarying Law . . . Heaven comes to mean very nearly the same as our popular conception of Nature."[55]

4. Xun views Tian (="nature") as available to human exploitation for arbitrary human ends.

Some of these quotations, such as Chen's "Man acts to control Tian (nature)," Jiang's "Control Tian (nature) and use it," and a number of comments of Li Di-sheng, affirm this.

5. Xun devaluates nature (or Tian), assigning it, in contrast to Mencius and Daoism, a negative value.

This emphasis is more to be found in Chinese authors than Western ones.[56] The argument runs: Xun held that human nature, the gift of Tian, was evil; hence he held that Tian is evil. Shryock notes this over 60 years ago: "In saying that the Nature is evil, Hsuntze either failed to understand Mencius, or he considered Heaven to be evil, or he had no place among orthodox Confucians. This conclusion is commonplace in China."[57] Even when not articulated, this implication, so unacceptable to Chinese sensibilities, may account for both the discounting of Xun Qing that occurred over the centuries, and for the fact that he appeared in civil-service examinations primarily in questions regarding "Kuang's doctrine," that human nature is evil.[58] One might note that the more recent version softens the conclusion that Tian is evil, preferring merely to say that, for Xun, Tian is morally irrelevant.

6. Xun views culture as a mere artifact, an imposition on nature.

This overtone is suggested in Tucci's use of the more derogatory term *artificiosa* to translate *wei*, rather than *artificiale*.[59] In the Zhou background it was assumed that culture was produced by sages; by Xun's times whatever old culture gods there may have been had been euhemerized into presumed ancient historical worthies, whose cultural gifts were in principle harmonious with Tian. The Daoists, however, posed the question: was it the elite culture that harmonized with the cosmos, or a much simpler, rudimentary, plebeian culture? The idea that much of the elite culture was an imposition on nature was prominent in Zhuangzi, the *DDJ*, and Daoists generally. Xun certainly affirmed traditional elite culture. The question for us is, then: did Xun's distinctive twist in dealing with the artificiality of culture agree with the Daoists in taking it to be an imposition on nature? Traditional interpretations are not always clear on this point, but seem to assume he largely did agree with them.[60]

We contend that all these theses are misleading, and some, to significant degree, in error. They will not be treated *seriatim* until our concluding summary, since they involve one another too closely. Instead, we shall first discuss some general philosophic problems relevant to understanding Chinese philosophy and especially Xunzi, then present material introductory to the *Xunzi* and the *Tian lun* essay. Chapters 6 and 7 introduce and present a translation, with commentary, of the essay; the commentary includes a few textual notes, discussions of the structure of the argument, evidence and argument to justify translations that are out of the ordinary, and considerable interpretation. Finally, the last four chapters relate the essay to other parts of the *Xunzi*, focusing on the relation of Tian to various ideas connected with or set against it, leading, we trust, to conclusions worth serious scholars' consideration.

2. Some Recent Work

Books on Xunzi in English, or for that matter in any Western language, are few, though many mention him, some at length. Dubs published, along with his translation of about half of the *Xunzi*, his *Hsüntse, the Moulder of Ancient Confucianism.*[1] These, dated 1928 and 1927 respectively, were for many years the chief sources in English on Xunzi. Aside from a few doctoral dissertations, occasional journal articles, chapters in various histories of Chinese philosophy,[2] and Rosemont's study of Xunzi's political theory in *Monumenta Serica*, there was little published that was devoted solely to the interpretation of Xunzi, save for Watson's very readable translation of about one-third of the corpus for Columbia University's Oriental Classics series, which was published in 1963.[3]

The situation is improving. In 1985 Antonio Cua published his *Ethical argumentation, a study in Hsün tzŭ's moral epistemology*;[4] then in 1988 appeared the first volume of John Knoblock's *Xunzi, a translation and study of the complete works*,[5] with the second volume out in 1990 and the third promised soon. This last bids fair to become the standard work, since it contains not only a careful, scholarly translation, well annotated, but also a wealth of historical, textual, and interpretive material, along with valuable apparatus. It is evident that no one in the West working on Xunzi will be able to do without it.

The text with which we are primarily concerned, the *Tian lun*, being *pian* XVII, has not yet appeared in this translation, but the references to it and other remarks in the first two volumes indicate clearly that Knoblock's interpretation will prove to be rather close to the tradition. This is as it should be, of course. A work entitled to become a standard ought not to skate on the precarious ice of provocative hypotheses; it ought instead to stand solidly surrounded by established scholarship, letting the *spermalogoi* flutter around it. In this respect, Knoblock's work is sound.

One contribution by Knoblock to the study of Xunzi especially needs to be mentioned: his development of a much fuller biography and chronology of life and writings than has hitherto been available.

Though it brings together many bits of evidence, both internal and external, and structures them around a theory of Xun Qing's philosophical development, it may seem to many to warrant more tentativeness than Knoblock's presentation expresses. This is especially true if one lacks the confidence Knoblock shows in some of his sources, or is not completely convinced by his theory of development. Nevertheless, his account is by far the best yet presented in the West. All of us owe him a great debt. If this book seems to quote him more often in disagreement than in agreement, that does not at all detract from our deep admiration for his work.

Another recent and refreshing book that deals extensively, though not primarily, with the *Xunzi*, and which contains in an appendix a translation of the *Tian lun*, is Robert Eno's *The Confucian Creation of Heaven*,[6] which, since it raises issues bearing directly on our interest, we shall discuss at some length. The book so delightfully agreed with some points we had considered our own departures, and so stimulated by its clear disagreements with others, that we were tempted to delay this project until we had more fully assimilated his work. The extent of our agreements and disagreements, and some of the grounds for our arguments, will be evident in the following pages.

In that book Eno treats the sequence Confucius-Mencius-Xunzi, developing a picture of "Ruism" (Zhou Confucianism) as "a rigorous, synthetic philosophy, which aimed to cultivate in disciples a comprehension of meaning and truth born of ritual skill mastery,"[7] rituals here including both music and dance, perhaps even ecstatic experiences. The ultimate aim of such mastery was to become sages, a state marked by intense concentration, a unified view of the world, a "sense of total control," and great "freedom and joy." One might attain anticipatory glimpses of this state in the actual participation in dance. These glimpses then were read back into historical sage-kings, and the latters' virtues and powers attributed to their having developed themselves in the same way. The chief function of Confucian philosophy, then, was to legitimize their practices in a world becoming increasingly naturalistic, a world in which "Ruists" were thought strange, ineffective, even pathetic.

Eno draws at least two important consequences from the picture he arrives at: (1) contrary to traditional interpretations, Zhou Confucians were not interested in achieving political power, office, or effectiveness; their political teachings functioned primarily to defend their practices and the hopes that supported those practices; (2) it is mistaken to try to achieve a conceptual understanding of *Tian* in Zhou Ruism, as it cannot be separated from the skills, the practice, the dancing of the Ruists: "we cannot," says Eno," . . . know what they knew or what T'ien meant to them," and "to know what this changeable notion was to Ruists over the early years, we would have to master Ruist skills and become Ruists."[8] In unfolding his theses, he lays out an account of the changes in the significance of Tian from the eleventh century B.C. to the third, an account that impinges upon our undertaking.

Disagreement with these first theses is dealt with in the notes,[9] but Eno's account of the decline of the significance of Tian during the centuries prior to Xunzi, upon which he bases his understanding of Xun's uses of *Tian*, needs at least summary treatment here, although more extended considerations also appear in the notes.

With regard to Tian, there are significant points to differ with. Two of his major claims are that "Tian," as a prime value term in Chinese thought, was in crisis in the third century B.C., and that, in consequence, significant communication using "Tian" by the Ruist community would have been useless except within the esoteric language of the community itself. Eno may not have intended his point to be that strong, but his argument seems to rely on attributing such weight to it.

This, Eno's logical thesis regarding Tian, is presented along with another, historical, thesis; the former may be expanded under several points: (1) that the word *Tian* in Confucian contexts shows "extreme instability" and is "employed without theoretical coherence," and, as a result, (2) it "must reflect the force of a coherent set of core interests that governed formulations of doctrine," whose (3) "free expression could only be impeded by the friction of a fixed concept" of Tian (p. 6); (4) this set of core interests was a set of ritual practices peculiar to the Ruist (Confucian) community, and (5) these practices were to "endow the individual with the skills needed to function in an ethical universe"; carried out fully, they would lead to sagehood.

Since we have already indicated our belief that *Tian*, like any prime religious term, was not at any time "a fixed concept," such that lack of "theoretical coherence" would result in "extreme instability," it would appear that Eno is making improper demands upon such a term. Thus, those parts of his thesis that depend on nonfulfilment of those demands are questionable from the very beginning.[10] To show our difficulties in satisfactorily defining a vague term, or distinguishing its "separate" uses, is one thing; to demonstrate that our difficulties with the term reflect patterns of error, immobility, or censorship the term brought about in its own milieu is quite another. Exhibiting the occurrence of puzzlement, even anguish, is not enough, and Eno hardly has done even that.

The rest of his case cannot be dealt with except within the context of his second thesis, an account of early Chinese history wherein he emphasizes the importance of ritual patterns, and their place in the success of the early Zhou regime, that led to its subsequent enshrinement in memory as an almost utopian age. This success he traces to "the institution of the kingship, the institution of hereditary succession to political office or social occupation, and the unifying force of a state religious system centered on the king and his god," Tian (Eno, 21). The legitimacy of the first two rested upon "the explicit claim that Chou rule was no more than an agency for the benevolent will of T'ien, and that government was, in effect, an organ for the discharge of religious responsibility."[11]

In elaborating this last, Eno surely overstates his case. One can agree that the early Zhou was enshrined in memory as an almost utopian age, but must then admit that whatever evidence there is for this shows also a similar enshrinement of the pre-Zhou ages of Yao, Shun, Yu, and Tang, none of whom were of the Zhou lineage. One can agree that "the Mandate of Heaven theory made the Chou king T'ien's executor on earth" without accepting "T'ien and the king were now nearly indistinguishable . . . T'ien was virtually the personal deity of the king." One can agree with "Only the king was permitted to have intercourse with T'ien through sacrifice" without accepting "In terms of function, T'ien was practically reduced to the king."[12]

Exaggerating the identification of Tian with the royal house of Zhou enables Eno to paint a picture of later Zhou history as a progressive delegitimation of Tian as the power and prestige of the Zhou sovereigns disintegrated. Having merged Tian into the kingship, having granted Tian no identity of its own, he cannot but read later complaints that attribute suffering to Tian's actions as the collapse of belief in Tian as morally significant:

> As long as T'ien remained linked to a strong human king, it was a just and discerning deity. Once the world of man degenerated into injustice and blind suffering, the king's god disappeared into the tradition of the sky god, terrific, unjust, and blind. As social values collapsed, so did the value of T'ien.[13]

These social values were all implemented through an intricate pattern of ritual formalities. As the pillars of the social system decayed, practice of

LI became more self-conscious, leading ultimately to the strong Confucian emphasis upon it as the basis for a stable society.

This last was undoubtedly true, but does not require Eno's previous positions. He ignores four important aspects of the king's sacrifices to Tian: (1) the very act of sacrifice implies a distance between the celebrant and the deity; (2) it implies the superiority of the deity to the sacrificer; (3) it implies the freedom of the deity to reject the sacrifice; (4) the king's sacrifices were primarily on behalf of the people, not the personal offerings of the king—he sacrificed primarily as *king*, as "Son of Tian," not just as a privileged individual. All these facts meant that if the sacrifice was not accepted (that is, blessings did not follow), it was either the fault of the king as king (and for all their personal characteristics, the later Zhou were not very successful kings) or an exercise of the freedom of Tian to determine how and when it would bless.

Eno interprets such an exercise of Tian's freedom to refuse to respond beneficently to the king's sacrifice as Tian's "disappearance into the tradition of the sky god, terrific, unjust, and blind." But Tian had always been the sky god, and floods, droughts, epidemics, and locust plagues undoubtedly occurred during the Early Zhou as well as the Later Zhou. And the sky god, as the High God, always was terrific—otherwise, why sacrifice to him? As for "unjust" and "blind," Eno is surely projecting Enlightenment expectations for deities back into very early history. To generalize so recent and local a bit of Western cultural history as Enlightenment ideology (though Eno seems to do it unconsciously), so as to make it apply to Zhou China despite the slimness of the evidence, seems rash indeed (although it is easy for us children of the Enlightenment to do so quite unaware).[14] The more usual response, in the history of religions, has been more like that of Job: puzzlement, sometimes fatalism, rather than "delegitimizing" the deity.[15] Eno would have done well to study Otto's discussion of "the negative divine,"[16] and note that it does not, in practice, negate the deity's moral functioning.

As to the indistinguishability of Tian and the king, it is clear that the Mandate of Heaven doctrine itself, at its very inception, distinguished the two. As Schwartz writes,

> At the core of the whole notion of the "Heavenly Mandate," which is to figure so centrally in the religous ideology of the early Chou, lies the centrality of Heaven itself. The high god's transcendent powers are by no means inextricably tied to the claims of any lineage. . . . If the late Shang dynasty had intended—as some evidence seems to indicate—to link the high god irrevocably to the fate of its own

> lineage, the early Chou founders were particularly bent on asserting the high god's transcendence of all such ascriptive relations.[17]

A king who has his throne only on sufferance by a deity is surely not identical with the deity; Tian, in the very doctrine itself, had reserved to itself the right to disown the Shang, and had certainly not resigned that right when it enthroned the Zhou. The legitimacy that the Mandate of Heaven doctrine gave the dynasty could only be a conditional legitimacy. The problem, as we have it hinted at in both Mencius and Xunzi, is rather, "Why is Tian taking so long to dump the ineffectual Zhou?"[18]

Eno's case, that "Tian" as a deity or prime locus of value collapsed as early as the eighth century B.C. and never recovered, and was so involved in a crisis of values during the Spring and Autumn and Warring States periods that it had no real moral function by Xun's time, or even Confucius', and had to be "invented" by the Ruists to bolster their unique practices, is itself unique and should require much better evidence than he presents.[19]

Further, Tian could never have been so closely identified with the Zhou king, since it had many other functions quite separate from those of the king. It was god of the seasons, counterpart (spouse?) of the Earth, and continued to give the benefits deriving therefrom, more years than not. It was, certainly long before Confucius, god of individual men's fate and even success. It was, as we shall advert to when discussing some general philosophically significant aspects of Chinese thought, the exemplary *shen* ("god"), not the exemplary *gui* ("demon" or "ghost")—something Xun implicitly acknowledges in the *Tian lun*.

There was, indeed, a hiatus in sacrificing to Tian from the overthrow of the last Zhou king until sometime in the early Han, and the reasons for this did include passing interest in Daoism, but otherwise they were more political than religious or philosophical. The restoration seems to have met with delay, rather than resistance. The paramountcy of Tian was readily granted, as if supported by lively tradition, especially in a Confucianism rooted in the classics (and competitive with Daoism). Schwartz comments:

> If the t'ien of the Chou people (whatever may have been his ultimate origins) was conceived of by the Chou founders as identical with the *ti* of the Shang, then one is profoundly impressed by the early emergence and relative stability of the idea of the high god as the heavenly counterpart in the cosmic order to the universal king in the human order and of the unique relation between the two. The relationship

remained intact in China's state religion until the revolution of 1911.[20]

Yet "Son of Heaven" indicated a *gulf* between the ruler and Tian, as well as a link. From the beginning, Tian maintained its own place at the top of the cosmic hierarchy, more or less independent of Confucian ritual or imperial success. (This is not to divorce religious concepts from ritual language, as will be discussed later on. One of Eno's strengths is his acknowledgment, even though it is somewhat reductionist, of their relationship.)

We have spent some time criticising Eno's theory of the abandonment of Tian-theology during the late Zhou because the *Xunzi* manifests much more continuity with the traditional view of Tian than his account admits. It has also given us the opportunity to stress some aspects of that traditional view that bear upon the interpretation of the *Tian lun*. Some reinterpretation there undoubtedly was, but nothing that could be considered delegitimization on the order claimed by Eno. Despite the many valuable and illuminating separate insights into the Confucian schools he gives us, I fear no historian of religion will be convinced by his rather simplistic account of the fall of Tian, or of any crisis of theodicy in the Zhou as drastic as he claims.

Despite this lack of nuance, Eno's work is welcome and important. His emphasis on music and dance in the *Xunzi* is an important contribution, and though there is less cause to stress that aspect in Mencius, Eno's including him as a part of the continuity of music and dance from Confucius to Xun requires more looking into. (Our treatment of the two-sided activity is rather oblique to his, but the affinity is there.) Many of his interpretations of bits of the *Xunzi* harmonize with, and sometimes go beyond, conclusions we have reached over the years. His work deserves thoughtful study, but also serious rethinking.

This long discussion of one thesis in Eno's book was sustained not because his work looms large in the literature on Chinese philosophy, but because Tian looms so large in Confucian philosophizing. Thus Taylor remarks, apropos of Confucianism,

> it is necessary to identify that element of the tradition that may be described as deeply and profoundly religious. This element revolves around the Confucian understanding of *T'ien*, Heaven, the traditional high god of the early Chou people. The religious core itself is found in the relationship of humankind to Heaven. Heaven for the Confucian tradition is not thought of, as some have argued, as an abstract

> philosophical absolute devoid of religious meaning. In the Classical Confucian tradition Heaven functions as a religious authority or absolute often theistic in its portrayal.[21]

Taylor goes on to point out that an absolute is not per se religious; that requires also a possible relationship between that absolute and the individual, and a specified way for him to move toward that absolute—in other words, a way of transformation or salvation. Eno is undoubtedly right in holding that the relationship to Tian *through the king* was seriously attenuated by the time of Confucius, and that the latter believed that his disciplines involved an approach at least oblique to the ongoing royal ritual involvement. But Eno fails to see two important things: (1) that the emphasis on self-development and on ritual and music are not only part of the *way* to relationship with the traditional Tian, but also a *celebration* of that way, and, indirectly, of its hoped-for outcome; and (2) Tian was never reduced to being nothing but a sponsor of royal legitimacy. Indeed, Eno's whole fixation upon legitimation smacks of the sort of sociological positivism that has never been able to give a satisfactory account of religious phenomena.

Taylor goes on to comment, "As this religious core is recognized, other elements of the tradition take on religious significance as they relate to this central meaning." This raises problems for the interpreter of the *Xunzi*, since its author has consistently been seen, as our quotations in the first chapter show, as nonreligious, even antireligious, but nevertheless in the Confucian tradition. It is interesting that Taylor, in the book we have been quoting, refers to Xunzi in only three places, in two of them only in passing. The other reference speaks of his place in the process that elevated writings the Confucians held important to the status of classics.[22] Apparently Taylor found the *Xunzi* recalcitrant rock from which to quarry material for building his argument—but undoubtedly he has read the *Xunzi* in light of the received tradition.

We have, then, an interesting dilemma: Xun Qing claimed to be a thoroughgoing Confucian. Nowhere in the *Xunzi* does one find any criticism of Confucius; in fact, it maintains that

> Confucius, on the other hand, was benevolent, wise, and free from obsession. Thus, though he studied the doctrines of the various other schools, he established his own school, taught the way of Chou, and showed how it could be put into practice, for he was not obsessed by old habits and prejudices. Hence his virtue is equal to that of the

> duke of Chou, and his fame matches that of the sage kings of the three Dynasties. (W 126)

When Xun criticizes other Confucians, it is always because they have either strayed from the tradition or been negligent in attention to it.[23] Nor do we have any indication that he was not thought, in his own time, to be a Confucian. Ch'en Shou-yi remarks,

> Obviously Hsün tzŭ was regarded by most of his contemporaries as a follower of Confucius, for despite the novel notes he sounded there was nothing in the thirty-two chapters of his book that contradicted or radically deviated from the teachings of the sage.[24]

The recognition that Xun was important in the establishment of the canon of Confucian writings as "classics" itself suggests he was no rejecter of religion. As Yang says, "Modern students of China who maintain the purely rationalistic view of Confucianism are not able to explain away the religious aspects of the doctrine without distorting the meaning of the original texts."[25] Xun accepted those classics; indeed, he was noted for being steeped in them.

I find it inconceivable that Xun Qing could have been so committed a Confucian, could have so revered the past, made ritual so central, and treated the ancient classics as authorities, and still have rejected the religious overtones those involve; yet the interpretation widespread in recent literature would require him to do just that. He uses them in his own way, for his own philosophical and polemic purposes, of course; but he so repeatedly treats them as central to the development of both one's mind and one's character, leading toward his goal of *shenming* sagehood—both of them reduced if stripped of their religious character[26]—that their music must have structured his thinking quite as much as their literal wordings.

As regards immersion in the classics, a comment of George Lindbeck is worth pondering:

> For those who are steeped in [authoritative texts], no world is more real than the ones they create. A scriptural world is thus able to absorb the universe. It supplies the interpretive framework within which believers seek to live their lives and understand reality."*

*George A. Lindbeck, *The Nature of Doctrine: Religion and Theology in a Postliberal Age.* Philadelphia: Westminster, 1984, 117.

It is worth noting that Xun never criticizes anyone for *holding to* the Classics,[27] nor does he ever suggest the latter might lead one astray (though reading them does require guidance). Someone who has never pondered what it means to live one's life in the light of authoritative scriptures, and who at the same time has a very "square" idea of what the religion of a thoughtful man with a critical mind would be, or someone who was not really concerned about Xun's religious sensibilities (as most of the interpreters I have studied seem to have been) could find it easy to expand Xun's criticisms of specific beliefs or actions into a wholesale rejection of piety. The question of those sensibilities, however, once carefully asked, demands more subtle treatment than it has usually been given.

It is significant that nowhere does Xun ever criticize any ancient worthy, or anyone he considers significant, for his religion. Nor does he criticize or reject any part of the "great tradition" of religious practices, only bits of the "little traditions." When he does criticize religious actions or ideas, it is always specific superstitions or beliefs, the sorts of things many a thoroughly religious thinker has criticized. To expand such retail criticisms into wholesale rejection, and then to allow such a presumed rejection to control the interpretation of ambiguous passages, seems unwarranted, most especially when those passages could imply a religious alternative quite as well as an irreligious one.

One further thought before leaving this topic: Eno discusses, quite properly, the several varieties of what might be called "naturalisms" (a word both vague and ambiguous) during the late Zhou, but in a way that implies they represented the major pattern of thought during that era. There does, indeed, seem to be a considerable seepage of shamanist influence up into the literate levels of society from the previously less-cultured strata or the previously less typically Chinese areas (Chu, Qi, Yen, Yue, as opposed to the original Zhongguo), which influenced the non-Confucian philosophies (except for Mohism). That influence is hard to assess, and there were probably other sources for the new schools (court astrologers, for instance). The schools do manifest more of an intellectual bent than shamanist ancestry alone would have bequeathed.

However, we have so little assurance of just when much of the *Zhuangzi* and the *Guanzi* were written or circulated, or how much influence the *DDJ* had before Xun's later years, or how demographically representative our sample of late Zhou literature is, or whether the attention given to these new schools was in any way proportional to their popularity, that one should not base an interpretation of third century B.C. Chinese thought on an assumption of some kind of dominance for naturalisms. The *Xunzi* certainly treats Mohism as much more important, and some of Xun's other targets are later identified with the Huang-Lao movement, which now seems to have been much more political, with interesting affinities with Legalism, than formerly thought. After all, Xun refers to Zhuang or Lao hardly at all; one can discern no affinities between his use of *yin*, *yang*, and *qi* 氣 with any special uses of the cosmologists, and his treatment of terms such as *xu* 虛, *jing* 精, and *shenming* seems distinctly different from Daoist usages.

Daoist influence on Xun, and upon terms he used, may well have been less, and more diffuse, than is sometimes claimed. Surely his criticisms of other Confucians, and Han Fei's listing of eight different schools of them,[28] would suggest that Xun hardly felt alone in a sea of naturalists.

We do not really know how widespread or influential naturalist ideas were by the end of the Zhou. So long as the *DDJ* was dated early, and it was held that most of the *Zhuangzi* and the *Guanzi* circulated widely a century or more before the Qin conquest, Daoism (in the broad sense that grades into other naturalisms) could be given a large place in our picture of Warring States philosophy. As things stand now, that rather traditional picture has become questionable. For instance, neither Mencius nor the Han author of the *Xingshijie pian* of the *Guanzi* seems to have been acquainted with the *Zhuangzi*.[29] Though much of the *Xunzi* is given to criticism of other philosophers' positions, it dismisses Zhuangzi with one sentence and Laozi with two. There were no doubt quasi-Daoist ideas "in the air," and a number of Zhou thinkers were labelled "Daoist" by later writers, but that was perhaps for their own intellectual convenience, rather than on the basis of firm and clear evidence.[30]

The appearance of Daoist opinions in the *LSCQ* shows there were such opinions, of course, and the *Guanzi* makes it probable they were represented in the "Jixia Academy" at some time, possibly when Xun Qing was there. Yet when he criticizes philosophers elsewhere identified as "Daoist," he criticizes their social and psychological doctrines. This has been taken to mean he agreed with their views of nature, and the *Essay on Tian* has been interpreted accordingly. It may simply mean, however, that he was not much impressed with their arguments, or was not much interested in the problems they addressed. In fact, it is striking that he so clearly rejects even raising those problems, and that the chief thrust of the essay most quoted as evidence for a quasi-Daoist view of nature in the *Xunzi* turns out to be, on close scrutiny, rather anti-Daoist.

Nevertheless, it is obvious that the nonreligious interpretation of Xunzi is not based on nothing. What is required is a careful examination of the relevant passages in the *Xunzi*. This we aim to do (in part), after a few further preliminaries.

3. Some Philosophical Issues

General Philosophical Problems

There are certain general problems in interpreting Chinese philosophy that deserve comment. Any philosophical literature assumes a great deal that "goes without saying," and those from a different philosophical milieu must beware both of basing their interpretations too much on their own assumptions and of missing assumptions basic to the text they are seeking to interpret. Some of our assumptions are necessary for us to come to an understanding at all; of these we can never be devoid. Some of the author's assumptions we may never be able to gain any feeling for; to that extent we are cut off from a complete understanding. Yet to say this is not to claim that our intellectual aims must be whatever his or hers were; we are, after all, using the text for our own intellectual purposes. It is only to insist that our aims are better served to the extent we are aware of our own assumptions, of the author's, and of the disparities between the two.

Cosmology

We have stated that the prime constructive aim of this book is to describe one aspect of Xun Qing's metaphysics—his idea of *Tian*. We assume that his over-all cosmology, in the narrow sense, was that generally held in his time[1]: that the sky was in some sense round, the earth square, that the heavenly bodies followed normal courses most of the time, although occasionally they might stray and produce an eclipse, a meteor fall, or a nova. These courses revolved about the pole star, which in Xun's time was probably still Alpha Draconis, the pole star of 1500 B.C., rather than Polaris, although by his time the movement of the pole toward Polaris should have been noticeable. The *axis mundi* passed from the pole star to the earth, nominally striking the earth where the monarch's throne sat,[2] so that, in "facing south" he had the backing of the universe, and could represent its order to the human world.

As all the other stars revolved around the pole star, so should everything terrestrial revolve around the Son of Tian. As the pole star did not move, but controlled the movements of all other heavenly bodies, so the true king should be able to rule *wu-wei*, without acting.[3]

There is ample evidence that this sense of a world structured around the pole star was reflected further in human affairs. The traditional, ideal model for the layout of a city was a square, with central north-south and east-west avenues, with the administrative offices at their intersection, facing south.[4] The north-south avenue, at least, was fundamentally a ceremonial route,[5] leading as it did to the domainal *sheji* south of town. (The hypothesis that *Dao* was originally the name of this ritual avenue, aligned with the north star and leading to the ritual harmonizing with the spirits, is attractive—though it is as completely devoid of supporting evidence as any other hypothesis regarding the origins of the word.[6]) In any case, the plan of cities ideally reflected both the alignment of Earth (square) with Tian (circular, but represented by the north star) and also the function of government, especially in its ritual capacities, as the nexus between the two.

Xun accepted the traditional dynamics of the interaction of *yin* and *yang*, treating them as general knowledge, needing no elaboration. They are mentioned only five times in the entire corpus, three of them in the *Tian lun*. The other two assign "observing the *yin* and *yang*" to shamans [*pian* IX] and remark [*pian* XIX] that "when *yin* and *yang* act upon each other, all changes are produced"[7]—about as general a statement as could be made.

As for the developing physics of *qi*, there is no trace of it in the *Xunzi*.[8] The word occurs some 25 times in the corpus, 22 of them referring to a person's emotional life or its manifestations, the other three to biological life—"when one loses his *qi* he dies" [*pian* XXI]. Xun may have held to *qi* as an explanatory principle for more than psychological and biological phenomena, as we find in the *LSCQ* and the *Guanzi*, but there is no evidence for it.[9] And as for the *wu xing*, the "five processes" theory, Xun mentions it only to reject it.[10] (The phrase "*wu xing*" occurs one other time in the *Xunzi* (*pian* XX), but there it is clearly used as Watson translates it: "When these five types of conduct . . ."[11])

It would be foolish to insist that explicit talk of the cosmos along the lines first introduced here was common in Xun's day, but it would be equally foolish to pretend that such deep-seated images of the universe could be easily overthrown by secular events or changes in political styles.

Basic cosmological models are very slow to change—it is doubtful that Copernican astronomy would have commended itself to the seventeenth century if it had not had the concomitant support of an upper-middle-class revolt against the hierarchies of feudalism and the expansionist imaginations generated by the discoveries of the preceding century (surely the best scientific evidence was with Tycho Brahe![12]). There was no such shock of discovery or sudden economic and social expansion, in the evolutionary pre-Qin changes, as visited Europe from 1450 on, nothing to shake the inherited cosmology or to rally an emerging and powerful class to incorporate some new view into their perceptions of the world.

As for other words that might refer to nature, the Daoist term *ziran*, or "what happens of itself," occurs in the *Xunzi* only twice, both times referring to the instinctive or "spontaneous" responses to stimulus that define our nature and require no effort.[13] *Yu*, the "canopy of heaven" (or the eaves of a house), with the overtone of "sheltering," occurs eight times. Three of these are in the fu (poem) on the clouds, and speak of them "wandering through the skies," and "filling the great canopy of heaven" (twice). One is a graphic variant for a different word. Another three say, "The myriad things inhabit the same world," "All the myriad things in the world," and the last, which is undoubtedly a later addition to the text, "The six directions in the universe." None of these seems to have any metaphysical significance at all.

The last occurrence of yu is in the binome *yuzhou*, a usual modern term for "universe" or "all of nature." Here the Sage "regularizing and dividing up the overall innate structure, conforms the whole universe to that structure" (a tentative translation of a puzzling and much commented-upon sentence).[14] This last clearly involves an important principle of order and significant metaphysical activity on the part of the Sage, and will receive further comment.

It would appear that Xun Qing had very little interest in the mapping of the cosmos. His dominant models or "root-metaphors" functioned within the cosmos, rather than referring to some whole. (We have already remarked on Knoblock's claim that *Tian* may be considered *the* Chinese word for "nature," and our doubts on that point.)

Cosmology and Sheng

It seems normal for an agricultural society to have identified nature with the processes of birth and growth. This is evident from the Greek *physis*, translated "nature," from *phuein*, "to give birth," as well as the Latin *natura*, from *nascere, natus*, "to be born" (whence "nascent," "native," "prenatal," "innate," etc.). There is a realm where things come to be without help; that is their nature, they do it "naturally."

Later, "nature" sometimes becomes the name of that realm, as in Stoic Greek and Latin. But as late as Aristotle, there was no "realm of nature," just the collection of things that functioned of themselves. Lucretius' poem, *De rerum natura*, was about "the nature of things," not "the things of nature." Gods, too, functioned according to their "nature"—Cicero wrote "On the nature of the gods." The totality of things was a collection of things, not a system; insofar as it was orderly, it was the "cosmos" (later, however, that was identified with *physis*); beyond order was Chaos.

The pattern that appeared in China was related, but different in form. There, *sheng*, the power or process of growth or giving birth, gained meanings extending to "life" and "to produce," to "fresh" (vegetables), and "sacrificial (life-giving?) animal." The original graph may possibly have been of a new sprout, but the other meanings appeared very early. It eventually produced a derivative, *xing*, sometimes translated as "human nature," but it contributed nothing toward words for "nature" as a collective. Apart from references to sacrificial animals (undoubtedly a specialized use), *sheng* is associated with two main poles of ritual importance: the family, through birth, and agriculture, through its sprouting and animal-reproduction involvements.

The existence of these two poles of existential importance for the Chinese presents the problem of how they were related. The ritual focus of the one was the cult of ancestors, wherein each family head was responsible to his immediate ancestors, presented (under proper ritual circumstances) in the ancestral tablets (*shenzhu*) in the domestic shrine. Through the clan head he was also responsible to the more distant ancestors, whose tablets had been removed from the domestic shrine to the clan temple. The hierarchic relationships were thus preserved and celebrated, and the status of the dead defined, though, as memory-images became fainter or were not present, the more distant members of the spiritual hierarchy became less definite, more impersonal (unless dramatized for memory by clan tales of exceptional deeds).

It is significant that there is so little identifiable mythology about the abode of the dead, although, as Allan points out, there are references to the "Yellow Springs."[15] This may be because one's ancestors, the only really significant dead, had a *ritual* presentation in the ancestral rites, and hence need for any imaginative presentation was lessened. The rites themselves were largely acknowledging, and thus encouraged only narrative about the living, not mythological narrative about the dead.

There may have been a time when the two poles, ancestral and agricultural, had close ties. During the Shang, the god *Shangdi* (who was later identified with Tian) functioned both as a rain and harvest god and as "first ancestor" of the royal house; remnants of this continued through later centuries, being part of the meaning of the title "Son of Tian." (In *pian* XIX, Xun acknowledges that "Royalty [sacrifices to] Tian as to their first ancestor").

For anyone lower than royalty, however, it appears that ancestral rites had no connection with Tian-rituals, or even with agricultural rites, except through the geographical proximity of altars of earth and grain (*sheji*) to clan temples.

The agricultural pole was differently organized. From very early on, the agricultural calendar was defined by state rituals, which were themselves calendared by the heavenly bodies—"the seasons." Authority over land carried with it ritual responsibilities to its gods, so the legitimacy of the local feudal lord was symbolized in his *sheji* or "altar of earth and grain."[16] This was spatially associated with his clan temple, but that connection with ancestry was qualified by another Earth altar, south of the domainal town, which represented the Earth as a particular locale, independent in significance, though not in ritual practice, of the ruler's lineage.

Although by Xun's times "possession of one's *sheji*" was guaranteed in fact more by military might or diplomacy than by ritual (though even warfare, especially earlier, was often a somewhat ritual matter), the old ideological basis had not evaporated. As the term suggests, the "altar of earth and grain" related the ruler to the processes of *sheng* as they functioned through the fruitful earth to produce life's necessities of food and fiber, with the corollary that a ruler's ritual business involved maintaining a proper relationship to earth and its productiveness. Thus, spring plowing could not proceed until the ruler, during the Spring Festival, had completed his own ritual plowing. Only if the earth was ritually addressed could it be cultivated; only if the ground was productive was a local ruler legitimated.

Earth, however, could not produce of itself. The mythology of agricultural peoples is full of analogies between farming and sexual intercourse, of the sky-father and the earth-mother, as in the Polynesian myth of the sky lying upon the earth to produce all other things, or reduced to metaphor in the use of sexual language, as in the Mediterranean area, where plowing and sowing—that is, penetrating the ground and depositing seed (Lat. *semen*, Gr. *sperma*, Heb. *zera'*)—were spoken of as a sexual act.

The active principle that makes production possible, variably represented as a sky god, a rain god, or a mountain god (where clouds appeared and rain "came from"[17]), was primarily, in China,[18] Tian or "Sky," acting through and in accordance with the seasons, as China has a relatively well-defined monsoon climate. So Tian as an agricultural deity has a certain priority over Earth; if the sky withholds rain, Earth does not produce.

Earth and Sky are thus the complementary foci of the whole natural process of production. The two unmixed hexagrams of the 64 in the *Yijing*, or *Book of Changes*, are described by Wilhelm as representing "nature in contrast to spirit, earth in contrast to heaven, space as against time, the female-maternal as against the male-paternal."[19]

"The valuable characteristic of Earth is its breadth," as Xunzi says,[20] and its breadth allows many local rulers and many *sheji*. There is, however, only one Tian, and its primacy required that it be ritually attended by only the "one man," the king. There are many fields, only one sky. Just as space must wait upon time for anything to happen, so the entire empire must wait upon the ritual action of the king toward Tian. His legitimacy as king is tied to his relation to the sky god upon which agriculture depends.

Human reproduction does not wait for the seasons (except perhaps in terms of the peasant rites described by Granet[21]). The agricultural rites, culminating in the monarch's worship of Tian, and the ancestral rites, dispersed eventually among the "hundred surnames," never could be unified. Xun recognizes this in his essay on ritual [*pian* XIX], when he remarks, discussing the bases of rites, "Tian and Earth are the basis of production (*sheng*), ancestors are the basis of the family . . . thus, as for rites, they serve Tian above and Earth below, and they honor ancestors."[22]

Both the familial order of ancestor worship and the agricultural order were thus hierarchic, with their levels defined sharply by rituals. Both were structurings of the basic process of birth or production, *sheng*, which was the characteristic process of nature. It is no wonder that insofar as nature was perceived as order—and order can be perceived in nature—it was perceived as ritualized and hierarchic. The seasons were the ritual patterns by which Tian regularly brought about the sequence of production, maturity, and death, and, insofar as there was order among the myriad things in nature, it was made up of ritualized responses to the seasonal ritual action of Tian, the highest point in the hierarchy, from which, ultimately, all originating action flowed and to which all orderly processes responded—as long as they followed their proper ritual patterns.

Outside these ritual patterns there would be disorder. Higher elements in hierarchy have more power than lower elements (otherwise there is no hierarchy). In earlier times, there was less emphasis on the higher powers' concern with order, much more concern with their freedom. In the exercise of freedom, any level may cause problems for those lower down. Thus, considerable divination recorded on the Shang oracle bones was directed to finding out which ancestor had caused a certain evil, in hope of placating it. The initiative and the power both rested farther up the hierarchy than with living humans, even royalty. Divination was not so much to find out a determined future as to discover the right way to act in the present crisis, or to find out whether a proposed action would violate some proper but possibly unknown form and invite disaster.[23] At the family level, an unreasonable father was to be obeyed; the son's problem was to find the ritually appropriate way to respond to his father's unreason. A number of Confucian passages treat this problem.[24]

The outlook so structured by ritual and hierarchy was hardly shared by those who found themselves near the bottom. "The LI do not go down to the mass of people." We do not know how far down the social scale the cult of ancestors reached by the end of the Zhou. The peasants had for centuries been kept in line by severe punishments and lack of alternatives. In the traditions that governed their lives they undoubtedly had their own "little traditions" somewhat parallel to LI, but not regarded as such by the elite, and their own forms of ancestor cult. As is usual in history, however, it was the elite minority, not the common majority, who left behind traces that survived long enough to become the materials for our constructions of cultural history.

It was not until long after the time of Xun Qing that China developed a systematic divine hierarchy to parallel the civil bureaucracy, one wherein Tian and Earth paralleled the emperor, provincial gods the provincial governors, district gods the district officials, city gods city mayors, and lowly precinct gods the lesser civic divisions. In such a system, numinous power (and virtue) was clearly defined and graded, and in that sense China could be said to have had a "national religion." Civic ritual defined civic gods, as gods always must be defined in ritual ways (one reason the antiritual Enlightenment in the West has never been able to come up with a viable "philosophy of religion").

This hierarchy of political gods (in later Chinese civil religion) reflected two basic Confucian sensibilities: that power and virtue are both hierarchical, and that power should be commensurate with virtue. One might ask help from a lowly precinct god toward success in a shady venture, but not the god of the city, still less the provincial god. The divine hierarchy narrowed to fewer, more virtuous gods at each ascending level, until it reached its acme in Tian, reflecting (or reflected in) the political hierarchy, culminating in the emperor, "Tian's son."

This later civil religion need concern us no further, except as an embodiment of something that had roots very early in the cultured Chinese consciousness, something also reflected in the concept DE, translated by terms ranging from "moral virtue," through "generosity to lessers" and "disposition" to "inner power," power that, in Daoism, unlike Confucianism, seems often to lack any moral or personal dimension. There are greater and lesser degrees of *DE*, whether degrees of power deriving from moral depths or of morality deriving from depths of power. The wedding of the two was related to a sense that *DE* only appeared in those who (or those things which) were authentically functioning in accord with their place in the cosmos, whether achieved ritually by Shang kings meticulously maintaining the sacrificial calendar, or philosophically by a Daoist sage shucking all the deceits and perversions of "respectable" culture.

It is significant that it was when Chinese society was working most effectively that it was most happily hierarchical. Antihierarchical Daoism emerged when the Warring States period pluralized what had been (in idea, anyway) a single hierarchical system, and remained always an intellectual refuge in times when hierarchy, and hence both order and morality, tended to be replaced by anarchy.

What this survey leads to is the conclusion that Xun, who accepted such a traditional cosmology, had no real interest in it. It formed a background to what he was interested in. This would accord perfectly with the conservative side of his character. Astronomy and cosmology had been the concern of court chroniclers and seers, not philosophers. Xun's purely psychological use of *qi* contrasts with Mencius' claim of possessing "flood-like" *qi* that, if nurtured, could "fill Heaven and Earth"[25]—a passage that continues to puzzle, but which suggests that Xun's criticism of Mencius for dabbling in the theories of the naturalists was not without foundation.[26] It also suggests that Xun was committed to leaving purely descriptive cosmology unchanged. The importance of *sheng*, productive process, as a descriptive dimension of the cosmos, *but not part of its moral dimension*, is in evidence in many places in the *Xunzi*, and especially in the *Tian lun*. This limitation of the scope of *sheng* is an essential part of his case.

Cosmology is not, however, all of metaphysics. The metaphysics of value holds first place as to human relevance. With the shift from the Spring and Autumn period, when local rulers vied to become hegemons who would stabilize the empire under the king, to the Warring States, when they already called themselves "kings" and sought to gain the empire for themselves,[27] adjustments in the metaphysics of value were called for. If actual rule was distributed among several warring states, where was the contact, the *Anknüpfungspunkt*, between the orderly value guarantees of Tian and the disrupted life of people on earth? (This was the problem Eno both exaggerated and oversimplified.) Xun's answer was "the sage," but the explication of that answer must await presentation of one of its prime expositions, the *Tian lun*.

Language and Its Uses

Speeches and writings, and languages and literatures, differ in the degree to which they rely on what is unsaid—what is assumed, what is in the context, what is extraverbal, what is traditional. Benjamin Schwartz observes, "The *written* language of ancient Chinese texts . . . relies heavily on situational context or the context of shared understandings."[28] Some of the "shared understandings" we may be able to divine, but often the "situational context" may escape us—we simply know too little about the ancient Chinese communicative situations, especially about the relations between oral and written communication.

The study of classical Mediterranean rhetoric, for instance, has shown that most, perhaps all, documents were written to be read aloud, and the significance of many written devices, such as *inclusio*, must be understood in terms of the demands made on listeners rather than on readers, who have the opportunity to reread.[29] A number of characteristics of ancient Chinese writings suggest that their milieu was in these ways parallel to that of the classical Mediterranean age.

Thus, when Graham remarks, "Most teaching and debate was oral, doctrine was what someone 'said' and 'I have heard . . . ,' and the issue of names and objects was always discussed in terms of the spoken, not the written,"[30] he suggests a number of questions not ordinarily faced in dealing with Zhou texts. How were they intended to be delivered? What demands did they make on the recipients? In what sense were they "books," for general circulation, or were they primarily in-house material for the use of students, to be accompanied by *viva voce* supplement? Were dialogues actually recorded, or was the "dialogue" always a literary device? What relationship was assumed between author (or reader-aloud) and the recipient(s)?

Further, we do not know how books were 'published' or circulated, or in what numbers—the need to recopy books after the Qin certainly so expanded the production of books in the Han that we cannot assume that even the scholars of Han had knowledge of the way books functioned in the Zhou. We do know that a number of writings ascribed to the Zhou period were really later pseudepigrapha, and there is reason to believe that Han accounts of literary production during the Zhou were exaggerated. (Should we believe literally Sima Qian's comment, "This was a time when there were . . . men who followed Hsun Ching in writing books and dispersing them throughout the world"?[31]) How were they copied, and by whom, and why? How were they circulated? If so widespread, why was the spoken word still so predominant over the written? Even the classics were to be *memorized*. This group of queries becomes especially important when, for instance, the question of the integrity of a treatise or the continuity of its thought arises. We shall advert to this when discussing the *Essay on Tian*.

Another problem, brought into focus recently, hinges on the observation that embedded in Archaic Chinese is a logic that "divides down" rather than "includes up"—individual things do not "exist"; rather, the world "has" them; and many nouns are "mass nouns" (such as our "mud," "water," or "cattle") out of which particular things must be distinguished either grammatically or contextually. This has been well discussed in general by Hansen, and more specially in Graham in relation to the absence in Chinese of a Western concept (or pseudoconcept) of "being."[32]

Other consequences, however, also seem worth noting. This dimension of language implies, and can be seen in practice to involve, that a more general term may not be simply a larger class of self-subsistent individuals, each characterized by some common property, but an indicator of an encompassing reality in which the individuals participate. This is not at all a Platonism, for the encompassing reality is not a timeless concept, but an image implying actuality.

Consider the Chinese family, based in now-dead ancestors who are not conceptually defined but are ritually acknowledged. They not only antedate but define the individual, who is the channel through which the reality, the family, passes on to his children. If he ignores his family, he has, in effect, compromised not only himself but, by not functioning properly as himself, compromised the other processes he interacts with. His lack of filial piety is a deficiency to the society, perhaps even the cosmos.

Though the modern Chinese man may at times feel his family is a restriction on his private identity, this does not seem to be the case for ancient Chinese, as far as the evidence available to us shows (unless the quest for physical immortality at the end of the Zhou bespoke a wish to be identified with one's *po*, or earth-linked "soul," rather than with one's *hun*, which could, under proper ritual circumstances, become an ancestral spirit). In general, however, it appears that one's family could be a problem, a burden, an irritation, but never something that did not define one's identity. This contextual understanding of the self (or lack of self) underlies many things in Chinese thinking, and we shall return to it.

This structure of language is also, of course, a determiner of thought, so that ancient Chinese thinking tends to be correlative. Since everything exists by participating in a determining context, which itself has a determining context, up to the all-inclusive matrix (the naming of which led through Dao to later Daoist speculations about *wu*, sometimes questionably translated "nonbeing"), everything participates to some extent in the same underlying and determining reality. Then any sort of thing may, to the sensitive eye, be an illuminating counterpart of something in some quite different area: the behavior of water may have metaphysical import in *Mencius*, 6A2 or moral import in *Xunzi*, XXVIII; animals or plants may embody moral indications; and, in the developed *wu xing* theory, colors, odors, and planets may be analogues to parts of the body, etc.

Xun's critical bent kept him from going off into this last overuse of correlative thinking, but he never departed from it in the main. Even his quasi-nominalistic theory of naming does not seem to have undercut his typically Chinese commitment to a correlative view of things. As Henderson remarks, "correlative thought is the most basic ingredient of Chinese cosmology."[33]

This correlative thinking meant that thought was not easily separated into isolatable departments. Keightley observes,

> metaphysics did not develop as a major category of Chou thought. This was not because later [than Shang] thinkers were uninterested in metaphysical problems. But it is because, I would suggest, metaphysical questions were viewed as religious (and, by extension, moral) questions. The nature of reality was not an existential question but an essential question. Since reality was pregnant with meaning, the nature of reality was always conceived in terms of what it meant. The

> study of reality without a study of its ethical significance would have had no meaning.[34]

The philosopher may need to adjust to Keightley's use of "existential" and "essential," but his meaning is not obscure.

We in the West have developed careful analyses of causation and distinctions among its kinds, so we are likely to be surprised when we find in the very first *pian* of the *Xunzi*:

> The emergence of every sort of thing must have its source . . . when meat rots, worms emerge; when fish is old it produces maggots; when a lazy and careless man neglects his character, disasters (celestial and terrestrial) are generated; . . . when corruptness and filthiness dwell in one's self, they invite resentment; when sticks are piled together, fire will go to the driest; when you level the ground, water will go where there is moisture; trees of the same species grow together . . . where a target is set up, arrows will arrive in it; where forest trees are thick, axes will arrive among them . . . when vinegar sours, gnats congregate. So there are words that summon catastrophe, there are actions that invite shame.

All these various kinds of consequentialities, so different to us, correlate in terms of the single idea of "inviting," from which Xun draws a moral: the Junzi should be careful of how he establishes himself.

This correlative thinking is based on a perception of the world as shot through with many sorts of influences, particularly qualitative interactions. Thus there is no theory prescribing limits to what may influence what, or the ways it may do so.[35] Such influences are to be *seen*, or at least accepted on the authority of reports that one credits. As Keightly puts it, "The thought of Chou and Han was more ostensibly secular, but the way the world worked, the logical links between its elements, was still partly mystical and symbolic."[36] We tend to demand general reasons where ancient Chinese simply accepted or denied on the basis of illuminating analogy.

Correlations important for Xun can be seen in the fact that the opposite of good government, *zhi*, is *luan*, "chaos"; the opposite of ritual, LI, is *luan*; and, at least by implication, *luan* is also opposed to Tian. He treats LI not merely as a means to good government; in an important sense it *is* good government. It is not merely the pattern of celestial routines; it *is* those routines—in some scarcely definable sense of "is." When Munro says Xun "projected" the idea of LI onto the motions of the heavens,[37] he is projecting our modern idea of "projection" onto Xun (and expressing our modern denial of LI in nature); Xun, however, simply *saw* LI in the heavens, and believed others could see it.

One aspect of this combination of "dividing down" in language and the corresponding "correlative thinking" is the function of parallel clauses or sentences in Archaic Chinese writings (and, presumably, their speaking). The meaning of a sentence often is not clear except in its conjunction with a parallel sentence. Without this, one may be at a loss to identify the use of some of the words or the precise grammatical structure.[38] This is in marked contrast to our belief that words can always be clearly defined by a dictionary, and a grammar book can teach us what we need to know about grammar. That is not to say that there cannot be Chinese dictionaries or grammars, simply that they must be different sorts of things from what we have led ourselves to expect. Traditional Chinese grammars have not been of great usefulness to Westerners, but the older objections to the traditional Chinese ways of "defining" words in dictionaries are now seen to be signs of our own parochialism. One might almost say that one who demands Western-type (that is, Aristotelian) "definitions" of Chinese words is in danger of cutting herself off from any real chance of penetrating classical Chinese.[39]

There is the complementarity not only of clauses and sentences in the written (and probably the spoken) style; there is also a complementarity in the uses of words. Thus, when Eno speaks of several sometimes "incompatible" uses of *Tian* in the *Xunzi*, one is entitled to wonder how much attention he has given to the complementary terms in each case. Was Xun speaking of Tian as the dialectic counterpart (in a sense neither Greek nor Hegelian) of Earth, or of humans, or of the ruler, or of *shen* (spirit), or of some other of the patterns of change in which it is involved?

Ricoeur has pointed out that true metaphor works reciprocally—in metaphor each pole influences the meaning of the other—and one might say the same for many important words in Chinese thought whose use is typically conjoint with this or that complementary term. Unlike Western philosophy, which has tried assiduously to avoid leaning on metaphor (although it always has), Chinese philosophizing can often be characterized as ongoing metaphor, because it sees the actual processes in the world as more akin to metaphorical relations than the West has of late been willing to admit.

That words function correlatively is not an idea unknown in the West, though it has had more than one guise. Long before Saussure, it was a common and useful practice, and still is, to define a term in contrast to its privative contraries. When first undertaking this study, we thought it would be useful to apply a typical Western version of this: "nature," or "the natural," could be elucidated over against its three obvious contraries, "the supernatural," "the unnatural," and "the artificial"—a device we have occasionally used in beginning philosophy classes. It is useful, if one wishes to discover just how someone is using a term, such as "nature," to get him to clarify his understanding of contrary terms. Whatever she includes under those, she excludes from the term—if she is being clear herself.

Although these three oppositions—"the supernatural," "the unnatural," and "the artificial"—proved not to be as useful for elucidating Chinese ideas of nature as was hoped, they at least show up nicely some aspects of the evolution of the concept of "nature" in modern Western thought. It was in the eighteenth century that it began to be held that "the supernatural," as a class of events or objects, was an empty class; and by the end of the nineteenth it was widely accepted, at least in academic circles, that "nature" did not need to be defined over against "supernature," since there were no supernatural events.

This has never been unanimous, however; and recently there has been a shift away from the word "supernatural" to words such as "numinous," "holy," "revelation," and "transcendence." That each of these bespeaks a significantly different understanding of "nature" in our culture is masked by the relative isolation that obtains among our different language-using communities—as, for instance, between different academic departments.

In the twentieth century, the replacement of "natural" as a clearly defined normative term has made considerable progress. In taxonomy, for example, definition of species by reference to an ideal "type-specimen" has been replaced by statistical ranges. Such development, extending into other areas, has made it difficult to maintain that anything factual is "unnatural." Thus, homosexuality has ceased, in proper academic circles, to be considered unnatural, but is taken simply to be a minority characteristic. If nothing is unnatural, another boundary for delimiting "nature" has vanished.

Even the well-established boundary between nature and "the artificial," between *physis* and *techne*, breached strikingly but temporarily by Woehler's production of artificial urea in 1828, is again stretched by laboratory production of trans-Uranic elements, which we can only postulate to exist "in nature" in supernovas. They are nevertheless still "elements," even though "artificial" elements.

This may seem like quibbling, since most folk are not aware of any unclarity when they read of "nature" in some popular publication, wherein the context is totally made up of terms about which they have the same comfortable feeling of clarity, or at least familiarity. But the translator of ancient Chinese is, by the nature of the task, dealing with terms functioning in a context that, even if not unfamiliar literarily, is not merely alien in the sense of nonnative, but far removed in time. Much of the context he or she perceives for the text must be of his or her own construction, without the controls that contemporary facts and uses provide in present situations.

To return to "the unnatural," "the supernatural," and "the artificial," it has become obvious that, useful as these may be in clarifying our own usages of "nature," when one tries to find crisp counterparts to them in ancient Chinese in order to clarify a Chinese concept of nature, one is trying to slice warm butter. A few distinctions may eventuate, but neither the knife nor the situation as a whole ends up neat. Nevertheless, at the end of this book, we shall fall back on this device as being as good as any available to our purposes.

Hierarchical Thinking

The classical Chinese society was hierarchical, and so was its worldview. It has been widely observed that basic to most Chinese thought, and especially to Confucian thought, was the assumption of hierarchy, if not bureaucracy. Keightley has traced the bureaucratic element back into Shang culture.[40] Schwartz, discussing the primacy of ancestor worship in Chinese culture, remarks that kinship roles are inevitably and naturally hierarchic.[41] Although this element has been widely noted, it is still difficult for a Westerner, as a son or daughter of the Enlightenment, with its commitment to uniformitarianism, to sense how deeply and subtly different the experience of a hierarchical world is from our own. A student of things medieval must have some grasp of this, but most of us would normally treat hierarchy as something *imposed* on an egalitarian world, and hence view it either as an arbitrary intrusion, or at best as a nonessential construct. This may cause us to miss some of its significance in thinkers for whom hierarchy *is* the structure of reality.

Xun's sense of hierarchy is evident all through the *Xunzi*, being manifested in terms of several different hierarchies: Tian, Earth, natural things; king, ministers, knights, and people; humans, animals, plants, and nonliving things; monarchy, dictatorship, precarious order, and collapse, and so forth—all of them hierarchies of value, as well as of fact. His ideal for the world was evidently one wherein the hierarchies of power and beauty were perfectly adjusted to the hierarchies of knowledge and worth. One might almost say that, for Xun, genuinely to exist was to occupy one's appropriate place in a hierarchy. The universe is made up of roles, roles are defined by LI, and LI are inescapably hierarchical.

For Xun, the very existence of Tian and Earth "embod[ies] the distinction between higher and lower." "The correct relationships between ruler and subject, father and son, elder and younger brother, and husband and wife . . . share the order of Heaven and Earth" [*pian* IX, W 36, 45]. "Two men of equal eminence cannot govern each other; two men of equally humble station cannot employ each other" [*pian* IX, W 36].

Hierarchical divisions are defined by LI: "Rites [LI] are the highest expression of the distinctions that make for order, the foundation of a strong state, the way to function with authority, the accordance of merit with reputation" [*pian* XV]. And "(By LI) Tian and Earth accord with each other, the sun and moon shine, the seasons progress," and so on down an order to "ten thousand changings without disorder" [*pian* XIX].

Hierarchy becomes especially evident in discussions of Tian, variously translated as "Sky," "Heaven," "the heavens," or (improperly, to my mind), as "nature" or "God." Tian was the Zhou name for the sky god, which they identified with the Shang deity Shangdi. This identification is often dated to the Zhou conquest, but there are indications that it was well prepared for in the Shang tradition.

There was a Shang god of "above," called "the Peak" (*yue*), giver of rain and good harvests, in opposition to the river god *ho* of "below." Both received sacrifices at the same level as Shangdi, the very ancient sky deity who apparently was also the kings' "first ancestor"[42]—a title that, from the Zhou on, was applied to Tian, also the giver of rain and good harvests. Thus, there were in the Shang good candidates for absorption into Tian.

When the mother of Zhou King Wen, a Shang princess, married into the Zhou ducal household,[43] she must surely have begun some identification of Tian with Shangdi, even if they were not already merged in Zhou thinking. No doubt she would have transmitted this identification to her child at an early age. We do not know whether the involvement of Zhou in the Shang sacrificial system, hinted at in the oracle bones, included the Di-sacrifices, but there is no reason to assume that the religious culture of the Zhou was so different from the Shang that the identification of Tian with Shangdi was a *tour de force*, rather than one of those equations of two deities so frequent in the history of religions. Allan's comment is apt: "Although various scholars have advanced the view that the theory of *tian ming* was a Zhou innovation, to the extent that such speeches were effective as propaganda, the Shang must have accepted their basic premises."[44]

Hierarchy implies significant gradations of power and dignity, and hierarchy requires a top.[45] There is no indication that in the elite culture of the Shang and Zhou any entity was more powerful or exalted than Tian-Shangdi (who was not even, like Zeus, subject to Fate). Even after centuries of euhemerization, Tian was still "the king's first ancestor," the highest possible office, and the recipient, in principle at least, of the highest ritual attentions, especially for rain and harvests. The very fact that no one but the emperor had the status (in theory) to address a sacrifice to Tian shows this.

Besides, Tian had a variety of other functions—it not only legitimated the ruler's authority (and in so doing relativized the claims of the Zhanguo "kings"), it caused the seasons, gave or withheld rain, caused Earth to bring forth, allotted spans of life, sickness and health, and success or failure. Since all these were basic to the existence and well-being of everyone, it is very unlikely that during the Zhou any general deposing or levelling of Tian down to the level of the things of nature could have proceeded as far as has sometimes been asserted.

It is this variety of functions of Tian that belies Eno's claim that the decline of the Zhou imperial authority seriously undercut the importance of Tian. His claim that "The debasement of the ruling king entailed the debasement of the ruling god"[46] might have been true if Tian had been identified as closely and exclusively with the political power as was Rome's Jupiter or the gods of Mesopotamia. But Tian's freedom to transfer the mandate was quite separate from its other functions. So long as the seasons followed one another and agriculture was possible, Tian's dignity did not depend upon the dignity of the ruling house, and so its hierarchic supremacy was not threatened merely by delay in transfer of mandate. Its *kindness* might have been questioned, for during the Warring States period it was surely at times "treating the people like straw dogs," but hardly its supremacy. After all, what alternative was there? As hierarchical thinkers in an agriculturally based society, for whom a hierarchical natural system was the ground of values, where else could they find a Highest? To put it another way, the problem of Tian in the late Zhou was a *religious* problem, not a problem *for* religion. (Our easy assumption that empirical naturalism is always a normal and ready alternative surely deserves serious questioning.)

In a cosmos unified in any great degree, even if that unification was aesthetic rather than conceptual, if Tian was the apex of the cosmic hierarchy, it would be the apex in some way of all hierarchies, whatever their degree of independence from one another. This fact made Xun's solution to the problem of "nature and morals" possible.

The Zhou Daoists, of course, in their plebeian-shamanist revolt against the existing social hierarchy, did manifest some strong antihierarchical tendencies. In particular, their rejection of the legitimacy of the civil and cultural hierarchy included a rejection of those aspects of Tian which had been held to legitimate (and to be reflected in) that system. But even they still thought in some hierarchical terms, demeaning Tian somewhat by placing the Dao above it, and granting both only the augustness of the spontaneous and communicable numinous powers of shamanism (which they sought for themselves), seen as implicit in natural processes.[47]

It seems psychologically impossible and logically improbable that a thinker so fundamentally and intensely hierarchical as Xun Qing would readily embrace an antihierarchical tendency in philosophy of nature unless he could see some advantage to it for ethics or social philosophy. But even when he distinguishes natural from human affairs, he always maintains an analogy between the two hierarchies, as we shall show, and a claim of a basic holism in their interrelation. So, in his one reference to Zhuangzi ("Zhuangzi was infatuated with Tian and did not understand humanity") in *pian* XXI, he not only is not commending Zhuang's thought, but implying that even the latter's understanding of Tian was vitiated by the one-sidedness of his perceptions (something he explicitly applies to "Laozi" at the end of the *Tian lun*).

Xun Qing was a systematic thinker, though not in the sense applicable to the great system builders of the West. The architectonics of his thought are implicit, but deserve explication. Some of his basic principles he of course shared with any Chinese philosopher, such as those implicit in the language (even in the later Mohists, despite their movement toward more nominalistic discourse) or in the extant styles of argument. Some others were equally rooted in the common ancient Chinese heritage, but made distinctively Xun's own in emphasis or in their relation to one another, and one may ask whether they have been sufficiently noted.

Three of his emphases—one could say his fundamental metaphysical commitments—may be taken as determining his position, given the world of his times as he observed it. First of all, like any Confucian, he had a deep commitment to order, though that commitment led him to positions that caused him to be seen eventually as a heretic within Confucianism. His idea of order was certainly not one of tight logical entailment, nor was it one of machinelike reticulation. As one more involved with "concepts by intuition" than "concepts by postulation,"[48] whose thinking never lost its rootage in a perception of the world as structured by metaphor, his idea of order was correlative, moral, and aesthetic. His most commonly used word for evil, *luan*, "disorder," points to what is disjunctive, immoral, and ugly.

A corollary to his commitment to order is apparent in his treatment of the orderly as in some sense the more real—the ancients could be models for the present because there was more order in the ancient world. Then, relationships were clearly defined, words were used properly, institutions were so ordered as to appear divine, and the classics possess their status to the extent they reveal that order and are capable of creating order in the scholar. The reverse side of this was his certainty that disorder—as he saw it, immoral and unaesthetic—was alien to the real character of the universe.

"Tian has its seasons, Earth has its fecundity, The Man has his setting-in-order function—these make it possible for them to make up a perfectly aligned threesome." The cosmos is a process wherein Earth produces its riches in response to the regular course of Tian, and should do so consistently, without causing disorder or harm. Natural changes and transformations should be the dynamic manifestations of an overall harmony, each action engendering its appropriate response.

Empirically, however, it is clear that this does not always happen. Committed to a principle that human disorder is a human responsibility, he refuses to lay its cause upon either Tian or the lower-echelon activities of *yin* and *yang* or the myriad things. Does the blame for disorder in nature lie with humans also? If not, why isn't the natural cosmic harmony perfectly evident? He refuses to assert, with the Daoists, that whatever is, is the natural order. In his lifetime, it was not orderly enough.

Xun's commitment to order manifests itself on nearly every page. His favorite word for governing was not *zheng* 政,[49] "government" or "to correct by law, force, or sanctions," but *zhi* 治, "to manage," "to put in order," "to heal." This contrasts with *luan*, "disorder," often juxtaposed to *zhi* as its opposite. It is striking that the *Mencius* uses the former once every 900 words or so, the latter once every 2400; whereas for the *Xunzi* the figures are every 240 and 390 words, more or less. Part of the difference is undoubtedly due to the narrative style of the *Mencius*, but that difference is nevertheless impressive.

Xun has other words for order and especially disorder; for instance, he uses 52 times the word *jian*, often translated "lewd" or "lewdness" because the graph pictures three women, but in its meanings of "traitorous" or "villainous" implying also breaches of order. He applies it to men, hearts, business, speech, and theories, often with emphasis and even relish. Xun lived in an age of social disorder, but so did the Daoists. His sense of the need for overall order, and of the threat of disorder, goes far beyond theirs, and is much more structural in content.

This bent toward order is reflected in his uses of the word *li*, (88 times in the *Xunzi*). Often translated "principle," it has in fact many uses, all of them rooted in the idea of an inherent order or the process of actualizing such an order. It may refer to the grain in wood or to the broadest cosmic order, as when Xun says, "Without the Junzi (the truly ordered person), Tian and Earth will not be orderly" (*pian* IX). The order *li* points to is inherent and basic; it is not just a tidy distribution of things or parts, but represents, in a way, what a thing is when it properly relates to its self and its situation in the cosmos (and, often, when it functions for the orderly good of humans). These two things involve one another, for in Chinese thought everything is what it is by virtue of external relations as well as internal ones (unlike things in Aristotle, where each being has its own "that which it continuingly was to be" (*to ti en einai*).

From the standpoint of the thing itself, this "essence," if one may call it that, this "what it is when it is really functioning as what it is," Xun, along with his contemporaries, may call *jing*, (sometimes written as *ching*). Again, unlike Aristotle and the West since Aristotle, this is not understood as formulable in a definition. In fact, it is not an object of formulation at all, but one of reference. One may "lose a thing's *jing*" (*pian* XVII) if it is not fitted into one's world properly, but where it should fit can be seen clearly only by sages, and can be learned only by one who follows closely in their footsteps.

That things were not in their proper places was abundantly evident in Xun's time, and there was no evidence that any current attempts to straighten out matters could do better than achieve the second-rate stopgap success of a "lord protector" or dictator. No natural amending process was apparent, certainly. Then must it be that Tian is unable to order nature? That would go against two other basic commitments, to hierarchy and to leadership. Hierarchy demands that Tian, the apex of hierarchy, move toward order. Leadership demands the possibility that there be some agent to bring such order about. And there must be such possibility, since there have been orderly ages, under sages, in the past.

As one who honored the regal past, Xun could not see the world except in terms of hierarchy, but the hierarchic structures he traced in the world were not perfectly congruent with the picture of the world held by his contemporaries. Further, his commitment to the principle of leadership led him into utterances that subsequent generations, especially recent ones, have systematically misconstrued.[50] The relation of leadership to achievement and maintenance of hierarchical order is what the *Tian lun* is all about.

One last note: frequently, in reading expositions of Xun Qing's thought, one finds what appear to be instances of what one of my revered philosophy professors liked to call the "nothing-but fallacy." That consists in trying to draw from a statement of the sort "A is B" the conclusion that "A is nothing but B." Thus, it does not follow from Xun's treating rituals as having psychological efficacy that he is claiming they have no other efficacies, or that, in saying a sacrifice is to be looked upon as a proper form, he is affirming that it is no more than a proper form.

This fallacy seems to arise most often under either of two sets of circumstances: where there is an antecedent expectation that the speaker will be reductionist, or where the reader would welcome such reductionism. Because traditionally he bore the label of being a maverick Confucian and a denier of the sanctities of Mencian orthodoxy, Xunzi was in the past usually in the first category; bearing the more recent conventional interpretation of being "naturalistic" in ways perceived to be attractively modern, he has lately been often in the second. Determining to what extent interpretation of Xunzi has committed the "nothing-but" fallacy may not be an easy task, but it is one that should be attempted.

4. The Text of the Tian Lun

The *Xunzi* consists of 32 *pian*, usually bound into 20 *quan*, or volumes (the history of this division need not concern us here). These *pian* range in size from more than 4600 words in *pian* XI to fewer than 600 in *pian* XXX. The entire corpus comes to about 75,000 words (Sima Qian credited Xun with "a number of tens of thousands"[1]), giving a mean size of slightly more than 2300 words per *pian* as we have them. The *pian* entitled *Tian lun* represents the median size of about 1700 words, and is situated in the middle of the corpus, the seventeenth of the 32. This centrality is no doubt pure accident, as the books have appeared in somewhat different order in different editions, including Liu Xiang's original one.

Pian XXVII to XXXII have been considered, at least since Yang Liang in A.D. 818, as materials most probably collected by Xun's pupils. Certainly, the last part of *pian* XXXII dates from at least a generation after Xun's death. There is no way of knowing whether any of the rest of this material comes from the pen of Xun Qing. Much of it consists of the kind of didactic stories that could well have been a large part of Xun's teaching material with his students. Not much of the same kind of narrative occurs in the earlier parts of the *Xunzi*; there, he often refers to such events without recounting the narrative, apparently assuming his hearers or readers were familiar with the story. This gives the main part of the corpus a more formal character than is found in these later *pian*.

Opinions differ as to how much of *pian* I to XXVI was written by Xun himself; no consensus appears on the horizon. Some would treat the whole corpus as a collection from a number of hands; others see no grounds for questioning more than a little. Nor is there agreement as to the order of writing. The most ambitious attempt at a chronology in a Western language is that of Knoblock,[2] who tentatively accepts the first 26 *pian* as from Xun, and distributes them in groups over several different periods of Xun's life as he reconstructs it. Knoblock has drawn together a great deal of useful evidence that cannot be ignored, but his use of that evidence is on occasion not convincing, especially at those points where he uses his dating of writings to support his theory of Xun's philosophical development, and then uses that theory to confirm his dating. This is made necessary, of course, by the lack of any external evidence for dating many of the *pian*. The only alternative to so precarious a chronology would be to abide with only a minimal scheme, dependent on those few *pian* wherein identifiable individuals are named or wherein there seem to be clear references to establishable external events—and these last establish only *termini a quibus*. Beyond that, the interesting problem of Xun's philosophical development is at the mercy of the critic's theory as to how it must have occurred.

The history of the text of the *Xunzi* is punctuated by two critical events, through which our only significant line of transmission passes. There was, first, the imperial order to Liu Xiang, in the second half of the last century B.C., to prepare an edition of Xun's works as part of the general revival of learning of the time, and possibly as a result of extensive changes in styles of writing. In his preface to the *Xunzi* Liu recounts that he had collated 322 *pian*, discarded 290 as duplications, and published the remaining 32 as one corpus.

On the basis of this rather pat arithmetic, it has been argued[3] that these were whole essays, not fragments or scattered sections, hence the collecting of Xun's work into *pian*—for a number of *pian* contain more than one piece of work—must have been done prior to the time of Liu. Graham, indeed, ends his account of Xun Qing's life with "he settled down in Lan-ling to edit his works."[4]

It is, of course, probable that the works were collected early by Xun's followers, else they would not have been transmitted to Liu. But that the latter's sources were just 322 *pian*, which required only the setting aside of 290 duplicates, is so improbable as to be unbelievable. It is much more likely that his report to the emperor was tailored to the emperor's reading, and that Liu had to make many more extensive collatory and textual decisions than it would have been appropriate to mention in an imperial memorial. It is thus difficult to estimate how reliable the texts were with which Liu had to work, or how much of our present text received its order at his hands. We do not even know which of his sources, if any, were pre-Qin, and so written in the earlier writing styles, or the probability that any such texts survived the "burning of the books."

A few passages in the *Xunzi* reappear in other ancient texts—the *HSWC*, the *Liji*, and the *Shiji*. These parallels have been adequately noted by Chinese commentators, but their precise value in determining the text of the *Xunzi* is open to debate. None of their variant readings, however, require significant changes in the text of the essay before us.

The second event was the writing of Yang Liang's commentary in 818; all editions seem to derive from his work, although some textual corrections have been derived from extended quotations from Xun in the somewhat earlier Tang *QSZY*. Yang reported that the writings of Xunzi available to him "contained doublets, were torn, tattered, with parts missing, and showed mistakes from inaccurate copying."[5] He wrote the basic commentary upon the text, one upon which all later commentaries have been based.

It is notable that Yang's commentary does not seem to quote from, or even presuppose, previous works on the Xunzi, though he quotes from commentaries on such classics as the *Odes* and the *Liji*. Yang does in many places report a *du* (a *Qere*, or oral reading not immediately suggested by the written text), but we are never told of any written source for such *du*, and are left to wonder whether they are Yang's own proposals or ones derived from an oral tradition. Occasionally, he seems to give a quote introduced by *huo yue*, "someone says," but this may as well be read, "if someone should say," since he does not treat such sayings as having any authority. In short, we are quite in the dark as to the history of *Xunzi* scholarship before Yang Liang, save as it may be represented in occasional quotations in works devoted to other topics.

A number of scholars have labored over the text since Yang, their work culminating in the celebrated nineteenth-century edition of Wang Xian-qian, but it still cannot be said that the text has been restored. External sources are meager; Xun was not quoted extensively, and what quotations we have are not necessarily accurate. Many corrections must, in the nature of the case, be conjectural, and, of course, one scholar's conjectures may be quite unconvincing to another, since conjecture arises from predispositions. Despite this, Dubs was willing to state that "In textual criticism the work is so well done that there is nothing to be desired, but in literary criticism hardly a beginning is made."[6]

Dubs wrote over sixty years ago, and much work has been done since he wrote, both on the text and in literary criticism. As to the latter, Chinese scholars such as Guo Mo-ro and Du Guo-shang have made important contributions, as have Japanese scholars. On the text, one must note particularly the work of Liang Qi-xiung, Liu Shi-pei, Gao Heng, and the recent edition of the *Xunzi* by Li Di-sheng, which the text given here follows in important respects. We have departed from it in a few places, accepting some suggestions of others. Any such changes are indicated in the notes.

Since we are dealing only with the *Tian lun*, further remarks will refer only to that text. The greatest textual change in Li's edition is the transposition of 13 characters to a spot some 49 words earlier. This change is worth some discussion, as there is no textual support for Li's solution. There is textual evidence of disruption, as the 13 words appear displaced by as much as 50 words in at least one edition, and not every edition has the same displacement. The most widely used English translations treat the passage in different ways: Chan follows Yang's text, Watson an emendation suggested by Wang Nian-sun, whereas Dubs eliminates the problem by rejecting the 13 characters as spurious, though he gives no argument for doing so. (Fang relegates them to the notes, but comments, "The text is confused; though they belong in this locus, [these 13 graphs] must be transposed."[7] We were delighted to find that Li's solution was identical with one we had been recommending to students for a time before his edition became available. He gives no reasons, but the advantages are evident. His transposition reveals the text to contain an impressive prose poem of three cantos. In his text, the lines are not as regular as is usual in Xun's poetry, so we have made bold to excise three redundant words (one of the excisions was already suggested by Yu Yue, and one other is of the same word in an analogous place in another line). This restores perfect meter without altering the basic meaning.

As far as word-by-word emendations are concerned, we have indicated such emendations in the notes to the text that accompany the translation, omitting notes for changes which merely reflect graphic variants, short forms, or common loan words. Where only explanation and no authority is given, the changes are my own submissions, which are, in fact, very few.

As to the integrity of the text, there is no consensus. There is one section of the essay, dealing with the Junzi and the petty man, that seems oblique to the main thrust of the essay. If it were to be omitted, the argument would go on with no evident interruption. Nevertheless, its first two sentences, taken by themselves, sound as if they did, indeed, carry the argument forward, so much so that they are often quoted along with the opening sentence of the essay to demonstrate its point. Later in the section there is a distinction between "what lies with Tian" and "what lies with us" that sounds deceptively like one of the chief distinctions in the essay, though on closer examination the similarity hides a genuine difference. It is easy to see that an editor would be led to include the passage in the essay simply because of those first two sentences and that later similarity.

However, when the reader discovers that those first two sentences are actually used in a way different from what appears at first glance, a more careful look is required. Our judgment in the matter is that the section in question is not so foreign to the main argument as appears at first glance, that such digressions are not foreign to Xun's style, and that the preferable route is to see whether the interpretations of the essay as a whole and of the questionable passage can be adjusted to each other. This we believe we have done.

One may note that Eno avoids all such decisions by taking the essay to be "an agglutination of a series of semi-independent short essays . . . Some sections also might be commentary inserts"; he then draws back somewhat with "I do not mean to imply that the sections of the "Treatise" all had different authors, although some might have."[8] Many *pian* in the *Xunzi* might seem to invite a similar judgment, but only in a few cases does there seem to be scholarly agreement as to which sections should be isolated as independent. Where there is continuity of thought, as in the *Tian lun*, it would be a better method not to be hasty to divide. And, of course, even division would not mean different authorship. There are grounds for thinking Xun incorporated earlier work into later, with no concern to make the seam invisible.

Even if Eno's claim that "The preponderance of evidence . . . points toward collective authorship" of the *Xunzi* applied to the first 26 *pian* quite as much as to the last six, each *pian* would still need to be considered as a separate case. There seem to be few grounds upon which to abandon either the overall unity of the *Tian lun*, even if the author included in it some previously existing sections, or its authorship by Xun Qing.

In terms of its placement in the text, the famous poem could be called into question, since it is interpreted to have no connection with what immediately precedes or follows. Since there appears to be no other place in the essay where it would fit, and because it is widely taken to emphasize and sum up the thesis of the work, it is not surprising that the suggestion it should be excised has gotten nowhere.

As to the question of smaller interpolations, opinions differ. In Guo Mo-ro,[9] in articles in *Gushipian*, and elsewhere, the occurrence of interpolations in the *Xunzi* have been suggested, a few of them in the *Tian lun*. Some of these are unconvincing, being presented with no supporting grounds, which leads one to suspect they were questioned because they seemed to conflict with some idea the critic thought Xun must have had.

Other cases are undoubtedly to be accepted; in one case, pointed out in our commentary, it is clear that glossing has occurred. Otherwise, the text has few problems, as compared with some other *pian*.

Translators, by and large, have treated the *pian* as a single whole. A noteworthy exception is Dubs, who indicates, by breaking his translation with a row of asterisks, that he considers the discussion of Heaven to end with the much-quoted poem and its summing-up sentence. He gives no reason for so doing, but it would appear he saw insufficient continuity of argument between the main body of the essay and the two or three paragraphs that occur after the poem. Since we will discuss at some length the relevant issues in the section on the poem itself, let it suffice here to point out that the subsequent paragraphs continue the thought of the paragraph preceding the poem, so that either a more complex critical adjustment than Dubs supplies is needed, or we must interpret the poem in the light of what precedes and follows it. Taking this latter tack, we include the final paragraphs in the essay, and do not take it to close with the poem.

Dubs, indeed, separates the two final paragraphs of the essay, treating them as two distinct "loose leaves," one dealing with the importance of LI and the other giving summary criticisms of four philosophers—Shen, Lao, Mo, and Song. One could venture that Dubs found grounds for suspecting this passage because these men are criticized not for their views of nature, but for views on ambition, desire, and rank, which seem to have nothing to do with nature. However, if it can be shown that such concerns, or concerns indicated by other possible readings, could have had significance for Xun's view of Tian, the paragraphs would make a fitting conclusion for the essay. We endeavor to show that such unity does in fact obtain.

In sum, in the absence of external evidence of lack of unity, it seems most appropriate to accept the implied judgment of Liu Xiang, the initial editor of the corpus, and to treat the received essay as one whole. This requires that it be allowed to interpret itself, in that we cling to no interpretation of one part that would make another part irrelevant or inconsistent. Such difficulties as may arise from this may lead us, as we hope, into a more complex, richer, and sounder understanding of what Xun Qing was getting at.

In the course of interpreting the essay, we shall naturally refer to other parts of the *Xunzi*, for clarification or for evidence. The question of the integrity and authenticity of the whole corpus must then arise. This is no place to argue that question, but the reader is entitled to some notification of the author's beliefs in that regard, so the following may be treated as assumed for the remainder of this book.

1. The entire *Xunzi* corpus does, indeed, reflect the school of Xun Qing, who himself determined its distinctive patterns of thought, though no doubt continuing some of his own teachers' emphases (whoever they were).
2. *Pian* XXVII–XXXII represent collections of material, much of which may not be from the pen of Xun Qing (some of it certainly is not). But it is close enough to him in thought to provide significant support to arguments derived from the content of other parts of the corpus, and enough influenced by his style to provide some, though lesser, support to arguments drawn from elements of the style of the rest of the corpus. The same may be said of those sections wherein dialogues involving "Sun Qing" or "Sun Qingzi" are reported in the third person.
3. Very few of the *pian*, such as I, XVII, XXI, and XXIV, contain only one essay, in each case by Xun himself. Others, such as XIX, XX, and XXIII, are nearly of one piece, there being some small section or two appended to or included within what would otherwise be one essay. *Pian* XXV and XXVI contain clearly demarcated, separate poems, probably all by Xun Qing.
4. More than half the *pian* in the corpus contain more than one piece of work, perhaps as many as ten in *pian* VIII. Xun's authorship of some of these may well be questioned, but each section must be treated independently. Dubs was undoubtedly wrong in rejecting *pian* III wholesale, for instance, when each of the four distinct essays it contains ought to have been evaluated by itself.
5. In the absence of clearly formulated criteria for judging authenticity, we shall venture to use *pian* I–XXVI with only occasional comment as to any variation in authority they may have.

Let this be a sufficient treatment of the general question of authencity. For our purposes, it will serve to take the *Essay on Tian* as indenfying Xun Qing as 'the man who wrote this essay.' Then the question of the authenticity of the other *pian* becomes, "Were they written by the same author who wrote this one?" As indicated, this author's answer to that question would be, for the most part, a guarded and tentative "yes."

The Title

Each of the 32 *pian* in the *Xunzi* has a title, 30 of them consisting of two words each. The exceptions are *pian* XXVI, a collection of five *fu* (unrhymed poems) and three rhymed pieces, which is simply named *Fu*,

"Prose poetry"; and *pian* VI, "Against the twelve philosophers" (*Fei shier zi*), whose title could hardly be shortened. We have no way of knowing how many of these titles go back to Xun Qing himself, though some of them very likely do not. *Pian* XXVII bears the title *Da lue*, "the large miscellany," and is obviously a grab bag of literary odds and ends. The titles of *pian* VII and of *pian* XXVIII through XXXII simply repeat the first two words of the text, a practice found in the *Shi*, *Analects*, and *Mencius*. Such a practice suggests the titles were added for their usefulness to later scholars, but are not likely to have been placed there by the author himself. Of the remaining 23, 19 have titles that are more or less apt indicators of their contents (though some, like that of *pian* XXIV, require emendation), and are not dissimilar to some of the subtitles that occur within essays; at least some of them may derive from Xun himself.

The other four, *pian* XVII through XX, are in a different category. They bear titles consisting of the word *lun*, "discourse" or "discussion," preceded by a single word: *Tian*, "Heaven"; *zheng*, "correcting"; *Li*, "ritual"; and *yue*, "music" respectively. In three cases the first word of the title is the same as the first word of the text, suggesting an easy way for an editor to give a title to an untitled text; in the case of *zheng*, the word does not appear until more than one hundred words into the essay, and then it occurs only twice more in the essay. Yet the several sections that make up the essay all claim to correct errors, seven of them beginning, "This generation's sophists say. . . ," the other four beginning, "Your master Songzi says: . . . ." Nevertheless, the title, like those of the other three, does not seem to fit Xun's style of titling, as exhibited in titles undoubtedly his, nor of general titling conventions in his time.[10]

We take this to be important, for if the title does not go back to the author, and is based, even in part, on the first word of the essay, it may have created expectations that misled generations of readers as to the real subject matter of the essay. Most notable is the fact that the discussions in the essay are not chiefly about Tian, but about the conditions for successful government, the full development of human possibilities, the limits of human responsibility, moral discipline, the proper attitude toward omens and sacrifices, the necessity of following LI, and the limitations of some prominent philosophers. Tian does figure in some of these discussions, once or twice in important ways, but hardly dominates the discussion.

We conclude, in fact, that Xun Qing would be quite surprised to see the title that has been given to the work, and would reject it as a determiner of the essay's interpretation.

5. The Occasion and Argument of the Essay

The Occasion and Purpose

The essay was no doubt written in response to some specific situation, but it seems quite impossible to divine what it was. The same is true if we seek to know the intended audience or readership. Some seem to have assumed that Xun's aim was primarily polemic, against some current supernaturalisms. Comparison with the style of clearly polemical passages elsewhere in the *Xunzi* quickly convinces one that cannot be so. It may have been a response to some paper presented at the Jixia Academy, but the essay is so expository and instructional that it seems more like an address to students, or a series or collection of such addresses, possibly called forth by students' questions. The story of Confucius and Zilu in *pian* XXVIII suggests a possible such scenario, if Xun were ever in a position similar to Confucius', as one passage in the essay might be taken to suggest he was.

Another suggestion is that some ominous event had triggered speculation that a new universal king was about to appear. By Mencius' time it had already been long evident that the Heavenly Mandate of the Zhou dynasty had run out. It is not hard to believe that the arrogation of the title king (*wang*) by the Warring States' rulers reflected some hopes on the part of each of them that they might gain that mandate, although their behavior rarely fitted the sagely requirements for dynasty founding that Confucian ideology advanced. Regarding such omens, Allan notes,

> Their [Jie and Zhou's] punishment, as in the Mengzi and the *Xunzi*, is Heaven-sent. But [in the Mozi] although the people wished to be

> ruled by Tang and Wen Wang and went to them, Heaven's will is demonstrated by supernatural omens rather than by the movement of the people. . . . At the end of the bad king's rule, for example, there were such ill omens as eclipses of the sun and moon, earth raining from the sky, ghosts moving about, the nine cauldrons changing places, and brambles growing in the roads (5/11b–13a, in SBCK).[1]

If the belief of the majority of even literate Chinese during the late Zhou was closer to that of Mozi on this point than to that of Mencius or Xunzi—which seems likely—it is reasonable to assume that any striking natural phenomenon would generate the question: Is it an omen of a new dynasty?

Available records of natural calamities for the third century B.C. are inadequate, but the Han era is better represented, and we can assume that the natural patterns did not change greatly with political change. Kirby cites Han records showing that between 200 and 7 B.C. there were 25 major floods, 12 major locust plagues; 9 epidemics, two of which involved the whole empire and lasted 13 and 5 years respectively; and 27 droughts, some involving the whole empire—a major natural calamity every 2.6 years, on average.[2] Zhou experience could hardly have been different. Such events must have caused suffering and disruption, and, along with the normal occurrence of eclipses, would naturally have been viewed as evidence of Tian's displeasure. In so indeterminate a political situation, they would also have spurred expectations of more positive indications of Tian's favorable disposition toward some new candidate for power.

Such a situation could well underlie several of Xun's emphases in this essay: the focusing on flood, drought, and epidemic in connection with Tian's Dao in the opening section and the discussion of rain sacrifices and eclipses later on; his emphasis on the distinction between humanly relevant and humanly irrelevant omens; his repeated rejection of any seeking to understand the ways of Tian, his characterization of doing so as "yearning," his relegating of concern for it, if at all, to underlings, not rulers; and possibly the striking departure from his usual modes of argument, namely, the patent lack of reference to any historical events or persons, other than the fundamental examples of Tian's appointment or rejection of Yao, Yu, and Jie.

Further, the fact that the prime candidate for supremacy was Qin, only a partial prospect by Xun's criteria (it encouraged agriculture and was frugal, but it did not foster LI) would account for his shift from the bald, bipolar Yao/Jie and Yu/Jie contrasts early in the essay to his more graduated scale later, when preparing to sum up. Qin could at best produce a Lord Protector, never one bearing Tian's mandate, a true king. His closing emphasizes that the latter would have to be committed to the whole Dao, the entire LI, implying what he says elsewhere more than once: to be a true king, it is the moral prerequisites that matter.

Such a suggestion assumes that the essay was primarily addressed to the question of omens, and impressive ones at that. But the actual discussion of omens starts from insignificant ones—a meteor or a tree noise, and never touches on the question of political succession, except to suggest, in a way not uncommon in the *Xunzi*, that, with suitable moral development, one may become a king, a dictator—or a failure. When he does deal with omens at some length, it is to stress the importance of omens clearly traceable to human causes, omens that portend doom.

Speculation as to what prompted the *Tian lun* thus seems fruitless. We can only guess what the occasion was. The situation for which Xun wrote, whatever it was, seems to have posed in some detail the questions: Which actions of men bring about a response in nature? Which omens are signs of Tian's response to human ways and actions? What effects do human actions, including ceremonial acts, have on natural events? What pattern of human action results in the optimum harmony between nature and humanity? Also implied is the issue between Xun on the one hand and Mencius on the other: what part does the natural process of birth and growth, *sheng*, have in establishing this harmony?

Place and Date of Writing

Even if one should see the essay as a response to some outburst of speculation following a series of prodigies or calamities interpreted as presaging a new dynast, that would not require us to put it after the final dissolution of the Zhou (249 or 256). That the Zhou line had forfeited the Mandate had been so evident for so long the point was not so much Zhou's loss as the unidentifiability of a successor.

As already noted, Knoblock has presented by far the most detailed chronology for Xun Qing's life available in English, one that takes into account a great deal of evidence. He would place the writing of the *Tian lun* between 275 and 265, when Xun was at the Jixia academy.[3] Such a date is reasonable as an absolute date, despite the fact that neither internal nor external evidence gives us much grounds for it. Indeed, dating of the essay must rely almost wholly on subjective judgments regarding the development either of Xun's style or of his thought, and disagreement with Knoblock on either point could lead to a different dating of the work.

One may, however, dispute on evidence Knoblock's placement of the *Tian lun* relative to Xun's other works. Thus, in *pian* XXI, which Knoblock places considerably earlier, Xun says, "Because Zhuangzi was prejudiced toward Tian he did not understand humanity," the only mention of Zhuangzi in the corpus. Knoblock takes this to indicate an early date, without giving any convincing reason. We do not know when Xun first heard of Zhuangzi—the *Zhuangzi* was not edited until long after Xun's death, and we know not what currency any of his ideas may have had at the Jixia. Xun's judgment in *pian* XXI would be so appropriate to the main thrust of the *Tian lun* it is hard to see why Xun did not include it there also—unless he had not yet heard of Zhuangzi. This would place the *Tian lun* before the *Jiebi* (*pian* XXI). Even this is a tenuous argument from silence, and, having abandoned Knoblock's chronology to that extent, we would still have no clear placement for it.

Knoblock allows considerable weight to his thesis that Xun's use of "the later kings" signifies later work than his use of "the former (or early) kings." In the *Tian lun*, however, we meet only with "the hundred kings," which includes both. We must conclude that dating the essay is a subjective process, though one might argue that the somewhat pejorative reference to the king of Chu suggests that Xun was not dwelling in Chu when he wrote it. One must be content with accepting Knoblock's suggestion of a Qi provenance.

The General Problem

In *pian* XIX (*Li lun*), Xun says,

> How can LI not be perfection? By it Tian and Earth proceed in harmony, the sun and moon shine, the four seasons pass in order, the stars and constellations make their orbits, the rivers flow, the myriad things prosper, likes and dislikes are disciplined, joys and angers are made appropriate; by it inferiors are made obedient and superiors made illustrious, through ten thousand changes there is no confusion; but deviation from it results in loss. When it is abundantly established so as to be perfect, nothing in Tian or Earth will spoil it or add to it. What is basic and what is derivative are then in accord; ends and beginnings correspond to each other; things are so formally perfect that differences are intact; under exhaustive examination everything has its justification.

This is one of Xun's several descriptions of an ideal state of affairs, wherein "Tian, Earth and humanity are perfectly aligned" (*can* 參); it is, of course, a state earnestly to be desired, and can be achieved, he holds, only by complete accord with the basic elements of the LI of the sages of antiquity, applied under the conditions of one's own time. Yet this description falls into three major parts: (1) those things which operate reliably: Tian and Earth proceeding harmoniously, the sun, moon, and constellations, and the four seasons; (2) those things which occur unreliably in the lives of men: likes and dislikes being disciplined, joys and angers being appropriate, inferiors obedient and superiors illustrious; and (3) those matters in between: rivers that may overflow or cease running, plants and animals that may not prosper, dry seasons that may not be dry, rainy seasons that bring no rain, strange, once-appearing stars, and other rare events.

That the first group were reliable or routine (*chang*) was common knowledge, and Xun could argue from that common knowledge. They constituted the area wherein LI was "abundantly established" most firmly and consistently, where the "deviation from it" that "results in loss" was slight or nonexistent. That in the second group such departure and loss occurred far too extensively was a dismal reality of the Warring States period, a practical and moral problem he attacked from a number of different angles. These two groups could easily be distinguished into the things concerning Tian (as presiding over the routines of nature)—that is, things wherein Tian strictly followed its Dao, its LI; and the things concerning human moral choices, things arising from the usually disordered way humans followed, or did not follow, their Dao. If these were all, distinguishing the roles of Tian and humans would be simple.

There is, however, the third group, comprising the irregularities and whimsies of nature and their human consequences, and the ways in which activities of humans upset the LI of nature. These posed the problem of where to draw the line: what part should be assigned to Tian (or its subalterns) and what to humans and their institutions? The effects of nature upon humanity are often evident; what were the effects of humans upon nature, and which ones would accord with LI, with the Dao? The essay faces this problem squarely, though admitting it to be very resistant to solution: "He (alone) is to be called The Perfect Man who is *enlightened* regarding the role distinction between Tian and humans."

Xun does not attempt to make clear to us where the precise distinctions lie; that would require both his being a sage and his turning us into sages, since only the sage can be clear about these things. He argues instead for the importance of the distinctions, and for our dependence on the sages for being able to conform to them, even though we cannot clearly understand them. Thus, discussion of the roles of humans and nature can only be, in the last analysis, a discussion of the importance of LI. Strange as this may seem to us, for whom philosophy of nature and philosophy of ritual have no apparent contact, it is the only way to make sense of the essay's wholeness.

It is clear that once we have discerned this three-part division, the question of whether to refer to Tian as "nature" has become complicated. When all is "aligned" so that *yin* and *yang* and the myriad things properly respond to Tian's Dao, so that they follow their own Dao harmoniously, all that is not human may be safely referred to as "nature"; but when there are "deviant emergents among things" and "portents arising among things from human disturbances," what we speak of as "nature" is not one system, but contains its own disorders, which cannot be removed in the absence of a sage, or at least a Junzi who "does nothing contrary to LI" (and so acts as a quasi-sage).

The Course of the Argument

Xun's first major thesis is, "It is disastrous to respond inappropriately to Tian's following of its Dao." He exhibits this by using the standard contrast between sage Yao and villain Jie. The one prospered, the other was destroyed, but neither event represented any special action on the part of Tian, whose supervision of the stars and seasons continued unchanged (Tian's *xing*). Jie failed properly to respond to Tian in the necessary way—following LI, that is, which fends off baleful spiritual influences, and which includes especially encouraging agriculture, which wards off famine, and concern for the people, which prevents epidemics. (For Xun, following LI includes both of these, just as famine and epidemic are included in "baleful spiritual influences.") As a result, starvation, illness, and harm inevitably resulted. Yao responded correctly in all these ways, with opposite results.

In these extreme cases, natural variables did not matter. If Tian (in its variable functions) sent flood or drought, extreme heat or cold, or baleful omens, Yao would still survive; if Tian sent instead the most salubrious conditions, Jie would still fall. Thus, these variables are not *sufficient* conditions for survival or destruction. (Xun does not mention until later the obvious fact that most cases would be intermediate between Yao and Jie, and in such cases these variables would certainly be causes contributory to success or failure.) Thus, it was a clear demonstration of the sagehood of Yu and Tang that the ten years of flood under the former and the seven years of drought under the latter did not bring the sorts of hardship they might have under a ruler only slightly less accomplished.[4]

Xun next addresses in more general terms the role distinction between humans and Tian, which only the "perfect man" can completely understand. He specifies Tian's part first. The "responsibilities" (*zhi*) of Tian, he states, are "to bring things to maturity without any special action, to confer benefits[5] without being besought"—Tian acting in its supreme *wu-wei*. The "perfect man" does not intrude upon or investigate Tian's work, but rather leaves Tian to its seasons and Earth to its fecundity, while he concentrates on the human task, doing his part to enable the three—Tian, Earth, and humans—to get into alignment. Not to do so would be to be delude oneself. (It is worth noting that Xun does not say humans must align themselves with a perfectly operating Tian-Earth pair. What goes on between Tian and Earth also needs aligning.)

Tian's working is spiritual and invisible; by it seasons pass, the myriad things spring up and mature. (Earth is not mentioned; apparently it, as *yin*, responds (*ying*) to Tian's *yang* advances (*gan*), and so participates.)

At this point appears another of Xun's topic theses: Though Tian works without any special actions, "The sage does act, he does not seek (or beseech) to understand Tian," and Xun goes on to specify such action. Though producing the human being is Tian's work, Tian provides at birth only a minimum of humanity—a body, life, emotions, senses, a mind to organize them, sustenance to choose for nurturance, and one natural prescription: accord with your species! All else depends on human action. Not to cultivate these toward a proper *telos* (as Yao did), but to disorder them (as did Jie) is disastrous.

The sage cultivates his humanity to perfection, making the work of Tian "expansively complete." Then the things of nature function perfectly; their activities are orderly, nurturing, and harmless. Only in this situation can Tian be said to be known, for it is clear that the sage's knowledge has meshed perfectly with the secrets of nature, and what he has done has harmonized with the invisible spiritual powers secrets beyond his ken and powers he cannot grasp. He knows his proper limits, that his knowledge is reasonably limited to what relates to human administration, including those parts of what we call "nature" that depend for their harmony on proper human response to Tian's initiative.

Xun has now laid out his principal theses: the only significant knowledge of Tian lies in the sages' perception of what must be done in society (which is embodied, insofar as it is available to us, in the LI-tradition), and this could be seen because under the sages the lower echelons of nature were completely responsive to Tian. Hence they functioned perfectly for humans' good (as they manifestly did not during the late Zhou, with its frequent droughts, floods, epidemics, and locust plagues).

Xun now takes up several apparent problems. Do Tian, Earth, and the seasons (the upper echelons of the cosmic hierarchy) have any relation to human order or chaos? Appealing to the examples of Yu and Jie, he argues they do not. He does not carry his argument down the cosmic hierarchy any farther than Earth, since he has already acknowledged that the myriad things may not behave, that floods and droughts, and the like, which ordinarily do bring disorder, and also untoward accidents of circumstance, do occur. He is not so much asserting the order of nature as he is locating its disorders. So he shifts back to the human functions.

The Junzi, as one developing himself toward alignment with Tian and Earth, and hence following their constancies, maintains his own constancies in the face of opposition and untoward circumstances, just as Heaven and Earth maintain their constancies in the face of human distress (the examples of human distress Xun gives are absurdly minor, compared with the actions of Tian and Earth they would require for redress). The Junzi progresses toward sagehood just because he focuses on what is within his province—what he can learn from the past and how he can discipline himself—and ignores what is in Tian's province, fortuitous "success" or "failure," mere happenstance.

The things in Tian's province include occasional unfamiliar changes (*bian*) that appear ominous, but such strange natural events, being outside the human realm, have no supernatural significance for us, and are not to be dreaded—they indicate no transgression or lapse on our part, nor any untoward consequences for us. Supernatural omens produced in more proximate nature disordered by improper human responses to Tian are, however, to be held in awe, as they presage chaos in the human realm. Thus, it is the human areas that may be disordered which should demand our attention, and the essay's rhetorical climax lies in his rhythmic intoning of these ominous signs that our misresponse to Tian calls forth, and which bode catastrophe.

This suggests a possible objection. LI prescribes a rain sacrifice in time of drought, and, when offered, it has been followed by rain. Thus LI itself apparently requires that men intervene in Tian's conduct of its work. Xun argues that Tian's beneficent action of sending rain is the same as it would be if we did not sacrifice. Rather than inviting misfortune by viewing the sacrifice as a way to get rain (and by so doing trying to meddle in Tian's area, to "compete with Tian's official responsibilities"), we should view the sacrifice as the proper formal and cultured response to drought, a way of expressing the significance of the occasion. Just as the ascending of the sun and moon signify Tian's supremacy in the hierarchy of magnificence, so the maintaining of LI and YI shows the elegance and culture of a state. Just as what happens to an individual, whom Tian has produced, depends upon Tian, so what happens to a state, produced by men, depends upon LI (including elegant rain sacrifices).

Then follows the famous poem, wherein Xun raises rhetorical questions regarding how Tian should be magnified and followed, what sort of attention should be paid to the seasons, and how one should accord with things and think about them, concluding, "How can yearning over the source of things compare with assisting what brings them to their fulfillment?"—which last is, of course, LI as cosmic harmony. "Therefore, if, neglecting human things, you ponder Tian's affairs, you will lose the very essence of things!" The celebration of LI turns into a warning about its neglect—as is frequent in Xun.

How, then, does one avoid losing that essence of things? One should take as the core of the Dao what the ancient kings found unchanging and sufficient, and apply it intelligently and thoroughly. It provides the chart for the ruler of the people, enabling pitfalls to be avoided. The many kinds of natural things represent their Daos only in part (at least until properly developed by a sage, or by following the sage's LI), and each single one only part of that. The foolish man represents only one part of one thing (not having developed himself, he is only an incomplete part of a humanity that itself needs "transforming" by the influence of a sage), and so he cannot know Dao. (Only the sage, who has "filled out" Tian's work, can fully do that; the rest of us must rely on LI.) So philosophers like Shen, Lao, Mo, and Song (all of them rejecting in one way or another the hierarchical structures basic to LI), in their arrested and hence partial development, need to conform to the Way of the Kings. Here Xun rests his case.

When the argument is so read, its continuity and progression are striking, and its coherence with the rest of the *Xunzi* more evident. Further, it does not put Xun in the un-Chinese position (prior to Buddhism) of depriving nature of its inherent value, or of setting humanity over against nature as its manipulator, with no obligation toward it. It makes the apparent alternations between speaking of nature and of LI more understandable, and undercuts the temptation to cut the essay up into poorly integrated fragments. Further, it undercuts the reading of Xun as a critic of basic Chinese supernaturalism (though it leaves him a strong critic of superstition, which is, of course, something quite different). This interpretation opens up Xun's refined sense of human involvement in the divine functioning of Tian, wherein he draws upon long-standing religious motifs in Chinese culture, but handles them in a unique and sophisticated way—which, apparently, those who came after him were not able, in their changed situation, to grasp.

We may thus outline the *Tian lun* as follows:

I. The nature and necessity of properly responding to Tian
   A. Yao and Jie as examples
      1. They got no special help from Tian
      2. Proper/improper responses the difference
      3. Tian simply follows its Dao
   B. The distinction between Tian's office and that of humans
      1. The general distinction
         a. Tian accomplishes without special action
         b. The perfect man respects the distinction
      2. The basis of possible alignment
         a. Tian's seasons
         b. Earth's fecundity
         c. Human setting-in-order
      3. Tian's seasons and Earth's fecundity
         a. Tian's *shen* creativity
         b. Tian's stopping point: humanity by nature
      4. The incompleteness of humanity by nature
   C. Human setting-in-order
      1. The crime of aborting Tian's work
      2. Its completion by sagely discipline
      3. a. The results: knowing Tian
         b. The sage knows the distinction
         c. The myriad things behave
         d. Limits to what the sage does

II. Four questions
   A. What do Tian and Earth have to do with order/disorder?
      1. Tian: nothing
      2. Seasons: nothing
      3. Earth: nothing
      4. (Quotation from *Odes*)
   B. Why isn't the Junzi favored by Tian?
      1. Tian and Earth aren't swayed by trifles
      2. The Junzi imitates their consistency

        a. External achievements lie with Tian
        b. Internal progress lies with us
    C. What about omens?
        1. Omens strictly in Tian's realm
            a. Things there deviate
            b. Such are not to be feared
        2. Omens precipitated by humans to be feared
            a. Eighteen examples
            b. Don't study them, work at LI
    D. What about rain after sacrifices for rain?
        1. No special Tian act involved
        2. Rites not manipulative, but celebrative
        3. Celebration is part of the cosmic pattern
            a. Sun and moon celebrate Tian
            b. Fire and water celebrate Earth
            c. Pearls and jade celebrate rank
            d. LI and Yi celebrate good government

III. LI as summary of all the above
    A. A poem celebrating the proper way of alignment of Tian, Earth, humans—that is, LI
    B. The LI of the Kings as the Way
        1. LI requires full application
        2. LI functions as a guide
        3. Incomplete philosophies won't do
            a. Four who fail
            b. (Quote from *Documents*)

6. On the Translation

The only translation to date of the entire *Xunzi* into a Western language has been that into German by Hermann Köster.[1] At times Köster's translation approaches paraphrase, and it has been considered tendentious (as every translation is, to some degree), but it wrestles valiantly with a number of difficult passages. Large parts of the corpus (approximately one-half in each case) have been translated into French by Belpaire, and into English by Dubs. Both need to be superseded.[2] When the third volume of Knoblock's complete translation appears, there will be available a careful, scholarly, and well annotated edition of the entire corpus in English, which seems worthy to supersede all previous translations for general scholarly work. However, we unabashedly offer our alternate translation of this one tractate as needing no apology in the face of Knoblock's weighty scholarship, on the grounds that it may present an alternative reading of the *Tian lun* that deserves consideration on its own merits.

Besides its appearance in the works mentioned, the *Tian lun*, as a single essay, has been translated into English a number of times. It appears among the ten essays translated by Watson and the three translated by Chan, both often alluded to in this book because of their wide availability and widespread use. There are also translations by Chai and Chai and by Eno, and a translation of about half the essay by Hughes.[3] All these have been consulted, as have many of the translations of significant passages from the *Xunzi* that appear in various secondary works.[4] References to some of these appear in both text and notes.

The present translation does not claim to be in any way a final correction of all or any of these translations, or that it should supersede them. Explanation of what it does claim to do must wait upon discussion of some aspects of the enterprise of translation itself.

The translator faces a text presented in a source language, and endeavors to produce a text in the target language that responsibly represents the original text. The original text contains ambiguities and elements of vagueness, as any text does. In the case of ambiguities, he or she must choose those alternatives which represent, in his or her judgment, what the author was trying to convey. In the case of vagueness, the translator should ideally present in the target language the same range of vagueness as he or she finds in the source. Languages being what they are, neither of these desiderata can be satisfied. In neither case ought the translator, without giving his or her readers sufficient warning, obscure, in the interests of clarity, those ambiguities and vaguenesses; nor should he or she introduce new ones where none were previously. These requirements cannot be satisfied, either. Thus, every translator, as the Italian saying goes, is a traitor to the original text: *traduttore e traditore*.

In the case of a modern language, the translator can at least find an informed native speaker of the source tongue to criticize her work. In the case of Archaic Chinese, that is simply not the case. Even Chinese of the old school, steeped in the Classics and in later literary Chinese, lived in a pool of language that melded the pre-Han dialects into one homogenized whole, which then went through a long evolution into classic literary and documentary Chinese.[5] Systematic knowledge of ancient grammar is still struggling to be born.[6] When an outstanding Western sinologist says,

> None of us yet knows classical Chinese . . . every word of even late literary Chinese seems a little vaguer than it really is. Again, we know too little about Chinese grammar . . . how can we tell whether it is a vague language or not?[7]

one less accomplished than he is tempted to throw up his hands.

Apropos of translating from Chinese into English, I. A. Richards remarks,[8] "The process becomes very complex. We have here indeed what may very probably be the most complex type of event yet produced in the evolution of the cosmos."

Richards goes on to list seven "sorts of work an utterance may be doing" such as indicating, characterizing, influencing, and the like. His list would have been longer had he not neglected the insights of existentialist philosophers, and not written before the work of J. L. Austin became widely known. Each of these "sorts of work" poses a separate question "we can ask of two utterances in two languages," and "any full utterance does all these things at once, and invites all of them in the comprehender."

It is clear the translator can rarely give satisfactory answers to the questions raised by all these various functions of language. We can only labor with a text in a way commensurate with our powers. A text presents two important limits; first, what the text requires, which one cannot transgress without omitting some of the straightforward significance of the text and its context. Second, what the text permits, beyond which one cannot go without adding something of one's own that is not supported by either text or context. The distance between these two limits varies from text to text, from sentence to sentence. The constraints in both cases are those of the author's words and syntax, and the context.

The meticulous academic is tempted to skate close to the safe shore of what the text requires, as the ice gets progressively thinner as he or she ventures into what the text may allow. The traditions of the "defensible translation" thus tend always toward the "most probable" reading of a word, or of the grammar of an ambiguous word order or particle, and toward that reading of the context to which one's discipline has habituated itself. It is rash to go against the conventional wisdom of one's own discipline, and there is good reason for not doing so. But the good of the discipline itself requires that occasionally someone should be maverick, and test the extreme limits of skatable ice.

Thus, the aim of this translation is to test how far a translation of the *Tian lun* can stray, in at least one direction supported by the rest of the *Xunzi*, from the accepted understanding of the essay, without transgressing the decencies of our present knowledge of pre-Qin vocabulary and grammar or the historic probabilities of what Xun Qing was likely to believe and wish to say. The former boundaries are clearly more objective than the latter. We have enough pre-Qin literary works to have established a high probability of reliability in our assays of word uses, and the grammar of most sentences, even when apparently ambiguous, presents clear-cut choices that exclude most other suggestible readings as impossible. *Hapax legomena* and anomalous sentences are few. The translator cannot be too venturesome in these areas, and we have, we believe, been responsible. Wherever we read an uncommon word use or claim other-than-obvious syntax, we supply justification from relevant literature.

The boundaries set by "what Xun Qing was likely to believe and wish to say" are much more subjective. The rest of the *Xunzi*, or at least those parts of it we can defensibly ascribe to Xun Qing, provide a control, but one that is itself subject to some of the same instabilities. Many things that might be read in the *Tian lun* are not touched upon elsewhere in the corpus; parallels in wording sometimes raise problems of their own, and the interpretation of some of the context can be affected by one's reading of the essay itself. Such problems are noted and our solutions given some justification in the notes.

As for the wider, historical context, it was a time of such a welter of ideas that any interpretation of Xunzi, even one assuming he was not a creative thinker and only selected from options presented to him, must place him within that context only in terms of what the interpreter finds in the *Xunzi*. We have tried to ascribe no ideas to Xun Qing that are inconsistent with that book, or would have been out of place in his milieu, as far as we can reconstruct it.

At one point, however, we have disagreed with part of a widely accepted version of that reconstruction. As already stated, we are committed to a "hermeneutic of suspicion" regarding our own modern tendency, based on the Enlightenment, to assume a natural "convergence toward naturalism" whenever thinking folk face difficulties in their traditional ideas. Such an assumption runs the dangers of overinterpreting some evidences and underinterpreting others, of underestimating the flexibility and fertility of inherited moral and religious ideas, and of oversimplifying the complexity of ideologically disturbed times. It also bespeaks taking an oversimple account of the intellectual history of the West to be some kind of universal norm.

The aim of so testing the boundaries was not merely experimental, but to make available to the Western philosopher interested in Asian or comparative philosophy, but not schooled in Chinese, an alternate reading of the *Tian lun* to enrich her own philosophical fertility. Also in view was the expectation that our work will meet with considerable criticism (let it not merely be ignored!) of value to the disciplines concerned.

In terms of standard translation theory, our version aims to be "dynamic" rather than "formal".[9] Except for keeping *Tian* and *Li* as "Tian" and "LI," there is no attempt to use only one English word for a given Chinese word, or to maintain as closely as possible the original order of words, or even of clauses. However, where a given word in one part significantly echoes the same word somewhere else, we have often not only used the same English word, but taken notice of the echoing.

The reader deserves to know our authorities. The text is our own, based upon Yang Liang (in the SBBY ed.), Wang Xianqian, Liang Qixiung, and Li Disheng, with a few emendations from Gao Heng, Liu Shipei and, rarely, others. These last are noted and reasons given. Other commentaries consulted are listed in the bibliography, and occasionally in the notes. Lexical work is based on Karlgren's *Grammata Serica Recensa*, *Cihai*, *Zhonghua Dazidian*, Schuessler, and the *Kangxi Zidian*; any other sources are noted. Extensive use has been made of the Harvard-Yenching concordance to check usage in the rest of the *Xunzi*, especially in *pian* I–XXVI, which have a reasonable case for their authenticity; and of sister concordances to other Zhou works as cited.

7. Translation and Commentary

The reader who has a limited command of Chinese may find it valuable to read this translation along with any of the more standard ones—Knoblock, if available; otherwise Watson, Chan, or Dubs—noting significant differences. Such will make the cogency of much of the commentary more apparent. It is, however, designed also to be read as it stands, with or without the commentary.

Since the title has been rejected as both a later addition and misleading, we do not translate it here.

[The nature and necessity of properly responding to Tian.]

1. As Tian maintains the constant routines of the heavenly bodies, it did no special act toward Yao's survival, nor toward Jie's fall. 2. If one [a ruler, such as Yao] responds [to Tian's initiative] by setting things in a proper order, good fortune follows. If one [a ruler, such as Jie] responds to it with disorder, misfortune follows.

3. If [a ruler], after encouraging agriculture, is frugal in use [of its produce], Tian then finds no occasion to impoverish. If, providing ample food, he requires labor only at the right times, then Tian finds no occasion to send epidemics. If, having cultivated Dao, he does not deviate from it, Tian then finds no occasion to chastise. 4. Hence flood and drought could not cause the people to starve,* nor could heat or cold cause them illness, nor uncanny occurrences bring them misfortune.

*Omit ko 渴 with *HSWC*.

5. IF [ANOTHER RULER SUCH AS JIE], NEGLECTING AGRICULTURE, IS PRODIGAL WITH ITS PRODUCE, THEN TIAN WILL HAVE NO OCCASION TO CAUSE HIM TO PROSPER. IF, BEING CARELESS REGARDING NECESSITIES, HE DEMANDS LABOR AT UNSEASONABLE* TIMES, THEN TIAN WILL HAVE NO OCCASION TO MAKE HIM AFFLUENT. IF, TURNING AWAY FROM THE DAO, HE BEHAVES FOOLISHLY, THEN TIAN WILL HAVE NO OCCASION TO BRING ABOUT BLESSINGS. 6. HENCE, HIS STATE WILL UNDERGO FAMINE, EVEN IF FLOOD OR DROUGHT HAVE NEVER YET ARRIVED; IT WILL SUFFER SICKNESS, EVEN IF [EXTREME] COLD OR HEAT HAVE NEVER YET OPPRESSED; THERE WILL BE MISFORTUNE, EVEN IF NO UNCANNY PHENOMENA HAVE YET ARISEN.**

7. SO, WHEN THE SAME SEASONS VISIT HIM AS VISIT A WELL-ORDERED AGE, BUT HE SUFFERS MISFORTUNES QUITE FOREIGN TO THE WELL-ORDERED, HE MUSTN'T BLAME TIAN FOR IT—ITS DAO IS JUST WHAT IT IS.

As Tian maintains constant routines for the heavenly bodies (*Tian xing you chang*)—literally, "Tian's course has its constancy"; *xing* 行, "course," is defined in *pian* XXII, "Rectifying Names," as "When we act on the basis of profit, it is called 'business' (*shi*), when on the basis of rightness (YI), it is called *xing*." *Xing* may receive two interpretations: (1) since in the *Xunzi*, it always (as a noun) is predicated of a moral or quasi-moral agent,[1] it could reasonably be read "(moral) conduct"; (2) in this one apparent exception in the *Xunzi*, in both the *Odes* and the *Documents*, and occasionally in the *Guanzi* and the *LSCQ*,[2] it pertains to heavenly bodies or to the seasons, and clearly means "courses." Since in most cultures, even in the West prior to the Enlightenment, the heavenly bodies were considered moral beings, there is no problem in reading *xing* as having both meanings here. Their constancy (*chang*) is a moral constancy quite as much as a behavioral one (*chang* often has a moral content). The question here is whether Xun intends the constancy of the *xing* to extend farther down the hierarchy of nature than the seasons. In light of what he says later, we think not. Lower echelons of the cosmic hierarchy *respond* to Tian's *xing*, but they are not part of it. There is thus no uniformitarian constancy throughout all of "nature" affirmed here.

The motions of the sun and stars, and the like, are Tian's visible *xing*, and their constancy has been apparent to every people; other effects of

---

*Read *ni* 逆 for *han* 罕, with Yu and Liu.

**Read sheng 生 for zhi 至, with *QSZY*.

Tian, such as determining the lifespan of individuals, would be invisible or at least more subtle, and *chang*, "constant," would be less applicable to them. Two significant consequences follow if Xun is speaking thus only of the heavenly bodies: (1) Xun is not making a novel claim about "Heaven's constancy," but is merely acknowledging what everyone in an agricultural society already knows; (2) Tian's *xing* does not include sublunary processes that might still be part of Tian's Dao, so that, contrary to commentators, *Tian xing* is not necessarily a precise equivalent to *Tian dao*; and (3), he is not making a statement regarding "Nature" as a whole, or enunciating any kind of nonmoral or deterministic "natural law" idea. Both these last imply that 'Tian' ought not be translated, at least here, as 'Nature,' attractive as that may seem to us. (4) The argument that follows must treat "floods and drought," and such, as falling outside Tian's *xing*, though produced by it, but not in any deterministically bound way. (This will be argued through later.)

However, even if one takes *xing* not to be so restrictive, but to include any process set in motion by the motions of Tian, the moral dimension of "walk" or "pattern of behavior" is still present. Nothing in the *Xunzi* asserts that Tian is *nonpersonal*, "having neither will nor thought," though much suggests that it, like any high bureaucrat, may be *impersonal* in the unswerving discharge of its duties (see p. 170f).

The usual translations, such as Graham's "Heaven has a constant course, neither maintained for sage Yao nor abandoned for tyrant Chieh,"[3] seem obvious but are questionable. (1) In the 26 *pian* of presumable authenticity, Xunzi parallels *cun*, "to survive" and *wang*, "to be destroyed," some 22 times, as applied to the survival or destruction of rulers or reigns, and often uses them separately to apply to such, but their linking as "maintenance/abandonment" of some process does not occur; (2) Yao and Jie (along with Shun and Yu, and occasionally Tang and Zhou Xin) are standard examples of rulers who survived or who were destroyed. These two stylistic facts make it extremely unlikely that he did not mean *cun* and *wang* to have Yao and Jie for their subjects. Also, (3) since it would make little sense to say that Tian "abandoned" its *xing*, as that should imply moral defection from its proper office, there would also not be much point in denying it.

(4) *Wei* is used more than once later in the essay to mean "specially act" or "act in behalf of" (as it does in the Daoist *wu-wei*, and Xun appears to be arguing against Daoism, among other things, in this *pian*), and that use fits well here. The contrast is between acting specially or exceptionally and following an established *xing*. Yao's security or Jie's downfall did not involve special heavenly events; they were grounded, if

in Tian at all, in its consistent general operations. (Yao and Jie here are hardly individuals; they are types of administration.) Xun neither affirms nor denies here (or anywhere else) the moral will or the moral involvement of Heaven, but here he does deny any preferential or *ad hoc* willings, at least in so important a matter as dynasty-maintenance. Tian, in short, in its astronomical functions, follows *wu-wei* perfectly, as befits that which is exalted—though, of course, it is the Confucian version of *wu-wei*.

Finally, (5) such a translation misses the logical point that Xun is arguing *from* Tian's constancy, not *to* it. He is arguing *to* the need for orderly governing according to LI (in his very broad sense of the latter); to do so he must assume his audience readily accepts the premise that Tian follows a constant course. In any agricultural society, nature's astronomical orderliness is at least as noticed as are the frequent meteorological disorders (which Xun also acknowledges as "flood, drought, heat, cold"). He clearly assumes such order need only be called to mind; it needs no argumentative support, nor does he give any. To take Tian's constancy to be a thesis he is offering for consideration is (1) to read him as doing what he explicitly disavows, speculative theology (we children of the Enlightenment, having separated philosophy of nature from theology, find it easy to overlook this point); and (2) to miss the fact that when he later specifies Tian's constancy, he points to the order of the *seasons*, not to anything lower in the hierarchy of nature.

Tian maintains constant routines—The text does not have "Tian's *xing* is constant," but *Tian xing you chang*, "Tian's *xing* has constant (aspects? elements? application?)" or "There are constancies in Tian's *xing*." In any case, *chang*, whose uses range from "usual," "customary," and "ordinary" through "routine" to "unvarying," can be taken as "moral constancy," quite as well as "unvarying"—certainly not as "eternal," which is not only a Westernism, but lacks the moral overtones carried by the word later in the essay. To take it here as expressing a mechanical or determined "order of Nature" would bring with it the onus of establishing not only (1) that the word must carry its strongest possible meaning of "unvarying," but also (2) that its extension here includes all of nature and (3) that here Xun excludes the moral connotations the word *xing* as noun carries for him in all other cases. Unless the context clearly requires it—and here it does not—that would be questionable. (As for "constant" alone, one may compare "a constant lover" with "a constant flow.")

The first clause might well be translated at the end of the complex sentence, as "Tian did not specially act. . . regarding Jie's downfall, since its pattern of conduct maintains its routine," for two reasons. First, it is not infrequent, in Archaic Chinese, for a preceding clause to be logically subordinate to its following clause, even in the absence of any subordinating particle. Second, the original order seems to have given the impression that the subject of the essay is the order of Nature, rather than the necessity of ordering the life of mankind—that is, the contrast between what Yao represents and what Jie represents. This was Xun's greatest concern, his most frequent topic, and clearly the emphasis of the essay as a whole—though it is viewed in terms of the two rulers' (representative) responses to Tian.

Responds—ying, response ranging all the way from reactions to stimuli (*gan*) through answering a question to the gratefulness and obedience appropriately called forth by the kindness (DE) of a superior. The primacy of Tian is never questioned. Response to it is what is crucial. The response here is obviously not a natural reaction, though Xun uses the same word for the spontaneous arising of feelings in humans in *pian* XXII (*Zheng ming*). There, however, it is a response to an "influence" or "stimulus," (*gan*). Here, he clearly means something much more complex, ranging from the farmer's response to the seasons to the sage's "above he has intercourse with Tian" of *pian* IX (*Wang zhi*).

Tian's DE is to transform and change by turns (*pian* III), which provides the requisites for human life. To such a DE, LI would require an appropriate and cooperative response.

setting things in proper order/disorder—one of Xun's most basic oppositions, *zhi/luan*. *Zhi* means primarily "good government," but secondarily "healing" or "establishing proper processes"; *luan* is "chaos," "disorder," or, occasionally, "sickness."

misfortune—Yang comments, "Good fortune and misfortune cause men to deny that Heaven loved Yao and hated Jie." Was he agreeing or disagreeing with that judgment? He was at least implying that Xun was here meeting a version of the problem of evil by asserting that good fortune and misfortune are not mere luck, but not arbitrary heavenly rewards or punishments either. They are consequences of performance. They thus fall under the category of *ying*, response, rather than acts of Tian. But Yang's comment is not inconsistent with Xun's idea that Tian's rewards are integral with our proper response, *zhi*, "setting in order," and its punishments integral with our improper response, *luan*, "disorder," rather than discrete "special acts."

The two words *ji* and *xiung*, 'good fortune' and 'misfortune,' however, do carry some numinous overtones, as Graham recognizes in translating them "auspicious" and "baleful."[4]

In paragraphs 3 through 7, Yao and Jie are clearly in view: Xun is not speaking of individual lives, but of the careers of rulers. Individual circumstances and an individual's span of life are not related to Heaven in the way he is discussing here, as he makes plain later and elsewhere. (See p. 110f. and p. 124)

agriculture—lit. "fundamentals," but Yang's interpretation is undoubtedly correct.

is frugal in use—Xun expands on his idea of "frugality in use" as a way of benefiting both ruler and people in *pian* X. He includes *jie*, "frugality" or "self- discipline" in his list of prime virtues in *pian* XXIV.

Tian finds no occasion to . . .—*bu neng*, often quite properly taken as "has not the ability," but used on occasion in the *Xunzi* (and elsewhere) for "does not avail himself of the opportunity" or "cannot bring himself to."[5] This is admittedly an unusual use for *neng*, which does usually mean "is able to," yielding the *prima facie* translation "Heaven cannot make you poor." Reasons for preferring the previous reading are given in the notes.[6] However, even if one prefers "cannot" as the reading for *bu neng*, the comments below to paragraph 4 of the translation still apply.

chastise—huo, as a verb, "to send down calamities."

Hence flood and drought could not cause the people to starve—translators differ regarding the precise force of *gu* here[7]; in the defensibly authentic *pian* of the *Xunzi*, initial *gu* indicates that what follows it is consequential to what precedes, not explanatory of it.[8] That consequential relation may be very tenuous, needing the translation "thus" or, sometimes, no translation at all, when the transition it indicates is amply signaled simply by the consecution of the sentences. (Explanatory *gu* does occur rarely in the *Xunzi*, but always within sentences or at the end, never initially.) Thus, we cannot take Xun to mean that the inability of flood, drought, and the like to cause harm is the *explanation* of why Tian "cannot" send trouble. If there is any explanatory relation, it is that Tian's lack of occasion explains the inability of flood and drought. This would be quite in line with his acknowledgment in *pian* XVI that there were nine years of flood under Yu and ten years of drought under Tang, two founding Sages, with no famines ensuing—reports he may have had in mind when penning this essay. (Though Xun doesn't mention it, the tradition implies that the floods came because of Tang's fault, but their harmlessness was associated with his sageliness[9]).

His statement indicates he distinguishes floods and such that may cause famine from those which do not, hot spells and cold periods that may cause epidemics from those which do not, and uncanny occurrences that may bring misfortune from ones which do not. Since this last distinction is one he develops later in the essay, any interpretation of this passage that would make it a denial of the effectiveness for evil of *all* uncanny occurrences must be wrong. However, it is more comfortable for us moderns to take the *gu* here in its minimal sense, omitting it from translation (as Watson does, W 79). Even in that case, if the sentence has any explicative reference to the preceding, it implies that flood and drought would indeed be, under different conditions, Tian's way of causing famine; heat and cold Tian's way of causing epidemics; and uncanny occurrences Tian's way of chastising—and those different conditions would involve differences in Tian's occasion for acting. If these good results simply accrue directly from the behavior stated in the protases, there is no point to the apodoses—indeed, to the whole conditional construction. To give it any force at all implies that the sentence it introduces follows from what precedes, rather than gives a reason for it; thus, it is Tian's position in the preceding sentence that explains the inabilities of flood, etc. to harm.

In any case, the conditional "if" of the preceding sentence still distantly governs this sentence, logically.[10] Xun does not suggest that there is so lawlike a consistency in responses to the constancy of Tian's *xing* that there are no conditional elements. Tian's following of its Dao may indeed result in flood or drought, heat or cold, or uncanny occurrences. These do not seem to be violations of its *chang*. Nor does he deny that through them Tian, under other circumstances, might send famine, sickness, and misfortune, but only that it will never do so under an appropriately sagely administration (as that of Yao). Here he affirms that uncanny aspects of the heavenly influences have no effect *under the conditions of suitable virtue in the ruler*. Compare Knoblock's translation from *pian* II: "A person who possesses these three qualities, though he be sent a greatly inauspicious omen, would Heaven have wrought his ruin?"[11] The conditional character of the innocuousness of omens is there clearly implied. What kinds of relations of cause or potency obtain among these things Xun does not specify. (But see the discussion of a relevant *pian* X passage below, p. 136)

uncanny occurrences—lit., "portentous prodigies," *yao guai*. On *yao*, see p. 117f. Dubs' "supernatural powers" and Chan's "evil spiritual beings" are defensible translations, but fit ill with claims that Xun did not believe in spirits, since he parallels them with "drought and floods, excessive heat or cold," facts with which he was well familiar. Although Xun did probably believe in spirits (as argued elsewhere), his elaboration, later in the essay, on the idea here calls for this translation.

unseasonable times—lit., "contrary, rebellious," on *Yu*'s reading.[12] Perhaps "unresponsive" or "irresponsible" (to Tian) might be closer to Xun's sense.

Tian will have no occasion to cause him to prosper—For the first time, the verb "to cause" (*shi*) is used of Tian. Previously, Tian would (not) "poor," "sick," or "misfortune," though flood, etc., would (not) "cause" famine, sickness, etc. In this more negative paragraph, "causing" or "employing" is predicated of Tian. I have no explanation for this. (Later on, Tian "droughts," but that may be simply "The sky non-rains.")

If. . . he behaves foolishly—wang, which implies even recklessness. For Xun, Dao and intelligence go together; abandoning Dao is an intellectual incoherence quite as much as a moral deviation.

Hence—see pages 83 and 87.

When the same seasons visit him—Xun surely is not predicting that every two rulers will experience exactly the same meteorological conditions (consider the years of flood in the case of Yu). One age may experience more or fewer of those exceptional acts of nature—extreme heat or cold, drought or flood—than the other, but these can be prepared for and ameliorated. The underlying seasons—the *chang xing* of Heaven—are the same. (Hughes translates quite differently: "observance of the seasons and good government go together, whilst calamities and good government are incompatible." Köster, however, treats this whole sentence as subordinate to the next, a procedure that makes good sense but seems less justifiable on the basis of the syntax.[13])

He mustn't blame Tian—"Blame," *yuan*, sometimes carries the overtone of an inappropriate response to acts of kindness by a social superior—one dimension of DE that is missed when it is translated always as "inner power." Tian's DE, as *pian* III implies, is to bestow the blessings of nature's changes (*bian-hua*) upon all under Tian; he who responds to Tian with *yuan* therefore does not "understand the decrees [of Tian]" (*pian* IV).

Its Dao is just what it is—a syntactically dense sentence: *qi dao ran ye*. The idea parallels "He who resents Heaven does not understand (its) decrees." Heaven's perfection requires that its decrees be utterly congruent with its Dao, which is perfectly (though not exhaustively) expressed in its *xing*.

An improbable but interesting translation would be to separate these last two clauses from what immediately precedes, and to treat them as a summary of all that has been said so far: "It is contrary to LI (*bu koyi*, "totally inappropriate"), to respond wrongly (*yuan*)[14] to Tian (that is, its kindness (DE), its alternately bringing about the seasons, etc.)—what it does is in accord with its Dao" (and hence beyond questioning by an inferior).

In either case, the burden of the whole section is clear: the problem is not how Tian's Dao works, or how Tian follows its Dao, or even what Tian can or cannot do in general, but the importance of how we respond to it.

[The distinction between Tian's office and that of humans.]

8. [THUS] ONE WHO IS CLEAR CONCERNING THE DISTINCT PROVINCES OF TIAN AND HUMANS MAY BE CALLED "THE PERFECT MAN."
9. "TIAN'S OFFICIAL RESPONSIBILITIES" MAY BE DEFINED AS: [1] TO BRING [THINGS] TO MATURITY WHILE NOT TAKING ANY ACTION, [2] TO BESTOW* WITHOUT BEING BESOUGHT. 10. SINCE THAT IS THE SITUATION, NO MATTER HOW DEEP HIS THINKING MAY BE, [THAT PERFECT] MAN DOES NOT EXTEND IT TO THINGS IN TIAN'S PROVINCE; NO MATTER HOW BROAD HIS ORIENTATION,** HE DOES NOT EXPAND IT IN THEIR DIRECTION; NO MATTER HOW SUBTLE HIS RESEARCH, HE DOES NOT EXTEND IT TO THEM. THIS IS WHAT "NOT COMPETING WITH TIAN'S PROVINCE" REALLY COMES TO.
11. TIAN HAS ITS SEASONS, EARTH HAS ITS PRODUCTIVENESS, AND [THE] MAN HAS [AN ABILITY TO] SET THINGS IN ORDER. IT IS THIS SITUATION THAT CONSTITUTES THEIR POTENTIAL TO BE HARMONIOUSLY ALIGNED. 12. GRAVE MISTAKES FOLLOW YEARNING FOR SUCH ALIGNMENT WHILE NEGLECTING THAT BY WHICH IT MAY BE ACHIEVED!

*Read *de* 得 as *de* 德.
**Read *neng* 能 as *tai* 態, following Gao.

This section begins with a fine example of *gu* used as an oral signal to hearers that a new section is being initiated. What oral clues were used to distinguish this use we do not know, but our own use of different inflections of "next," for instance, to indicate the degree of separation or consecution we are affirming, would be an apt example.

Thus—gu often means "therefore," and most commentators and translators so take it, treating this sentence as the conclusion of the preceding paragraph. It does not seem to sum up or explain what precedes; rather, it points ahead to what is coming. Therefore, we take the sentence as a topic sentence for the discussion that follows, which first introduces the distinction between Tian and humans and soon after deals with how to become a perfected man. In that case, *gu* cannot be taken as "therefore," but rather as a particle introducing a new paragraph, as is not uncommon in the *Xunzi*. It then needs no translation. We have included it here in brackets just to acknowledge its presence in the text.

the distinct provinces of Tian and humans—fen, "provinces," is basically "to divide." In the *Xunzi* it often indicates social distinctions in rank or responsibility, even "duties," properly assigned according to LI. For Xun, civilized life requires divisions of labor, responsibility, authority, and dignity, as his criticisms of Modi reiterate, and he refers to such divisions as *fen*. It would be rash to exclude *a priori* any of those dimensions here, though the idea of Tian's authority seems less present to his mind than its area of work and its responsibilities (he later speaks in ways that suggest Tian's higher dignity).

and humans—It is natural for us to take "humans" as a collective here for humanity. In light of the way in which this whole section focuses on the Sage (possibly still Yao), who, as the top of the human hierarchy and "perfect man" sums up humanity, it might be better to translate as "The Man," just as the king could be referred to as "the one man." Xun is thinking of natural action as summed up in Tian, and human action as summed up in the Sage, as hierarchical thinking tends to take the top as in some way including the whole. It is the Sage, after all, who can become "aligned" with Tian and Earth.

the perfect man—*zhi ren*, "the man who has arrived," or "the ultimate man." The phrase occurs elsewhere in the *Xunzi* only in *pian* XXI, where it is clearly equivalent to "sage." Cf. *Zhuangzi*, *pian* 33 (probably later than Xun Qing): "He who does not depart from the ancestor is called the Heavenly Man; he who does not depart from the Pure is called the Holy Man; he who does not depart from the True is called the Perfect Man."[15]

The distinction between Heaven and humans is not at all easy to make. Apparently, most interpreters of Xun are themselves sages, since they so easily point out just what this distinction consists in! The distinction, as Xun's work taken as a whole shows, is clear only to those who base their disciplined and informed action upon spiritual enlightenment (*shenming*), which arrives only after unlimited open-mindedness and complete self-knowledge, extreme discipline, and reverent waiting. It would be patronizing for any interpreter to claim for herself such achievement, which Xun reserves to the sages. (It is doubtful that Xun considered himself to be a sage, though he had no doubt he was a very enlightened Junzi.)

Here Xun uses his strongest definition-formula (*fu shizhiwei*)[16] to answer a question fundamental to his case: What is the proper scope of Tian's activity?

official responsibilities—*zhi* 職, "duties of office," what LI distinguishes (by *fen*, as above) from others' duties. The hierarchic, bureaucratic image is maintained. Tian, the first and highest of the three (Tian, Earth, humans) has certain functions reserved to itself, in accord with the cosmic LI.

The four words *bu wei er cheng* that make up [1], *to bring things to maturity without taking special action*, are found in *DDJ*, 47, applied to the sage. They are surely as apt here, applied to Tian. Tian, like the sage-king, rules by *wu-wei*—cf. *pian* XVIII, "When [Yao and Shun] faced south and judged the empire, all living people were moved, obeyed, and yielded to their influence" (Dubs, 198, 202); and *An.*, 15.5, "Wasn't Shun among those who ruled by *wu-wei*? What did he do? He merely faced south gravely and reverently." The human world's orderly functioning was its response to the sage's *wu-wei*. In this sense the sage "follows Tian."

Buwei, "not taking any special action," here refers back to the initial sentence and forward to later discussions.

to bestow without being besought—Qiu usually means "seek" or "ask for," but it was early the name of a request for rain,[17] and in the old bronzes *qiu nian* meant "to pray for a good harvest."[18] Since both rain and harvest were special functions of Tian, and Xun soon speaks of "seeking" (or "beseeching") knowledge of Tian, and then discusses rain sacrifices later on in the essay, we use "beseech" here. It is not clear that the two uses are as separable in Xun's Chinese as in English.

Graham translates, "What comes about without being done, is got without being sought, these we say are in Heaven's charge."[19] This is beautifully clear and seems apt, but has difficulties: (1) it takes the *doing* and *seeking* to be *ours*, but the first half of Xun's definition (*bu wei er cheng*), as it appears in *DDJ*, 47, applies to the activity (or inactivity) of the sage, who "knows without traveling, sees without looking, accomplishes without doing." If Xun's reference to "Laozi" at the end of the essay indicates he knew the *DDJ*, the parallel would suggest that it is Tian's doing (and being besought) that are in mind. (Even if the phrase was one in general use to express the Daoist idea of *wu-wei*, the stress is on the agent's manner of (non)acting.) (2) It is unclear whether *fushizhiwei* would nominalize four verbal clauses in this way; (3) what follows stresses the mysteriousness of the doing rather than what is done; and (4) it begs the question of a logical subject for *wei*: to restrict all 'doings' to humans does not match the way Xun talks about many natural occurrences; and to restrict all Tian's actions to "nondoings" raises many questions.

The second half (*bu qiu er de*) is also not quite clear. Li suggests that it means Tian does not *ask* Earth to bring forth, but who would say that it does? Other commentators lay out the results of Tian's discharge of its office, as Xun presents them later, but none, taking *qiu* to mean "seek," gives any satisfactory account of why Xun says what he says here. As noted already, *qiu*, "to seek" or "beseech," was, in both Shang and Zhou, the name of sacrifices for rain or harvest, and Xun, later in this essay, uses it in a specific reference to a beseeching for rain. Hence, we make bold to take it as a passive. A certain problem then arises, as his acceptance of rain sacrifices indicates he held that a sage would offer them. Since he does deny that *beseeching* Tian has any effect on its accomplishing its natural ends, (since it does that without any special action), this would seem to mean that sacrifice is rather the appropriate acknowledgment that Tian does in fact do whatever *de*, which is usually translated as "attain," indicates. Our tentative move here is to take *de* to be a graphic variant for its cognate DE, which can mean "the bestowing of gifts from a superior to an inferior (to which the inferior should respond appropriately)." One may compare Knoblock's note to *pian* X, regarding the DE of the Junzi: "Such *de* inner power bestows *de* kindnesses on the people, for which they feel a debt of gratitude."[20] Since Tian's seasons are what bestow life and its support, and sacrifice without request is an appropriate response to Tian's kindness, this is an attractive move, but one for which more defense would be welcome.

Defining Tian's official job description in this way means that beseeching would be a transgression of the proper assignment of roles (*fen*) to Tian and humanity. Begging Tian would be a form of "competing," urging one's own will over against Tian's following of its Dao, and hence acting contrarily to the sort of complying that is fundamental to the Chinese concept of the moral person.[21]

No matter how deep . . . broad . . . subtle—There is some ambiguity as to what these are attributes of. Chan, Dubs, Köster, and Chai follow the main commentatorial tradition and refer them to the things of Tian; Watson, following Zu and Tao (with Liang), refers them to the sage's understanding. We prefer the latter, in light of "the greatest wisdom resides where he has no concern" that comes later.

not competing with Tian's province—The various emerging Daoisms each treated some aspect of traditional elite culture, and hence most of Confucianism, as "competings with Tian," and probably considered their own speculations to be "deep," "expansive," and "subtle." (Xun meets the same kind of claim in *pian* XIX (*Li lun*) by insisting that the meaning of LI is "deep," "expansive," and "lofty".) Here he is holding his philosophical ground: "competing with Tian" can only be defined if the respective provinces of Tian and humans are first delineated, and only the "perfect man," the sage, who, even when not the source of the LI, at least understands it fully, can do that.

harmoniously aligned—Can is often translated as "triad" or "threesome," its other meanings of "accumulate," "examine," etc., not fitting. However, its use as a name for part of Orion, the three stars of whose belt are in line, suggests that "aligned" is closer to what Xun has in mind.[22] Such alignment, or harmony, is the aim of every school but the extreme Legalists; Xun insists that its basis is economic order, based on LI, as the proper response to Tian (as fully *yang*, it initiates; as high, it is to be harmonized with). During the Zhanguo period, the world was certainly out of line!

consists in the fact—Xun uses a definitional formula here that, under Cua's analysis,[23] would carry the force of "only in terms of Tian's seasons, Earth's productiveness, and human government can one meaning fully speak of the possibility of aligning the three"—a forceful rejection of any attempt to attain harmony with the cosmos that is not rooted in good government. In Xun's mind, of course, that means conforming to ritual, LI, which for him is not only the foundation of orderly government, but the deposit, within the tradition, of the insight of the past sages, who were perfectly aligned with Tian and Earth.

Earth has its productiveness—cai, "wealth," here used potentially, "its ability to produce wealth." That is the aspect of Earth that is most dependent on the seasons and which most concerns government.

the man has an ability to set in order—usually "humans," but here in particular the sage-king. Xun does not seem to believe that ordinary humans, without a sage, can really align themselves with Tian and Earth. "Be" is preferable to "become" (neither being explicit in the text), since such harmony is, for Xun, the norm—it is the *da shen* of Yao, the fulfilment of Heaven and Earth as well as of humans.

The final *yi* indicates this is a perfectly general truth.

that by which it may be achieved—Obviously, the means include good government by LI and YI, but what follows implies that there are also spiritual requirements, fulfilled by someone who "completes Tian's work" by achieving sage status. It is the activities of Tian and Earth that humans by their own activity can unite harmoniously with, not Tian's height or Earth's breadth (the other characteristics most commonly attributed to them), or any more intuitive or mystical attributes. The Daoists yearned for an alignment they hoped would come naturally if elitist dogmas were abandoned; the Naturalists yearned to discover the hidden harmonies lying in the alignments of nature. Both, for Xun, contributed to the chaos of the age.

[Tian's seasons and Earth's fecundity.]

13. THE ORDERED STARS PURSUE THEIR COURSE,
THE SUN AND MOON IN TURN GIVE LIGHT
THE SEASONS FOUR GO MARCHING BY,
WIDESPREAD THE WIND AND RAIN'S LARGESS

(These lines are rhymed. They are possibly a quote familiar to Xun's audience.)

14. EACH OF THE MYRIAD THINGS ACHIEVES THAT HARMONY WHICH LEADS TO ITS PRODUCTION, AND EACH ATTAINS THE NOURISHMENT THAT LEADS TO ITS MATURATION. 15. NOT SEEING THE ACTUAL WORKINGS, WE SEE THE EFFECTS, AND FOR THIS REASON [THE AGENTS] ARE PROPERLY CALLED SPIRITS; EVERYONE KNOWS WHAT [IT IS THAT] CARRIES [THE PROCESS] TO COMPLETION, BUT NO ONE

KNOWS THE UNOBSERVABLE [THAT IS AT WORK]; FOR THIS REASON IT IS PROPERLY CALLED TIAN.

The courses of the stars, the shining of the sun and moon, and the succession of the seasons Xun refers directly to Tian. He does not tell us whether he refers *yin-yang* transformations to Tian or not—they seem often to be responses to these antecedent activities, constituting a lower level in the hierarchy of nature. (Lack of rain, however, may be from Tian—at least "Tian droughts" in paragraph 46 (p. 119ff.), and there were rain sacrifices addressed to Tian, as well as to the Spirits of mountains or rivers. See Chapter 8 for further discussion.)

It is surely *yin-yang's* seasonal activity that is in view here—*yin* cold and *yang* dry changing into *yin* wet and *yang* warm, with wind and rain their proper consequences—in a normal year. (Xun is not here concerned about floods, droughts, and other deviations, wherein things do not "attain harmony" or "receive nourishment.") This is all part of, or a consequence of, "Tian's seasons." Earth's productiveness is complex and yet harmonious; when things function as they should, each thing finds its needs and fills its place—analogous to the functioning of LI in human affairs.

for this reason it is properly called (fu shi zhi wei)—Here again Cua's analysis is clarifying. Xun is maintaining that acting as the invisible cause of visible effects is both a necessary and a sufficient condition for being acknowledged to be *shen*, "spirit," and something that brings (at least such natural objects) to completion without observably acting qualifies to be called "Tian." (He has, in fact, defined the *office* of Tian as functioning in just that way, in section 9.) This does not require that Tian be the immediate or proximate agent, any more than a ruler's acts must be those done by himself, rather than through a chain of command.

Is the parallelism in section 15 of the text synonymous or synthetic? The previous parallel, in 14, was the latter, setting "production" over against "maturation." The translation deliberately suggests synthetic parallelism here by taking *shen*, "spirits," as plural, indicating the lesser subordinate forces involved directly in the production of each of the myriad things, and Tian as singular, as the power whose office it is to oversee the whole process. If the parallelism is taken as synonymous, then, since in English Tian must be singular, *shen* must be taken so, too, despite the fact that a multitude of *shen* were commonly identified with processes involving the myriad things.[24] *Shen* may be taken as adjective, of course, and attributed to Tian. This poses no problem, since in a hierarchical cosmos, if there is a spirit dimension at all, there should be a highest locus of spirit, and for this Tian would be, for a Confucian, the only candidate. *DDJ*, 39 says that the *shen* can persist only if they attain shamanic powers (*ling*)—which would not be tightly bound to Tian—but such ideas seem most un-Confucian. (The *Analects*, *Mencius*, and the *Xunzi* do not even use the word *ling*, except in proper names). However, since in Chinese singular and plural are not necessarily distinguished, and since Tian is dealt with here as anything but localized, and since this is not a context in which distinguishing one spiritual force from another would be significant (it has no ritual involvements, for example), it would be best to let the vagueness of the passage beget an equal vagueness in our minds. On any interpretation, it affirms that *shen* is to be predicated of Tian, whether simply or eminently.

The wider parallelism, involving both 14 and 15, implies that the springing up of a thing is due to its own *shen* (or its *sheng*, "life?"), but its maturation is due to Tian. Living things may spring up, but they mature only if the seasons, for instance, cooperate. The distinction between *being alive* and *being perfected* is reflected even at the level of the myriad things. It does seem unlikely that here Xun is speaking of the ultimate perfection (*cheng*) of things he soon attributes to the activities of the sage, because he immediately goes on to speak of the further completion of Tian's part in the process, which he must also have in mind here.

Yang notes that some claim the text should read "called Tian's work" (adding *gong* after *Tian*), but rejects it. Wang Niansun (according to Wang Xianqian) accepts the addition. The latter apparently agrees, noting that *Tian gong* occurs three times in the passage immediately following. Liang demurs, but Li opts flatly for adding *gong*, in line with his strong scientistic stress. On rhetorical grounds, we agree with Liu and Liang in rejecting the suggestion.[25] Xun's argument certainly stands well enough without adding *gong*. Ascribing *production* to spiritual forces and *completion* to Tian fits Xun's sense of hierarchy well—even Jie might in some sense produce, but only a Yao can complete.

We end the paragraph here, as the next sentence appears to be a title for the following section. Watson and Köster, however, follow the Chinese paragraphing (which is recent) and include the following sentence with what precedes. Dubs, Chan, and Chai avoid the problem by not paragraphing.

(Tian's stopping point: Humans by nature)

16. [BUT] THE SAGE ACTS! HE DOES NOT SEEK [OR BESEECH] FOR KNOWLEDGE OF TIAN.
17. TIAN'S FUNCTIONS HAVE BEEN CLEARLY DEFINED; WHEN ITS WORK HAS RUN ITS FULL COURSE AND OUR BODIES ARE COMPLETE, OUR SOULS COME TO BE.

(Now comes a detailed inventory of what has been produced in a living human body, as it comes pristine from Tian.)

18. WHAT ARE TO BE CALLED "THE FEELINGS AS TIAN PRODUCES THEM" ARE DESIRE, AVERSION, DELIGHT, ANGER, GRIEF, AND JOY, THEN STORED UP WITHIN US. WHAT ARE TO BE CALLED "THE SENSIBILITIES AS TIAN PRODUCES THEM" ARE THE EAR, EYE, NOSE, MOUTH, AND BODY—EACH HAS WHAT IT IS RESPONSIVE TO, AND THEY CANNOT INTERCHANGE THEM.
19. WHAT IS TO BE CALLED "THE RULER AS TIAN PRODUCES IT" IS THE MIND, WHICH RESIDES IN THE CENTRAL CAVITY SO AS TO ORDER THE FIVE SENSIBILITIES.
20. [THE MIND] MAKES USE* OF THINGS NOT OF ITS NATURAL KIND IN ORDER TO NURTURE ITS NATURAL KIND; THIS IS TO BE LABELED "NURTURANCE AS TIAN PROVIDES FOR IT."
21. WHAT IS TO BE CALLED "GOVERNMENT AS TIAN GIVES IT" IS THIS: TO ACCORD WITH WHAT PERTAINS TO ONE'S NATURAL KIND IS TO BE BLESSED, TO GO AGAINST SUCH IS TO MEET CALAMITY.

---

*Read *cai* 財 as *cai* 裁, with Yang.

(In the case of humans, Tian produces (*sheng*) them but does not complete (*cheng*) them, so the argument must move from *sheng* to other processes:)

22. What may be called "the greatest of misfortunes" is this: so to darken the ruler Tian gave, so to abandon the nurturance Tian provided for, so to disorder the sensibilities Tian gave, so to violate the mode of government Tian provided, so to mistreat the feelings Tian gave, that one aborts Tian's work.
23. The sage, however, clarifies the ruler Tian gave, sets straight the sensibilities Tian gave, sees that the nurturance Tian provided for is adequate, follows the mode of government Tian has produced, so that he perfects Tian's work.
24. When he has arrived at that point, then he has come to know what is the scope of his own actions and what is not.
25. What then follows is that as Tian and Earth perform their functions the myriad things act as their servants; the latters' courses are completely ordered, the nourishment they provide is completely apt, their emerging causes no injury. It is **this** situation that should be called "knowing Tian."
26. [Thus] the greatest skill resides where [the sage] does not act, and the greatest wisdom resides where he has no concern. As for any interest in things of Tian, he has already observed their possibilities for setting times. As for interest in things of Earth, he has already observed their possibilities for suitable crop development. As for interest in the seasons, he has already observed their possibilities for managing the calendar. As for interest in yin and yang, he has already observed their natural harmonies*' possibilities for governance. Letting underlings observe Tian, he himself observes (attends to) the Dao.

The sage acts! He does not seek (or beseech) for knowledge of Tian. This sentence seems to have occasioned some unease among translators, for, as usually read, it is not syntactically smooth, nor does it seem to fit well the flow of thought of either the preceding or the following paragraph, nor to accomplish a transition between them. Translators Watson, Graham, Eno, Köster, and Hughes, and Chinese editors Liang and Li, in-

*Read *zhi* 知 as *ho* 和, with Wang Niansun.

clude this sentence with the preceding paragraph, though Eno treats it as a quotation apparently thrown in at the end of a section he doubts was in the original text. The traditional Chinese texts do not paragraph, nor does the H-Y text. Dubs and Chan run the two paragraphs together, and thus avoid a decision. However, as we translate it, it makes a perfectly fitting title for the next section, interpreted as follows:

> Having dealt with Tian's seasons and Earth's fecundity, Xun now turns to man's ability to set in order. His part in the eventual harmony comes about only if he acts. Since he is not Tian-and-Earth, he is unable to produce or complete without effort. Tian follows its Dao effortlessly; humans do not so follow their Dao (until they reach perfection). So knowledge of what special action makes for "completion" must guide human effort along the lines of what truly "sets in order."

Other interpretations translate the sentence variously: Watson's "Only the sage does not seek to understand heaven" is perhaps typical, taking the first *wei*, 唯, as "only" and the second *wei*, 為, as "acts as one who." Graham, however, reads that *wei* as "to deem," resulting in "Only the sage may be deemed to refrain from seeking to know Heaven."[26] Both such readings seem to ignore the interplay of *wei* as "act" and *qiu* as "seek" (or "beseech") in paragraphs 9 and 46, which would suggest that *wei* should be read here as we do.

Further, the sentence, taken in any of these extant ways, is puzzling. Can Xun really mean to claim that *everyone* but the sage seeks to know Tian? And if he does, what is the point of injecting that idea here? He has just said that everyone already knows Tian as the cause of the myriad things' maturation, and nobody knows it by watching it work. He has not implied anywhere that seeking to know Tian is wrong, only that it may be wrongly or excessively pursued. And surely the sage, part of whose perfection is the perfection of knowledge, knows Tian! The sentence simply demands some other reading. But if one takes *wei* here as "to act (specifically)" or as "to exert effort" as we did in the lead sentence of the essay (and as akin to Xun's use of cognate *wei* in his discussions of human nature), the sentence makes an entirely appropriate title for the whole next section. Its initial particle *wei*, 唯, usually translated "only," can also function readily as an introductory word for a new topic, translatable by "but," or, indeed, may be treated as needing no translation.[27]

but—Reading the initial *wei* here as "only" has surely confused the understanding of this sentence, since the section concludes by saying the sage *does* "understand Tian," which is preceded by discussion of what action the would-be sage takes in order to achieve such knowledge. As for *wei*, it is one of those words, like *gu*, that can function merely to introduce a new section. Though it may be omitted from translation, we have acknowledged its existence with "(but)."

Tian's functions have been clearly defined—lit., "Its duties established." The idea is that Tian's work has a clear stopping place. When our bodies are so complete that our soul comes to be, Tian's productive function ends.

souls—the same word (*shen*) as "spirit" above, but here it denotes what Aristotle called *psyche*, the animating function.

come to be—The basic meaning of *sheng* seems to have been "to sprout," then "to give birth," but by extension it includes all the natural productive processes (and sometimes artificial ones also). Since we interpret Xun's disagreement with Mencius to be largely over the question of the limitations of the natural processes represented by *sheng*, "born" would be an appropriate lead-in to later discussions. The production of humans is the final accomplishment of Tian's official work, its *zhi* that is distinguished from human effort. The living human body is all that can be achieved by Tian through the natural processes of *sheng*, "giving birth, producing."

as Tian produces them—The text simply says "Tian feelings . . . Tian sensibilities. . . ," and the translator must divine the connection. We take it as privative: "as far as Tian's activities, taken by themselves, can achieve"; what is present in our 'human nature,' our *xing*. Though often taken as "the natural emotions," etc., the emphasis is not so much on their naturalness as on their unfinished state. It is not that Tian has done a poor job—its responsibilities of office have been perfectly discharged; it is that that is as far as Tian's process of production (*sheng*) goes. The things listed are not normative; it is worth noting that Xun does not mention YI, "the sense of duty" that in *pian* IX he says sets humans above animals, and which Mencius claims has at least its first "sprouts" in our nature, our *xing* 性. For Xun, it is now up to humans to make something more of themselves.

Eno (296) takes "Tian" here to mean these primal human gifts are "Tian-like," hence their moral potential is being affirmed. It seems rather, in the context of natural production, that what is being stressed is not their potential, but their moral deficiency. Their eventual "Tianlikeness" is a result of *hua*, a transformation, and the potentiality for transformation is, in Xun, always referred to an agent, not the patient (except, of course, for *yin* and *yang*, whose very nature is to be in constant transformation).

stored up within us—In *pian* XX, Xun says "humans cannot be without joy," and "joy must have its expression." Of the other emotions, he tends to say they are evoked by externals. His sage is joyful, whether other emotions occur in him or not. We return to this primacy of joy in Chapter 11.

the ruler as Tian produces it—For Xun, qualifications for rule are intellectual and moral. He soon remarks on what needs to be done to the mind along those lines. Merely as natural ruler, it is liable to all the sad disorganizations he refers to in *pian* VIII, XXI, and XXIII. Nevertheless, properly cultivated, it can become, as in the sages, divine. In *pian* XXI he says, "As for the mind, it can be host to divine manifestation (*shenming*) because it is a ruler, the ruler of the body."[28] This is something far beyond what it is "as Tian produces it." Nevertheless, Tian does give it, and, in the nature of things, provides for humans' part in bringing order, "rule," to the cosmos.

The mind, as "ruler," is to "produce order" in those areas where Tian "cannot"—but it is produced by Tian, presumably for just that purpose. It is clear that in the *Xunzi* mind holds a special place in the economy of the cosmos.[29]

the central cavity—"Mind" and "heart" are the same word. The mind has spatial location. Xun knows no nonmaterial, spaceless mind, which has the correlate that for him "material" is not by definition "nonmind."

The mind makes use of—reading *cai* as "makes use of," as we do elsewhere,[30] and then taking its subject, "the mind," as continuing from the previous sentence. Xun several times speaks of the sage or the perfect Junzi "making use of" (*cai*) the myriad things. Since not everything is edible, "makes use of" implies "deciding."

not of its natural kind—Xun undoubtedly considered cannibalism to be unnatural, not something that could be from Tian, but the main thrust here is that making decisions about the things of nature is a basic and proper function of the mind—done perfectly, of course, only when the mind has reached its full development. Translating *lei* as "species" is too specific; "natural kind" is preferable.

nurture . . . nurturance—"Nourish" is too narrow, since Xun often links clothing and shelter with food as natural necessities. Therefore, Eno's felicitous suggestion of "nurturance" is embraced.

An important consequence of this sentence, as leading to the next, is that Tian bestows on humans that which enables them to be "the noblest beings under Tian" (*pian* IX), and so endows them with the function, in all propriety, of using other species toward that good of humanity that is also the overall harmony of the cosmos. In *pian* IX, humans' supremacy under Tian is a function of YI, a moral faculty; here, it resides with the mind (*xin*). We may assume that the "uses" that the mind, when functioning properly, makes of "other species" toward nurturance of its own species accord with the sense of appropriateness present in YI. The reflection in humans of Tian's DE is not the *xing*, "nature," but the mind; yet the mind is not given in its fullness in the *xing*, the "nature," and does not (contrary to Mencius) attain its fullness just by spontaneous development of the *xing*.

Eno takes *xin*, "mind," also to be the subject of *wei*, "deems," so that the mind calls things "good" that accord with its species. This idea may be present, but stating it in that way invites us Westerners to read into the passage a subjective theory of the nature of good, which surely is not present.

government as Tian gives it—lit., "Tian's governing." Context tells against any generalization that would make this contradict traditional notions of the authority of Tian in other contexts. Xun is leading up to what *humans* must do to complete Tian's work.

government—not Xun's usual "setting in order," *zhi*, but *zheng*, "government," which implies encouragement by rewards and especially correction by punishment.

blessed . . . calamity—Appropriate English words are hard to find. *Fu* and *huo*, though often merely "happiness . . . misfortune," are also linked with "sent from Tian," and both are written with the "sacrifice" radical. It is hard not to feel Xun carefully chose these words, rather than his frequent *ji . . . xiung*, just for this overtone.

Aborts Tian's work—Possibly archvillain Jie is in mind here. He is said to have done all these things; his fall required no special act of Tian—he did it all himself. Humans can destroy Tian's work as well as expand it. Sima Qian uses *gong*, here "work," to refer to the residual moral power inherited by an unworthy descendant from a worthy ancestor, enabling him, though unworthy, to administer with some effectiveness. If such an idea should be present here, it might mean that Xun held that, as Tian "bears" (*sheng*) humans, the mind receives some DE or *gong* that it may build on to become worthy, or may squander, as Jie did. This may be, but if so, it would be not so much innate as communicated by inheritance from the moral disciplines of an earlier generation, so that Xun's difference with Mencius would still hold: there is no significant natural moral endowment that can be independent of someone's moral effort guided by LI.

The order here is not the order of first exposition, nor is it quite the reverse. The mind is mentioned first, as befits Xun's emphasis on education. Finally, the emotions themselves are perverted. Apparently the "evil" he ascribes elsewhere to humans' nature can be made much worse by wrong human activity. Deviation from the proper course of completion of Tian's work is both possible and evil.

The Sage, however, clarifies the ruler. . . perfects Tian's work. This is, of course, a summary of Confucian curriculum: training the mind by correcting language, careful discussion, and study of the *Documents* and *Annals*; setting straight the sensibilities by LI, moral discipline, careful observation of people and affairs; caring for the feelings by studying the *Odes* and music, and such, and so doing what is best for one's humanity.

perfects Tian's work—quan, "complete, whole," used causatively. In what sense is it still Tian's work? Is it just that Tian provided the raw materials, or is it that Tian, like a master, turns the work over to his apprentices to finish? Or is it neither, or something in between? One's answer depends largely on two things: (1) one's antecedent expectations as to what Xun is about, and (2) one's interpretation of the "cannot" in statements such as, "Tian can give birth to creatures but cannot order them" (*pian* XIX, W 103; see the discussion on p. 153ff.). We perceive in the contrast between "aborting" and "perfecting" Tian's work a genuine teleology, whether it should be spoken of in terms of Tian's "intention" or of some less-than-personal "nisus" Xun gives no clue. In any case, the sage's "perfecting" is a perfecting of the cosmos, not simply of himself or the human lot, and the goods achieved go beyond merely human security. Order and perfect accordance of the cosmos to LI, to its Dao, is a good that includes, but cannot be reduced to, human happiness.

he has come to know the scope of his own actions—Taking *suo* with its original connotations of "space" and final *yi* as having perfective force: At last, the distinction between Tian and humans has become clear to him, in all its complexity. This "knowledge of Tian" is the intellectual side of being aligned with Tian-and-Earth.

What then follows. . . (the myriad things') courses are completely ordered. . . nourishment is apt, their emerging causes no injury—This is the climax of the whole section: the ideal harmony of nature and man. In the very first passage of the essay, under Yao's type of sagely government, "floods and drought could not cause famine" (because "their course was completely ordered" and "the nourishment things provided was completely apt)"; "heat and cold could not cause sickness" (because that "nourishment was ample"); the "emerging" of heat and cold or "uncanny visitations" "caused no injury." The sage himself, of course, followed Dao. All this because Yao "filled out" the work of Tian.

The implication is that though Tian's *xing* is constant, the conduct of the myriad things under Tian will deviate unless there be a sage-king whose "intercourse with Tian" attracts, awes, or inspires them to be "obedient servants." Xun's idea of the sage "transforming like a god" thus goes far beyond mere "model-emulation."[31]

as Tian and Earth perform their functions the myriad things act as their servants—Chan has, "Thus he rules heaven and earth and directs the ten thousand things" (Chan 118), taking the logical subject of the sentence to be the sage.[32] The sentence reads, literally, "Then Tian Earth officials *er* myriad things serve-as-servants *yi*." One issue in interpretation is whether "officials" implies being *under* a superior or *over* an underling. We take the "serve-as-servants" to imply the latter, especially since the particle *er* tends to subordinate the first clause to the second, in which case the functioning-as-officials of Tian-and-Earth is antecedent to the obedient serving activity of the myriad things. This would suggest that until the sage appears, their rule is not sufficiently effective, just as Xun says: "Tian can give birth to things but cannot rule them . . . the world's myriad things wait for a sage; only then are they organized" (*pian* XIX).[33]

their courses are completely ordered. . .—Commentators from Yang on (with the possible exception of Liang) take the antecedent of *qi* to be the sage, yielding "His actions are completely ordered; his nourishment of the people is completely appropriate; his life is without injury" (W 81), apparently because seven preceding *qi*'s have all referred to him. Yet the immediately preceding grammatical subject is the myriad things, and the one before that, Tian-and-Earth. We take these clauses to be elucidations of the immediately preceding sentence, so that *qi* here refers to the myriad things, which otherwise could deviate, fail to nourish, or cause injury.

That the discussion of the sage's knowledge is immediately resumed is no problem: that is the overall context within which this smaller context functions. Our interpretation, however, places these clauses and the preceding sentence within the "what is not his scope of action" that immediately precedes them, and which is the chief burden of what follows. The "perfect man's" sagehood not only attracts the people to be "transformed," but also attracts the lower levels of nature to fulfill their proper natures, their *jing*, their "essences," and thus to accord with *li*, the basic functional structure of things.

the greatest skill. . . the greatest wisdom—There is disagreement whether it is the sage's skill and wisdom, skill and wisdom in general, or Tian's skill and wisdom that are here spoken of. Grammar gives no clue; context seems to favor the last.

already. . . already—Yi. . . yi implies it is accomplished. The sage has reached the limits of propriety in investigating nature; there he curbs his interest, possibly lest he "compete with Tian."

possibilities for setting times. . . for crop development. . . managing the calendar. . . governance—The grammar here is unusual and parsing must be tentative, but what Xun means is hardly in question. Putting it into English in a way that does full justice to the text is difficult, however.

calendar—Calendars were agricultural, but also ritual. The civil, and largely the ritual, calendars were lunar, but agriculture, tied to the seasons, had an implicit solar calendar. As rulers had responsibility for rituals upon which their subjects' agriculture was held to depend, adjusting the ritual calendar to the actual seasons was an important matter; hence the sage's concern for celestial index points for timing his agricultural ritual responsibilities. As long as agricultural seasons were initiated in the proper ritual manner, he need have no further concern for celestial patterns.

appointed experts—Cosmology, before Xun's time, was a concern of court astronomers and archivists, not philosophers. Apparently, the growing philosophical interest in it was something Xun did not share.

observe . . . observe—Fortunately, *shou* bears the same ambiguity as does "observe": "to keep watch over" and "to practice (some observance)." This fact turns the edge of Liu Shi-pei's comment that this sentence says "Tian and Dao are not the same," a comment that Li Di-sheng parlays into "it says Tian is *ziran* and not *shen*." However, to set "keeping watch on Tian" over against "observing Dao" contrasts the actions involved, rather than the objects of those actions.

Although made up of three distinct parts, the essay to this point has presented a well-organized and focused argument. Next follow four sections that could be independent of one another, although they appear to be answers to four questions, only three of which are stated, that might arise in response to the argument so far. The relevance of the first, third, and fourth of these is apparent; that of the second much less obvious. The possibility that it might be an interpolation has already been discussed under the topic of the integrity of the essay. Since, despite its apparent adventitiousness, it does add to the total argument of the essay, and since such only partially relevant digressions occur not infrequently in the *Xunzi* (and much ancient literature), there is good reason for including it.

After all this discussion of the positive side of his thesis, Xun now finds it necessary to remind the reader of its negative side, since otherwise there may obtain the impression that Tian's part in the perfect situation called "knowing Tian," embodying Tian's superior skill and knowledge, would imply some heavenly involvement in good and bad government. This first question has three parts.

27. ARE ORDER AND DISORDER [MATTERS OF] TIAN? 28. [WE] MAINTAIN: THE ORDERLY COURSES OF THE SUN, MOON, STARS, AND THE ASTRONOMICAL REFERENCE POINTS WERE THE SAME UNDER BOTH YU AND JIE. YU BROUGHT ORDER AND JIE DISORDER. TIAN IS NOT [THE DIFFERENCE BETWEEN] ORDER AND DISORDER.

29. THE SEASONS? [WE] MAINTAIN: PLANTS SPROUT AND MATURE IN SPRING AND SUMMER, THEY ARE HARVESTED AND STORED IN FALL AND WINTER—AND THIS WAS THE SAME UNDER YU AS UNDER JIE. YU BROUGHT ORDER AND JIE DISORDER. IT IS NOT THE SEASONS.

30. THE EARTH? (WE) MAINTAIN: THINGS GAINING ROOTAGE IN THE EARTH LIVE, THOSE FAILING THAT DIE—AND IT WAS THE SAME UNDER BOTH YU AND JIE. YU BROUGHT ORDER AND JIE BROUGHT DISORDER. IT IS NOT THE EARTH.

31. THIS IS WHAT THE ODE MEANS WHEN IT SAYS:

"TIAN MADE THE HIGH HILLS,
KING TAI CULTIVATED THEM;
WHEN HE HAD DONE THIS,
KING WEN SERENELY ENJOYED THEM."

The first sentence is, literally, "Order/disorder is Tian?" (*zhi luan tian ye*). The interrogative *ye* does not presume either an affirmative or negative answer, so the question need not be taken as a challenge by a disputant. The absence of *zai*, "*resides with*," may indicate that the question is not about Tian's *office* or *proper function*. It probably should be read, "Then just what *is* Tian's involvement in order or disorder?" His answer limits Tian's relevance to that of its astronomic regularities (its *xing*). The next question shifts the topic to the seasons, as if one is then no longer talking about Tian itself, but, as consequential to Tian's direct activity, something lower in the natural hierarchy. The third question moves still lower, since it is through the seasons that Tian fructifies the Earth.

We maintain—Though *yue* is often translated as "it is said," Xun not infrequently uses it to state his conclusions, which is the only fitting reading here.

Astronomical reference points—The precise meaning here is unclear, and commentators differ (cf. Watson's "heavenly auspices"). There is no problem with the general meaning, however.

It is noteworthy that only astronomical events are here referred to Tian. Clearly "Nature" as a translation would be inappropriately broad, whereas "sky" would hardly fit the question. Eno concludes that "Tian" is used here quite differently from earlier occasions, implying even different authors.[34] Considering the "soft focus" of many Chinese terms, we fail to see any significant problem. Uses we see as different, even incompatible, need not seem so amid different "forms of life." Xun seems to have felt no difficulty with differing uses of "Tian" in the rest of the *Xunzi*. (See the discussions of Eno at several places.)

No claim is made that the seasons were precisely the same under Yu and Jie—it is that the requirements for human response were the same. If he had made a claim for equality of seasons, the switch from Yao to Yu would raise a problem, for Xun maintains elsewhere that there were nine years of flood under Yu, who avoided famine, apparently, by having already ample grain stored up[35]; nowhere are such floods reported under Jie. (Of course, Xun may not have yet known of the account of the floods during Yu's reign—it may have been a late tradition not in his sources and not yet widespread; or master Xun may have nodded.) Nevertheless, one may guess that emphasizing harvesting and storing fitted his purpose, rather than any idea of invariant seasonal climate. Whatever seasons come, they are to be responded to properly.

Again the theme of agriculture, which must assure good rootage for its crops. It is not Earth, but bad farming practices, that cause disorder. He soon lists them among human disturbances of nature that have ominous results.

It is worth noting that though Xun here distinguishes the seasons from Tian and from Earth, he does not carry his argument down to still lower-level activities such as *yin* and *yang*, or floods, droughts, epidemics, and the like, which certainly had helped cause disorder in his own time. This might be laid to style, three parallels being enough. Yet it suggests we should not extrapolate his argument down into those lower realms. In light of his later discussion of natural omens, he could hardly claim a uniformity at those levels. If he had intended to have the argument apply in the meteorological realm as well, Yu's floods would still be a problem.

things gaining rootage in the soil—Eno takes it, "He who acquires land is able to live," which is textually possible but contextually awkward. Land being acquired or lost is no function of the Earth, but providing rootage is. Xun spoke earlier of encouraging agriculture, and later speaks of poor plowing and weeding losing crops. Xun's argument is plain: neither Tian's constant *yang* activities (its *xing*) nor Earth's constant *yin* passivity correlates with order/disorder in the social sphere.

The problems in translating the quotation from the *Ode* do not obscure its general thrust. King Tai was a celebrated ancestor of the founder of the Zhou; King Wen was his grandson. In Xun's model of history, theirs were times of peace and prosperity. Eno's suggestion (296) that this quotation was "to reinforce the notion that people create the world through effort" seems to miss the point that Xun never says *people* create an orderly world; it is the sage who does so—both Tai and Wen were such. And it is not just through effort, but because the sage has a peculiar relation to Tian (and Earth) that he is able to bring the hills into successful and fruitful cultivation—partly by his proper ritual observances.

(If the poem that forms our paragraph 48 is to be resituated, immediately following this *Ode* quotation would be the only place it would fit in well with the argument. However, following an *Ode* quotation with a poem would not fit Xun's patterns of closure at all.)

The second question is unstated, but must be something like, "If all Tian does is to rotate the seasons, and not reward virtue, what is the point of the Junzi 'following Tian'?" or, reaching back farther in Xun's exposition, "If the whole world responds happily to the sage, why aren't there evidences of the Junzi's local world responding pleasantly to him?" These are like the two sides of a single question. Or possibly some "petty man" had asked, "If you're so smart, why aren't you rich?"

32. [JUST AS] TIAN DOES NOT ABANDON WINTER BECAUSE OF HUMANS' DISLIKE OF COLD, AND EARTH DOES NOT ABANDON ITS EXTENSIVENESS BECAUSE OF HUMANS' DISLIKE OF GREAT DISTANCES, [SO] THE JUNZI DOES NOT ABANDON HIS WAY OF ACTING JUST BECAUSE OF PETTY MEN'S CLAMOR. TIAN HAS A CONSTANT DAO, EARTH HAS CONSTANT DIMENSIONS; THE JUNZI HAS A CONSTANT SUBSTANTIAL CHARACTER. WHILE THE JUNZI FOLLOWS HIS CONSTANCIES, THE PETTY MAN IS BUSY TRYING TO EVALUATE HIS (THE JUNZI'S) ACCOMPLISHMENTS. THIS IS THE MEANING OF THE ODES' "WHY BE UPSET AT WHAT FOLKS SAY?"

35. THE THOUSAND CHARIOTS THAT FOLLOW THE KING OF CHU ARE NOT TO BE DEEMED [A SIGN OF] WISDOM; THE JUNZI'S EATING GREENS AND DRINKING

WATER IS NOT TO BE DEEMED [A SIGN OF] STUPIDITY. THESE ARE HAPPENSTANCES. BUT EVEN IN SUCH CIRCUMSTANCES, IT FOLLOWS THAT [THESE THINGS] STILL DEVOLVE UPON US: TO KEEP IN MIND* THE [BEST] AIMS IN LIFE, TO ENRICH OUR MORAL POWERS AND CONDUCT, TO BROADEN OUR KNOWLEDGE AND OUR DELIBERATIONS, AND, WHILE LIVING IN THE PRESENT, TO EMULATE THE ANCIENT MODELS.

36. THUS, THE JUNZI, REVERING THE THINGS LYING WITH HIMSELF, DOES NOT LONG FOR THE THINGS THAT LIE WITH TIAN. THE PETTY MAN, NEGLECTING THE THINGS LYING WITH HIMSELF, LONGS FOR THINGS FOR HIMSELF THAT REALLY LIE WITH TIAN. SINCE THE JUNZI, REVERING THE THINGS THAT LIE WITH HIMSELF, DOES NOT LONG FOR WHAT LIES WITH TIAN, HE PROGRESSES EVERY DAY. SINCE THE PETTY MAN, NEGLECTING WHAT LIES WITH HIMSELF, LONGS FOR WHAT LIES WITH TIAN, HE RETROGRESSES EVERY DAY. THE ONE PROGRESSES FOR THE SAME REASON THAT THE OTHER RETROGRESSES, SO THAT WHAT SHOWS UP THE DIFFERENCE BETWEEN THE TWO CAN BE SEEN JUST HERE.

The first two clauses have been quoted as Xun's declaration that Tian and Earth are disinterested in human affairs. They are, however, such everyday common sense there would be no point in proposing them as theses. Surely one could believe in all kinds of interventions without embracing these two! His argument is obviously *from* the stability of Tian's seasons and Earth's expanse, taken for granted, *to* the appropriateness of the Junzi's moral character—he acts like Tian and Earth, which do not yield to any human who would "calculate (their) accomplishments." If there is any implied affirmation regarding Tian and Earth, it would seem to be that it would be at least as far *beneath* Tian and Earth so to be influenced by human desires as to abandon their Dao as it would be for the Junzi to abandon his. Otherwise the moral analogy is lost. A further implication is that it is in each case the *moral* course for each to do as it does. Thus, to point out Tian-and-Earth's lack of responsiveness is an assertion of their moral character, not a denial.

the Junzi—the first mention of Junzi in this *pian*. The term occurs seven times in two paragraphs, and then only once (with possibly a different re-

* Reading *xin* 心 as *zhi* 志, with Wang Nian-sun.

ference) in the rest of the essay. This may indicate this section was formulated separately, and included at a later stage.

his constancies—Qi hardly refers back to Tian and Earth.

his accomplishments—One might expect "his," *qi*, to refer to the petty man's own accomplishments, but the following quote suggests that Xun means those of the Junzi—which leads much more naturally into "the Junzi eats greens and drinks water" (signs of unemployment) in the next paragraph, and which makes more sense of the quotation from the *Odes*.

why be upset—This ode is now lost; Yu and Liang would precede this quote with five graphs from a second quotation of it in *pian* XXII to read, "If I don't transgress LI and YI . . ." One may wonder why the preceding six more are not included. They mention being true to high antiquity. Probably Xun expected his hearers to be familiar with the *Ode*.

Our records do not tell whether Xun Qing was disappointed, and temporarily impoverished, by not receiving an appointment from the King of Chu, but this paragraph invites such a guess. Alternatively, it may be a reference to the story, recorded in *pian* XXVIII,[36] of Confucius' difficulties in Chu, where he and his disciples did have to survive on greens and water. The implication would be that the king of Chu was unwise in not employing Confucius—or Xun.

happenstances—In *pian* XXII (*Zheng ming*) Xun defines *ming*, "fate" or "decree (of Tian)," as "unexpected occurrences which one meets with" (Watson 140), not as a new interpretation, but as its ancient and established reference. Later in this *pian* he quotes, "the fate (*ming*) of humans rests with Tian." He leaves it unclear how he relates these to each other, allowing interpreters considerable leeway. Here, however, he is acknowledging that success, failure, and such "lie with Tian."

It would be a mistake to equate the distinction (in job descriptions) between Tian and humans, introduced near the beginning of the *pian*, with the distinction here between "what lies with Tian" (*zai tian*) and "what lies with oneself" (*zai ji*) in this very personal situation. The former distinction is in a sense cosmological, and only the sage can be clear about it; here, however, the issue is personal and moral, and the Junzi can know the outlines of "what lies with oneself," as given in 35—in short, to work toward sagehood, toward an eventual understanding of the more profound and much more difficult distinction between humans and Tian. He also accepts the fact that his chances of success, even of survival, "lie with Tian."

[What about omens?]

(Now the discussion goes back to the relation of Tian to social and political life. Omens were taken to presage dire events, though merely local omens would hardly presage vast events. The question asks about relatively small omens; Xun's answer expands the range greatly.)

> 37. A STAR FALLS OR A TREE MAKES A NOISE, AND ALL THE COUNTRY FOLK ANXIOUSLY ASK, "WHAT KIND OF THING IS THIS?" I MAINTAIN, "NO [SPECIAL] KIND OF THING." THEY REPRESENT TIAN-AND-EARTH'S CHANGES, YIN-AND-YANG'S TRANSFORMATIONS, DEVIANT* EMERGENTS AMONG THINGS. IT IS APPROPRIATE TO THINK THEM WEIRD, BUT DREADING THEM IS AN ERROR.
>
> 38. BUT CONSIDER [INSTEAD]: THE SUN AND MOON UNDERGO ECLIPSES, THE WIND AND RAIN MAY BE UNSEASONABLE, ANOMALOUS GROUPS OF WEIRD STARS MAY APPEAR. IN NO GENERATION HAVE SUCH THINGS NOT BEEN FREQUENT. WHEN RULERS ARE ENLIGHTENED, GOVERNMENT REMAINS STABLE, AND THEN THERE IS NO HARM DONE EVEN IF ALL THESE ARISE AT THE SAME TIME; WHEN RULERS ARE BENIGHTED, GOVERNMENT IS [ALREADY] PRECARIOUS, AND THEN THERE IS NO BENEFIT EVEN IF NONE OF THESE THINGS OCCUR.
>
> 39. AS FOR THE FALLING OF STARS AND THE GROANING OF TREES, THEY ARE BUT [PASSING] CHANGES IN TIAN AND EARTH, MUTATIONS OF YIN AND YANG OR DEVIANT** EMERGENTS AMONG THINGS. IT IS APPROPRIATE TO THINK THEM WEIRD, BUT DREADING THEM IS AN ERROR.

---

*See first note on p.78.

**See previous note.

Xun does not deny significance to all omens; he makes a clear distinction between those which do presage human misfortune, and hence are to be held in awe, and those which do not, and may only be deemed weird.

a tree makes a noise—lit., "cries (like a bird)." Commentators differ as to whether this refers to the groaning of branches or the sounds of birds in the tree, but seem to agree that it probably refers to the sacred trees planted by shrines, whether official *she ji* or popular shrines. In any case, such things clearly were widely taken to be ominous.

what kind of a thing is this . . . no special kind (*shi ho ye*? *wu ho ye*)—cf. Graham: "*ho ye*, 'What is it?' . . . One asks of the object . . . 'What tree is this?' 'What bird is this?' . . . and answers with the kind . . . comparable with Aristotle's species rather than essence. . . . When *ho ye* is used it is generally in requesting an enumeration of the kinds, . . ."[37] Xun is stating that such events are each unique, so they are beyond explanation. Though he does class them, to our logic, as harmless events, that is not for him a *lei*, a "natural kind."

variations . . . transformations (*bian . . . hua*)—Tian and Earth can be involved in only superficial changes (*bian*); yin and yang, however, undergo fundamental transformations (*hua*).

deviant emergents among things—We follow Liu Shipei in reading *ni* for *han*, on the grounds that Yu points out the same graphic error in paragraph 5, and that the change better fits the argument.

changes . . . transformations . . . outcomes—Xun grants that such events may happen at different cosmological levels: variations among the stars occur at the level of Tian-and-Earth, but are superficial changes (*bian*). Tian causes transformations, but does not undergo them.[38] Transforming, however, is the normal mode of activity of *yin* and *yang*, which can undergo radical intermutations; things (*wu*) such as trees produce outcomes such as sounds. Nowhere does he suggest that these have specific explanations, nor that anyone should seek such explanations, nor that explanations would be by reference to any lawlike statements. In fact, it appears, rather, that he is saying that just *because* they are natural events, they have no explanations. They are things of which "everyone knows their effects, no one knows the nonmaterial *shen* or Tian (that lies behind them)"(paragraph 15). Least of all does he suggest that offering more detailed explanations would better allay folks' fears. The world is just as it is; it is enough to know what impinges upon humans' province and what does not.

it is appropriate—ko sometimes means "is not a violation of LI"; "possible," a frequent translation, does not fit. Xun's emphasis seems to be that deeming them weird is quite fitting.

dread—wei; the original graph was of a demon holding something. Xun may use the word for the awe appropriate to the presence of some *tremendum*,[39] as in "Fear him as a theophany" (*pian* XVI), although he also uses it enough times in a more secular way to make it clear he did not reserve it for dread of the supernatural. (In most languages, religious terms get degraded into common intensives.) Here, however, he intends to stress that whatever *shen* may be present in these natural phenomena, they do not imply any numinous threat to humans.

an error—fei, "it is not true." That such things are to be dreaded apart from the question of orderly government is a mistaken idea. Dread should be reserved for things worthy of dread.

eclipse—One of the *Odes* speaks of eclipses as "of very evil omen," since by "not keeping to their proper paths" the sun and moon "announce evil."[40] "Not keeping to their proper paths" declares errancy, not law-abidingness. Incidentally, the *Ode* would not affect Xun's argument, since it also says, "All through the kingdom there is no (proper) government."

generation—Possibly "age"; since *shi* designates no particular stretch of time, and Xun's point stresses the frequency of such phenomena rather than their infrequency, "generation" is more apt.

frequent—chang, obviously not used to mean "regular" or "predictable," but "frequent" (on *QSZY*'s reading, see note[41]). Tian's *xing* has its *chang*, its regularity, but there are also, at the lower levels, events that are *chang* only in the sense of "common." The constant *xing* of Tian does not exclude such exceptional departures—there is no hard determinism, no strict laws of nature. Nor does Xun venture any statement as to the relative probability of such deviations. (Though the text seems to read *bu chang*, "infrequent," the *bu* negates the following verb (a case of "neg-raising"), not the *chang*.)

eclipse—The *Chunqiu* records 26 eclipses. As Sivin points out, ancient Chinese astronomy, unlike Babylonian and Egyptian, was never equatorial, so the inclination of the ecliptic to the equator was not important. Hence eclipses could never be viewed as predictable,[42] and no chance for a mechanical interpretation ensued. Thus, eclipses were always *bian*, temporary exigents, as unpredictable as wind and rain.

Tian and earth . . . yin *and* yang . . . *things*—Xun returns to his first trivial examples, as if he is not willing to say that eclipses and the like are merely "changes in Tian and Earth, mutations of *yin* and *yang*," etc. He also maintains his hierarchical universe, using different verbs to refer to phenomena at different levels. Tian and Earth cannot mutate, they can only manifest temporary changes; *yin* and *yang* undergo transformations; but things can suffer "deviant emergents" (reading *ni* for *han*, with Liu, corresponding to the same textual emendation in paragraph 5). "Rebellious arrivals" might be too strong, although one cannot read it out *a priori*.

Zhi, "to arrive," is the verb he predicates of "flood and drought" in the first section and (following Yang) of "omens and weird events."

weird—guai—not so much "improbable," as "producing feelings of the uncanny." Xun does not say they are to be treated as if they were ordinary phenomena; what he denies is that they should produce foreboding, as if they indicated consequences for humans.

That such events might have some explanation seems to be ruled out. If any such explanation had human relevance, it would have had a moral component, and the sages would have so indicated.

[Humanly precipitated supernatural omens.]

The textual problems in the following paragraph have been discussed in Chapter 5. We translate here the text as amended, the emendations indicated by footnotes.

40. IF, HOWEVER, THE THINGS THAT HAPPEN ARE SUPERNATURAL MANIFESTATIONS CAUSED BY TERRESTRIAL DISORDERS IN THE HUMAN REALM, THEN ONE MAY BE FILLED WITH DREAD.

41. WHEN POOR PLOUGHING HAS INJURED CROPS,
WHEN POOR WEEDING CAUSES THE HARVEST TO BE LOST,
WHEN GOVERNMENT IS PRECARIOUS AND LOSES THE PEOPLE'S ALLEGIANCE;
WHEN FIELDS ARE UNKEMPT AND HARVESTS ARE BAD,
WHEN GRAIN IS EXPENSIVE AND PEOPLE STARVE,
WHEN CORPSES* LIE IN THE ROAD;

THESE ARE WHAT ARE TO BE CALLED SUPERNATURAL MANIFESTATIONS CAUSED BY TERRESTRIAL DISORDERS IN THE HUMAN REALM.

42. WHEN GOVERNMENTAL MEASURES ARE UNENLIGHTENED,
WHEN OFFICIAL DECISIONS ARE UNTIMELY,
WHEN AGRICULTURE IS NOT INTELLIGENTLY ATTENDED TO;

*Omitting *ren* 人 as superfluous and unmetrical.

When exactions of labor are unseasonable,
When* cows and horses interbreed,
When the six domestic animals produce prodigies;**

These are also to be considered supernatural manifestations caused by terrestrial disorders in the human realm.

When LI and Yi are not cultivated,
When men and women are not properly separated,
When males and females are lewd and disorderly;

When*** fathers and sons doubt one another,
When superiors and inferiors are out of touch with each other,
When invasion and disaster arrive together;

These are what are to be considered supernatural manifestations caused by terrestrial disorders in the human realm.

(End of unrhymed verse)

44. Portents such as these are born from human disorderliness. If all three sorts are precipitated together, the state has no security at all. The reason for these portents is very close at hand, but as visitations they are very grievous. They may be considered weird, but they are also**** to be dreaded.

45. [Our] tradition says, "The books give no explanations for strange things in nature." Instead, they set aside such useless topics for discussion and such unimportant objects of investigation, excluding them from the things it sets out in order, such as the right relations of ruler and minister, the affection of father and son, the distinction

---

*Omitting *ze* 則 as superfluous and unmetrical.

**This whole stanza, 12 graphs, occurs 56 graphs later in the received text.

***See the first footnote above.

****Reading *Yi* 亦 for *er* 而, with Wang.

BETWEEN HUSBAND AND WIFE—PATTERNS TO BE CUT AND POLISHED DAILY, AND NOT NEGLECTED.

When the dislocation of the text is properly corrected (as in Li's edition), and when three unnecessary intrusions into the text are excised, the three paragraphs, 41–43, though unrhymed, have an impressive rhythmic structure: 30 graphs in each of three stanzas, distributed as six four-word lines followed by a six-word line—something obviously to be chanted with solemnity. These three cantos are the dramatic climax of the persuasion: Xun is clearly expressing awe here, not skepticism.

We moderns, who have so thoroughly isolated (in thought) the human realm from both the natural and the supernatural realms, are tempted to note that, with two arguable exceptions (domestic animals interbreeding and also producing prodigies), all the listed "omens" are simply results of bad administration, and conclude that Xun calls them "omens" only metaphorically or satirically. In light of his understanding of the interpenetration of the natural, the supernatural, and the human, and his less conceptually defined sense of causation, he would undoubtedly not understand our doing so; in his context, our grounds for thus being reductionist would not hold.

As already pointed out, Xun does not deny significance to all omens; he makes a clear distinction between those which do presage human misfortune, and hence are to be held in awe, and those which do not, and may only be deemed weird.

Supernatural manifestations caused by terrestrial disorders—yao, appearing in the text with the "supernatural" radical (which also appears in the *Shuo wen* entry), rather than the more usual "woman" one. Watson's "human portents" empties the word too much of both its natural involvements and its clear supernatural implications: that disorders among earthly things involve disturbances in the spiritual realm, and spiritual causes intervene in producing the earthly consequences. Cf. *Zuochuan*, VII, 15: "When the seasons of Heaven are reversed, we have calamities *zai*; when the productions of the earth are reversed, we have prodigious things *yao*; when the virtues of men are reversed, we have disorders *luan*. It is those disorders which give rise to the calamities and prodigious things . . ." (Legge, V, 328). Such calamities are caused by disturbance of natural things; Xun precedes *yao* with *ren*, "human," to indicate he is referring to those disturbances of the order of nature which are caused by humans. See below under paragraph 40.

supernatural manifestations, etc.—See preceding note.

born—sheng, "are born" or "arise from." He does not say humans *cause* them; *sheng* primarily refers to the actions of Tian and Earth and their extensions, and only occasionally, and metaphorically (as when a sage 'produces' LI), to human causal activities (save for giving birth, of course).

reason—shuo, ought perhaps be translated "explanation," but that could smuggle in Western ideas of the nature of explanation that would be misleading here. He does not mean that the phenomena can be brought under some inclusive law-type statement, or conformed to some conceptual model, etc., but that the human behavior that precipitated the specific dislocations in terrestrial affairs which have disrupted the orderly cosmic spiritual processes can be identified by anyone who knows LI.

visitations—zai, "calamities," often taken as sent from Tian (cf. *Shuowen*, "Lightning is called '*zai*' (written with a different graph) also written '*zai*' (as here)").[43] Xun's emphasis on the *proximity* of the cause (occasion) seems nicely to contrast to the *distance* of the source of the outcome (Tian). It would be quite in his style to do so—if we grant him any numinous overtones to his use of *zai*.

Our tradition—Since it was characteristic of, though not unique to, Xun's branch of Confucianism to single out certain books as authoritative, we presume he refers to "the books" as those accepted within his school's tradition.

The books—HSWC's selection from this section precedes this sentence with, "The calamities of Tian are hidden in (the time of) their coming." This would not suit Xun's argument. Yang takes the books to be the "Six Classics"; Xun, however, seems to recognize only five (he bypasses the Yi).

Eno takes *shu* verbally: "prodigies . . . should be recorded but not explained."[44] Although the Classics do record some prodigious things, Confucius did not discuss them (*An.*, 7.12). Mentioning the recording of prodigies would seem to be contrary to Xun's argument here, although his claim that they have occurred in every age could imply that they were recorded.

to be cut and polished daily—an echo of *Ode* 55: "There is our elegant and accomplished prince—/ As from the knife and file,/ As from the chisel and the polisher!"[45] Cut and polished gems were signs of rank and honor, hence, in theory, virtue.

The emphasis on these dimensions of LI leads into another question: LI prescribes traditional sacrifices for rain in time of drought; are these transgressions of the line between Tian and humans? And when Tian responds, isn't that *wei*, "special action?" As Wang Chong was to ask later, "If, before the proper time of rain has come, somebody unreasonably prayed for it, and if Heaven recklessly sent it down, it would be on a level with a prince yielding to solicitations."[46] By emphasizing the untimeliness of the praying and the "recklessness" of Tian's response, even the skeptical Wang seems to allow that timely rain sacrifice and responsibly sent rain from Tian would simply be an appropriate correlation of ritual with natural event.

[What of rain after rain sacrifices?]

46. When we sacrifice for rain, it rains. What sort of thing is that? We maintain, no special sort of thing. It's just like the rain when we don't sacrifice. We "save" the sun and moon when they undergo eclipse, we sacrifice for rain when Tian [has sent] drought, we engage

IN DIVINATION AND THEN DECIDE SOME MATTER OF GREAT MOMENT. IT IS WRONG TO REGARD [THESE THINGS] FROM THE STANDPOINT OF OBTAINING SOMETHING FOR WHICH WE BESEECH, BUT RATHER AS THE PROPER FORM. THUS, WHEREAS THE JUNZI SEES THEM AS THE PROPER FORM, THE POPULACE SEES THEM AS [INFLUENCING] SPIRITS. IF THEY ARE SEEN AS PROPER FORM, GOOD FORTUNE FOLLOWS; IF SEEN AS [INFLUENCING] SPIRITS, MISFORTUNE FOLLOWS.

47. [JUST AS] OF THE THINGS IN THE PROVINCE OF TIAN, NONE OUTSHINES THE SUN AND MOON, OF THE THINGS IN THE PROVINCE OF EARTH, NONE OUTSHINES WATER AND FIRE, [AND] OF NATURAL OBJECTS, NONE OUTSHINES PEARLS AND JADE, [SO], OF THE THINGS THAT ARE HUMANS' PROVINCE, NONE OUTSHINES LI AND YI.

48. BUT IF THE SUN AND MOON DID NOT RISE HIGH, THEIR GLOW WOULD NOT BE RESPLENDENT. IF WATER AND FIRE DID NOT COLLECT, THEIR WETNESS OR SHEEN WOULD NOT BE EXTENSIVE. IF PEARLS AND JADE ARE NOT BROUGHT OUT WHERE THEY ARE VISIBLE, THE EXALTED STATUS OF KINGS AND DUKES WOULD NOT BE EXHIBITED. SO IF LI AND YI ARE NOT GIVEN SPECIAL ATTENTION BY A STATE, THEY WILL NOT PELLUCIDLY MANIFEST ITS MERIT OR NOTEWORTHINESS.

49. THUS, "A MAN'S FATE RESIDES WITH TIAN," BUT THE FATE OF A STATE RESIDES WITH LI. AMONG THOSE WHO GOVERN, HE WHO SURPASSES IN LI AND PROMOTES MEN OF WORTH MAY BE A KING; HE WHO IMPOSES LAW BUT YET LOVES THE PEOPLE MAY BE A LORD PROTECTOR; HE WHO LOVES GAIN AND USES FREQUENT DECEIT WILL RULE ONLY PRECARIOUSLY; WHILE HE WHOSE DARK AND EVIL WAYS INVOLVE SUBVERSION AND THE PLAYING OF FOLK AGAINST EACH OTHER WILL BE [UTTERLY] OVERTHROWN.

Paragraph 46, concerning rain sacrifices, is usually taken as quite separate from its immediate context, which allows it to be read as a statement of religious skepticism. Yet both the preceding paragraph and those following emphasize and recommend LI, and this should also be taken as doing so. Xun's emphasis is not to disvalue rituals, which he holds in high regard, but to reject viewing them as mere instruments for manipulating spiritual things, which would be, interestingly enough, trespassing on or "competing with" Tian's proper sphere. Rituals are not technologies; they are, as he makes plain in many places (especially in *pian* XIX), celebrations, acknowledgments of deep things, necessary elements in the development of persons and peoples, participations in the whole of things. As any thinking religionist knows, superstition consists largely in treating religious rituals as technologies, ways of manipulating situations (as did

Mozi). For Xun, they are ways of responding, of affirming relation, and of celebrating, which are quite different things, things central to genuine culture.

What sort of thing. . . no special sort—On the question, see gloss on paragraph 35. His answer is that rain after sacrifice is to be classed with any other rain, not with the sacrifice.

sacrifice for rain—the great rain sacrifice *yu*,[47] important enough to be recorded 19 times in the *Spring and Autumn Annals*, and hence a rite with ample Classical documentation. Together with eclipse rituals and "matters of great moment," these were rites involving the highest levels of government, responses to situations significant for the whole people. As one who revered the classical past, Xun could not have taken these things to be matters of scorn, but as essential parts of LI and of the kind of personal and social culture it represented.

when Tian has sent drought—The text says simply, "Tian droughts." We might prefer "The sky doesn't rain." It is doubtful Xun would see any difference. The rain sacrifice was a sacrifice to Tian, as one, sky or not, that could be addressed.

we engage in divination—Divination undoubtedly had at least Neolithic roots. It does not appear to have been so much an attempt to "get what you seek" as an attempt to "know Tian." Consider Allan on Shang sacrificing, "Shang divination was an attempt to verify that the ritual offerings were received and satisfactory and that there would therefore be no curse."[48] That is, they served to affirm that a proposed course of action was "acceptable to the universe." Late Zhou was not Shang, but rituals are very conservative, and accounts of divination in the *Zuochuan* are illuminated by Allan's interpretation.

something for which we beseech—de qiu. As pointed out already, *qiu* was anciently the name for a rain sacrifice,[49] though we have no way of knowing whether Xun knew that. All three times the word appears in this *pian*, it is in a context of Tian or "knowing Tian." It is difficult to assess how much to make of that, but also difficult to ignore it.

proper form—"Elegant culture (which harmonizes with Tian and Earth)" would be perhaps too weighty a reading of *wen*, but certainly much closer to Xun's point than Dubs' "glossing over the matter" or Unschuld's "purely ornamental."[50] For Xun, *wen* usually is a serious matter, and nearly always means much more than mere "ornament"—it was Modi's failure to understand *wen* that was his chief blindness. The polarity between *shen* and *wen* here, and the related polarity between superstition and religion, we discuss in chapter X. Suffice it here to say that Xun is affirming religion as over against superstition, not rejecting it. This is somewhat more evident as we treat this last paragraph as leading into the following section, which is an expansion of its last two sentences.

The two paragraphs, 47 and 48, of this next section are made up of balanced but unrhymed clauses. In meaning they follow directly from the preceding one. The great rain sacrifice is part of *wen*, the proper embellishment of the life of humans, the cultural aspect of LI. Taking it as utilitarian[51] rather than as celebrative misses his point, just as treating pearls and jade as having utilitarian rather than celebrative functions would. Fire and water have many uses, but Xun alludes here only to their functioning to ornament Earth, and to what they must do to perform that function. He ignores any causal functions of the sun and moon, and instead treats them as Tian's ornaments, fitting for Tian's exalted status—but they, too, must perform properly to that end.

The same is true of fire and water as evidences of Earth's elegance. As these complete and proclaim with their brilliance the exalted status of Tian and Earth, and thus bring to fullness their place in the scheme of things, so, also, do pearls and jade fill out the status of kings and dukes, and LI and YI bring the order that harmonizes the human realm with everything else—so that all together manifest the beautiful appropriateness that calls forth Xun's fascination with LI: "How is LI not absolutely perfect? (By it) Tian and Earth are harmonious, the sun and moon are luminous, the four seasons are orderly, the star groups have their procession, the rivers flow, the myriad things prosper" (*pian* XIX). Thus he affirms that the rain sacrifice is to be seen as *celebrative* worship of Tian, rather than as the manipulative "worship" of the *do ut des* of popular religion. See chapter 10.

of the things. . .—Zai Tianzhe here means "the things in the heavens." Earlier in the essay Xun used *zai Tian* to mean such things as success in one's profession or the length of one's life, things "in Tian's realm" in quite another sense. This suggests he did not classify these two sorts of things as being as different as we would take them to be.

Sun, moon, fire, and water have natural functions not under humans' control, but for the proper fulfilment of the functions of pearls and jade or LI and YI, human effort is required. Pearls and jade may be natural objects, but here they lie within the orbit of humanity, as objects of human effort and ornaments of human distinction. Tian and Earth may make them, but only humans fit them into the true scheme of things. It is LI that allots their proper places. The same may be true of other natural objects. Hence discrimination of nature's part from humans' part is subtle and difficult.

outshines—ming, "bright," "clear"; but it may also carry overtones of "manifestation" of spiritual things, as in *ming shen*, "spirit manifesting itself," *shenming*, "(localized) manifestation of spiritual power," or, applied to objects in religious rituals, "what ritually acknowledges spiritual presence." These seem to be continuous, not disjunct meanings, but the attenuated, secular meanings are much more common. Nevertheless, "pearls" and especially "jade" often convey overtones we would consider esoteric. To write off such correlative involvements *a priori* would be reductionist.

Xun's idea of the hierarchy of order that obtains in the cosmos is here illustrated: the courses of the heavenly bodies are constant; they do not fail to display Tian's glory; fire and water are less predictable—Earth's grandeur is not always displayed. Pearls and jade are produced rarely, and have no function while buried in water or earth, and LI and YI are wholly subject to the choices of humanity.

exalted status . . . exhibited.—More directly, *insignia of rank* (*bao*), literally, "precious," but occurring in the ode *Song gao*, in "I give you the great [jade] sceptre/To be your treasure [*bao*]" (Waley, *Ode* 137). There it clearly means "insignia of office," evidence of worth, authority, and dignity.

pellucidly manifest—The word is "white" (*bai*), which means both "pure" and "evident." Xun undoubtedly intended neither overtone to be missed.

In paragraph 2 Xun set Yao and Jie over against each other, as polar opposites. Here in paragraph 49 he presents gradations of security in government, without any comment as to what Tian "cannot" do—in perfect parallel to several similar statements elsewhere. For the rest of the essay, he is done with the ideal polarity, and wishes to concentrate on the practical gradations of following LI.

This paragraph (49) has been thought a digression, and perhaps spurious. Similar utterances occur elsewhere in the *Xunzi*, suggesting that he was willing to settle for a Lord Protector if no true king should arise. He might well have considered it an appropriate explication of the previous sentence.

A man's fate resides with Tian etc.—This sentence occurs also in *pian* XVI. There are no textual grounds for excising it here. Xun's characterization of *ming*, "fate," as "unexpected event" in *pian* XXII seems consistent with what is said here. As regards life span, a human is a *wu*, a natural thing. It is only in regard to their moral-political being (which in *pian* IX is based on their YI, their "moral capability," which humans alone of natural things have and which gives them their unique dignity "under Tian"[52]), that their fate depends upon LI.

The following poem, of six rhymed lines followed by a moral (not just the "that's what it means" that Xun appends to quotations from the classics), occurs between two paragraphs exalting LI, and should either be read in that context, placed somewhere else in the essay, or excised. Since there is no other promising location for it, and its content clearly accords with the essay's overall thesis, the first alternative should be followed. This suggests the poem is primarily about LI, not technology.

(Each of the first five lines of this poem has a distinctive structure, not found anywhere else in the *Xunzi*, nor have we found a parallel anywhere else. Each runs

A *er* B *shu-yu* C *er* D,

with A, B, C, and D being in each case a verb-object clause. The most obvious logical reading would be, in each case,

(A *er* B) *shu-yu* (C *er* D),

where *shu-yu* is a double interrogative particle asking for preference between the alternative preceding it and that following, giving "Which is preferable: B under conditions A, or D under conditions C?", which would accord perfectly with the typical parallelism present. However, there can be grammatical parallelism without congruent logical parallelism, and such a reading, though surely the most obvious, misses two important facts: (1) that in each case "C *er* D" is an explication of an alternative possibility of A, and (2) that although in each case Xun is recommending "C *er* D," in every case A is not something he denigrates, but rather something he elsewhere either practices or recommends. Thus, although on syntactic and literary grounds the reading noted first may appear preferable, the logic of the lines should be read as

A *er* [B *shu-yu* (C *er* D)],

as we here translate them.)

[LI as summary of all the foregoing.]

50. WHEN "MAGNIFYING TIAN," WHICH IS BETTER:
(MERELY) TO CONTEMPLATE IT,
OR TO TURN THINGS INTO WEALTH* BY NURTURING THEM?**
WHEN "FOLLOWING TIAN," WHICH IS BETTER:
TO SING ITS PRAISES, OR
TO MAKE USE OF WHAT OCCURS*** BY CONFORMING IT TO A PATTERN?
WHEN "ATTENDING TO THE SEASONS," WHICH IS BETTER:
(MERELY) TO AWAIT THEM, OR

---

*Replacing *zhi* 制 with *zai* 財, with Wang Niansun, to rhyme.
**Reversing *wu chu* 物畜, with Gao.
***Omitting *tian* 天, to maintain meter.

TO EMPLOY THEM PRODUCTIVELY BY RESPONDING TO THEM?
WHEN "HARMONIZING WITH THINGS," WHICH IS BETTER:
(MERELY) TO PRIZE THEM, OR
TO TRANSFORM THEM BY MANIFESTING THEIR POTENTIAL?
WHEN "THINKING ABOUT THINGS," WHICH IS BETTER:
(MERELY) TO NOTICE WHAT THEY ARE ON THEIR OWN, OR TO AVOID LOSING THEM, BY MAKING THEM CONFORM TO THEIR UNDERLYING RATIONALE?
(IN SHORT,) WHICH IS BETTER: TO DIRECT YOUR CONCERN TOWARD THAT WHICH GIVES BIRTH TO THINGS, OR TO ASSIST* WHAT BRINGS EXISTING THINGS TO FULL COMPLETION?

THUS, IF, NEGLECTING HUMAN MATTERS, YOU DIRECT YOUR THOUGHTS TO TIAN (ALONE), YOU WILL LOSE WHAT IS REALLY ESSENTIAL IN NATURAL THINGS.

magnifying Tian—Da, here "to deem great," like *gadlu* in Psalm 34: "Oh magnify the Lord with me, let us exalt His name together (King James Version).

turn things into wealth . . . by nurturing them—reading as in the footnote, but reading *cai* as 財 rather than 裁, with the text in *pian* VI, VIII, and IX.[53]

what occurs . . . conforming to a pattern—our reading of the clause *zhi ming*, omitting the *Tian* in the given *zhi Tian-ming*, as explained below. The phrase occurring in the text has been translated as "control nature's course," which, though a popular reading, is difficult to support (*zhi* has overtones of an already-existing pattern[54]). Nowhere else does Xun use *Tian ming*, although he has just said, "The *ming* of a man lies with Tian." In *pian* XXII he defines *ming* as "unexpected occurrences one meets with" (W 140); these together remind one of those cases in the *Zuochuan* wherein the sudden death of a figure is tied to his questionable character. That, however, is little help. Although what *ming* means here is far from

*Reading *you* 有 as *you* 友.

certain, we tentatively accept the extension of Xun's *pian* XXII definition to include whatever happenings involve us. (Incidentally, under such a reading, restoring *Tian* to the text would make little difference.)

The phrase *zhi Tian ming* that stands in the text is puzzling, once one has questioned Hu's well-known translation. Relegating justification elsewhere,[55] let us summarize here how our tentative solution was reached. (1) *Zhi* is to be read as indicated, "to bring into the proper pattern"; (2) "Tian" is to be omitted as a gloss; (3) the definition of *ming* just discussed is used, as referring to "new situations that arise"—not necessarily in nature, narrowly defined, since we have no grounds for restricting *ming* to the areas we would readily call "natural." (In the *Zuochuan*, evil folk can meet unexpected death by human agents, not just natural ones.)

(The circularity of assuming a technological interest on the part of Xun, using that assumption as a basis for reading so puzzling a phrase as *zhi Tian ming* as "control nature's course," and then justifying the attribution to him of such an interest on the basis of that reading is patent.[56] Arbitrarily to expand the *pian* XXII definition so as to include all natural events, taking this to imply a tacit "Tian," reading that as "nature," and from that to argue that for Xun *Tian* can be equivalent to "nature," is equally circular.)

Are we here liable to a *tu quoque*, in translating the phrase as we do? Doesn't that imply a "technological interest" on the part of Xun Qing? Not quite. Our penultimate line reads "assist[57] what brings them to full completion." Xun has already said that such final perfection is the "completion of Tian's work," and the preceding phrases ("nurturing," "manifesting their potential," "conform to the underlying rationale)", together with the following "what is really essential" present the goal not as human dominance over nature, but as nature's own fulfilment. One of the meanings of Xun's much-used word "order" (*zhi*) is "to heal," and the aim of healing is to bring accord to the thing healed, not some private aim of the healer. Thus Xun's aim is not "to control nature's course" but "to assist things in finding their place," so as not "to lose their essence."

to transform them (*hua*)—not merely to change them (*bian*), but to translate them to another (probably higher) state; to "transform the people" means to bring them into obedience, security, and prosperity.

what they are on their own—things left to the processes that brought them into being (*sheng*), such as the functions of a human "as Tian gives them" in paragraphs 18–21. Xun speaks in *pian* X of things in nature "not having (their) proper place," and in VIII and IX of things, under sagely rule, "attaining (their) proper place" (*yi*). He clearly excludes making the spontaneous (dis)order of nature normative, as Daoists suggest. The "underlying rationale" of things is not implemented spontaneously (as by *sheng*), but requires the sage's "completing the work of Tian," which "produces" but "cannot order."

their underlying rationale—li, often translated "reason" or "principle"; originally probably "to mark out fields," but later "to carve jade according to its veins"—not following the veins could ruin the jade. Since Xun often associates it with "use," and associates it with things (parallel to associating *wen*, "cultured pattern" with people), it may imply for him an inner structure *toward usefulness*, that is connected to the underlying LI of the cosmos.

essential—(*jing*), sometimes written as *qing* (cf. Graham, Disputers of the Tao, 417)—"the word which, with the reservation that it is independent of Being, is comparable with Aristotelian essence," but (99)—"I therefore prefer to use constructions with 'essential' rather than translate *ch'ing* directly by 'essence'."

neglecting human matters—of which LI is paramount. "Neglecting your humanity" is possible and attractive, but seems rather improbable.

[LI, the Dao of the Kings, is the Way.]

51. What was unchanging in [the rule of] the hundred kings is sufficient; consider it to be the core of the Dao. And when one situation ended, and another arose, they responded to it in terms of that core. Applying that core intelligently, they caused no confusion. But if one does not know this core, he does not know how to respond to change. The broad outlines of this core have never failed to this day. Confu-

sion arises from their mistaken application, orderly government from their most detailed application. If you focus on what is effective in this Dao, you can follow it successfully; but you cannot operate with just bits and pieces of it. If you miss its way entirely, you will be seriously off the track.

52. Those who wade in waters chart the deep places. If the chart isn't clear, they fall in. Those who govern people have a chart—the Dao. If they are not clear about the chart, chaos results. Those who lived by LI are the chart; setting LI at naught is putting one's age into darkness (to darken an age is to increase its disorder).*

53. Thus, when Dao is perfectly clear, the difference between what lies outside and what within will be clearly charted. When this distinction between what is obscure and what is quite evident has been stabilized, the people's pitfalls will have been eliminated.

54. Each sort of thing (as they appear in) the world presents only one incomplete part of Dao; any one thing represents only one incomplete part of things in general. A foolish man, though he represents only an incomplete part of one thing, may deem himself to know the Dao, but he has no such knowledge.

55. Though Shenzi took later ideas into account, he took no notice of earlier ones; though Laozi took yielding** into account, he took no account of enlarging*** one's scope; though Mozi took equality into account, he took no account of inequality; though Songzi took limiting desires into account, he took no account of developing them.

56. If there are late ideas, but no early ones, the entire populace has no key to their situation. If there is yielding,** but no resolute development,*** the worthy and the unworthy would be indistinguishable. If all are equal, without inequalities, administrative orders could not be given. If desires are diminished, with none being developed, the populace could not be transformed.

57. When *The Documents* says: "Follow the kings' Dao, whether it involves actions you like or not; follow the kings' road, whether it involves actions you hate or not," that's what it means.

---

*The last five graphs (translated in parentheses) are undoubtedly a gloss, though there is no textual ground for excluding them.

**Reading 詘 as *qu* 屈, with Liang.

***Reading *xin* 信 as *shen* 伸, with Yang.

the hundred kings—Xun speaks variously of "former kings" and "later kings," distinguishing them, in *pian* V, only by the amount of historical data available about them. Here (and a dozen other places) he includes them all—"the past (sage-)kings." Knoblock dates the use of "former kings" as early and "later kings" as late. That is at least possible, but sheds no light on "the hundred kings." It is also possible that Xun's use conformed to the polemical needs of the moment, as Modi's appeals to the Xia and proto-Daoist appeals to even earlier figures certainly antedated the beginning of Xun's career. As he has, in this essay, appealed to Yao and Yu ("former") and Tai and Wen ("later"), and here assumes an identity in their essential policies, nothing can be made of the epithet here. Probably it should just be translated "the ancient kings." (Since he restricts "king" to those he approves (*real* kings), tyrants like Jie would not be included, no matter how ancient).

knew how to respond—Pian XXXI (*Aigong*) quotes Confucius as saying: "He may be called a great sage who knows exhaustively the Great Dao, who does not lack resources when responding to changing conditions. . . ." (for a fuller translation see note[58]). *Pian* XIV (*Zhengshi*) remarks, "To cope with a crisis among the people, the very first principle of good government is to respond to changed conditions according to YI." Xun speaks of "responding to changing conditions" 15 other times, and it is YI (moral common sense, the *aisthesis* of the *phronimos*) that guides the application of unchanging LI in a changing world. This fact alone should turn the edge of the charge of rigid authoritarianism that some have aimed at Xun Qing.

outside. . . within—Wai nei often refer to men's affairs and women's affairs; some have taken the two words to distinguish Confucian ethics and Daoist mysticism. Neither use would fit here. In terms of the rest of the essay, they appear to refer back to what lies outside the human sphere—the obscure work of Tian—and what lies within the Dao of humans—the disciplines and institutions of LI, as clearly delineated by those "perfect men" of the past, the sage-kings.

the people's pitfalls—Folk in the Warring States period were floundering, misled by false charts wrongly indicating where the dangers lurked, seeking to find firm ground by listening to those who would trespass on Tian's turf. Only those who lived by LI, and did not compete with Tian, could safely be followed.

Each sort of thing. . . presents. . . only part of the Dao—taking *wu* as used in the *Zuo*, "sort of thing." "Thing" can include matters social and political as well as material. When Xun criticizes six philosophers in *pian* XXI (three of them represented here), he says that Dao,

> while embodying what is constant must embrace all changes. Just one corner is not sufficient. (These) men of limited understanding, considering one corner (alone), could not yet recognize (what was really the case), and therefore, thinking it sufficient, made much of it.

Dao is not completely embodied until the sage orders the whole world. Compare *pian* X: "The myriad things being in the same world, have different makeups; (even) when not in their proper places their uses exist"; and in IX: "The myriad things in the cosmos, and every man alive, wait for a sage; only then will they be (properly) organized (*fen*)." The Dao of humans, which for Xun is inseparable from LI, completes natural and social things as one harmonious whole.

foolish man—one who has not developed himself according to the disciplines of paragraph 23; as undeveloped, he is still only "one incomplete part." Rival philosophers, not yet being complete men, could hardly have complete philosophies. How could they "know Dao" when they have not followed the way that leads to "knowing Tian?"

Shenzi—Shen Dao, who, according to Thompson, was born in Zhao about 360, was a celebrated member of the "Jixia Academy" in Qi before 300, wrote a book, and left or died before 285.[59] Hanfei (*pian* 40) quotes him as saying, "Yao as an ordinary person could not have ruled three others," and treats him as a forerunner of legalism. Of existing fragments attributed to him, one reads, "The *Songs* are bygone aspirations, the *Documents* bygone exhortations, the *Annals* are bygone undertakings."[60] *Zhuangzi* 33 says he "laughed at the world for honoring worthy men" and "disparaged the great sages of the world,"[61] but that is a later account. In *pian* XXI Xun says of him that "being beclouded by 'law,' he did not understand (the ancient?) worthies."

Laozi—"the old philosopher"—probably a legendary character. No reliable historical identification of such a philosopher exists. We do not know whether this reference derives from the *Zhuangzi*, where the name appears 22 times (though never in the authentic *nei pian*[62]), from the *DDJ*, widely attributed to a Laozi, and which, as already noted, contains a phrase identical with one in paragraph 9 of the *Tian lun*, or from oral tradition about such a character or his teachings. That Xunzi knew the *DDJ* is more probable than that he knew the later chapters of the *Zhuangzi*. That he had heard oral Daoist references to a "Laozi" is even more probable.

yielding . . . enlarging one's scope—(qu . . . shen), literally "crouching . . . standing tall," but when coordinate, often "contracting . . . expanding." DDJ 38 treats Confucian virtues as contractions of natural humanity; Xun's theory of education stresses how they expand man beyond his "nature" and make him "worthy," and this essay has sketched out how the "perfect man" has "completed Tian's work." Lao's partiality lay in his ignoring the way humans (and things) can be developed beyond the limits of natural endowment.

Mozi—apparently Xun's favorite opponent, named in eight different *pian*, attacked at length in X and XX. So well known that further comment is unnecessary, except that in *pian* XXI Xun identifies Mo's chief failure as "he did not understand *wen*," the elegant form of truly civilized life.

Songzi—also known as Song Xing, Song Keng, and Song Yong. He was apparently contemporary with Mencius. Xun criticizes his views in *pian* XVIII (probably early), more briefly in XXI, and, conjoined with Mozi, in VI. Probably the long section on desires at the end of XXII was also directed against Song. *Zhuangzi* 33 says of him and his companion Yin Wen, "To outlaw aggression and abolish the use of arms—these were their external aims. To lessen the desires and weaken the emotions—these were their internal aims."[63]

Xun apparently sees these four ways of being one-sided toward the Dao as dangerous; the Legalists (in the broadest sense) rejected traditional wisdom, the Daoists were too passive, the Moists thought they could have egalitarianism and order too, and Songzi would deprive social life of richness and motivation. All rejected LI.

no key to their situation—The text says merely "no door" (*men*), but this use of *men* as "the way out of a predicament" is attested at least in the *Yi*. Xun often claims that only the time-tested standards of the past can be relied upon to correct the present; other claims (as those of the Legalists) are purely arbitrary.

could not be transformed—Watson's note, "Because they will not be attracted by the hope of reward" mistakes Xun's idea of popular transformation, which he nowhere bases on hope of reward—except for rewards due to worthy officials. The people are to be moved primarily by the moral power and example of the sage-king, acting almost miraculously, "as if he were a god (*shen*)." Desires come into the picture in two ways: (1) the official's rewards already mentioned, which are, of course, things a refined and learned man would desire, and (2) the sensitization and exquisite discrimination ("multiplication") of desires that is itself part of the discipline leading toward the scholar, the Junzi, and eventually the sage. In paragraph 25, "the sage sets straight the sensibilities Tian gave." The people at the bottom can be transformed only if there is a rich, elite culture at the top. One is reminded of John Dewey:

> The formation of a cultivated and effectively operative good judgment or taste with respect to what is esthetically admirable, intellec-

> tually acceptable and morally approvable is the supreme task set to human beings.[64]

Xun Qing would no doubt largely agree.

Xun holds every one of these men to have an insufficient grasp of the principle of hierarchy and what its undergirdings must be. Indeed, every one of them was, in one way or another, a critic not merely of traditional hierarchic patterns, but, at some point, of the basic principle of hierarchy.

The Documents—Shujing, V. iv. 14, part of the "Great Plan" (*Hong fan*).[65]

the kings' Dao—Xun has already claimed that this is sufficient, as it was for Yao, to guide a ruler into achieving what Xun indicated at the very beginning that Yao did—an agriculture that provided plenty and was independent of flood and drought, an administration of the people that freed them from epidemic disease, and a harmony of things with Tian that would never be threatened by any spiritual visitations, presumably the same ideal state he characterizes somewhat differently in *pian* IX and calls *da shen*,[66] "the highest spirituality" or "the maximum of order."

8. Some Interpretive Issues

Several crucial issues of interpretation arise during translation of the *Tian lun*. Many issues have been resolved in the commentary, and should need no further treatment, but a few call for more integrated and compact treatment to establish clearly the lines of thought we find in the essay.

Following Dao as the Inclusive Condition

First, the logical and rhetorical force of the two compound conditional sentences needs clarification: "If (a ruler), after encouraging agriculture, is frugal in use, Tian then 'cannot' impoverish," etc., and "If, neglecting agriculture . . . then Tian 'cannot' cause prosperity," etc. In the first case, the third thing Tian 'cannot' do is "chastise"; in the second, it is "bring about blessings." "Impoverishment" and "epidemics" are included in "chastising," and "prospering" and "being whole" in "blessings," so the basic conditional is "If, having cultivated Dao, he does not depart from it, Tian 'cannot' chastise; if, turning away from Dao, he behaves foolishly, Tian 'cannot' bring him blessings."

Do these mean that if a ruler does "depart from Dao," Tian *can* chastise; if he ceases "turning away from Dao," Tian can bless? In strict formal logic, of course, denying an antecedent leaves the consequent indeterminate, but rhetorically that tends not to be so. If Tian categorically cannot chastise or bless, there is no rhetorical point in stating any conditions. It is possible, of course, if one identifies Tian with "nature," to say that Xun is simply stating the natural conditions for prosperity or penury; this is fine as long as one limits one's attention to agriculture and corvee schedules. But Dao for Xun contains many hints of moral, ritual, and spiritual disciplines with their own hardly naturalistic consequences, and it is clearly cultivation of Dao that he is primarily commending. Thus, we conclude that the conditions for escaping all these evils include nonnaturalistic ones, and, given the degree of correlation Xun maintains among the physical, moral, and spiritual, we have no leave to limit ourselves to the simpler and more attractive naturalistic interpretation.

This becomes especially clear in what follows: "Hence" (in consequence) "flood or drought could not cause starving, nor heat or cold cause sickness, nor uncanny occurrences misfortune." In a questioned passage in *pian* X Xun asserts that "although under Yu there were ten years of flood and under Tang there were seven years of drought" there were no starving people, apparently (from the context) because the rulers had stored up sufficient grain. This is a perfectly satisfactory naturalistic explanation, so long as we do not raise the question, "Would Yu have had enough grain for 20 years of flood?" If the size of the harvest and the extent of the flood both depend upon Tian, then Yu's success did, indeed, depend on what Tian was "disposed to do." That the extent of the flood depended upon Tian is suggested by the tradition that Yu tried to cleanse himself of the transgression that brought on the flood.[1]

Further, how does one account for "uncanny occurrences" being "unable to bring misfortune" in a manner appropriate to the literary parallelism with "flood and drought?" Must we make the move Knoblock does concerning the passage in *pian* II, which he translates as "A person who possesses these three qualities, though he be sent a greatly inauspicious omen, would Heaven have brought his ruin?" and then says in a note that Xun changed his mind about this before writing the *Tian lun*? Why must the *Tian lun* be interpreted as contrary to this statement, just to maintain a traditional reading of it, especially when there is so little evidence that *pian* II was much earlier than the *Tian lun*? A more just conclusion would seem to be that, for Xun, flood and drought were correlates to, and, in cases wherein Dao was not followed perfectly, involved with, "uncanny occurrences," if not, indeed, themselves being such.

If flood or drought can bring famine, except under conditions of following Dao, then the parallelism requires us to read that uncanny occurrences can also bring misfortune, except under the same conditions. Here a naturalistic reading becomes impossible. The best that could be said for it would be that Xun is referring to the omens arising from human activity, which he discusses later. To them we shall return.

One aspect of our difficulty is the preciseness of our Western concept of cause. When discussing correlative thinking, we quoted a series of apparent cause-and-effect statements that Xun treated as parallel; each could, indeed, be a metaphor for any other. This does not mean he did not recognize mechanical causation or biological motivation; it is that he did not distinguish them the way we do. In consequence, it is misleading to impose our distinctions upon him. For him, the way that floods can be accompanied by famine is quite correlate to the way that uncanny occurrences can be accompanied by misfortunes; else he would not trust the parallelism. To say, then, that he did not trust common sense is specious; this *was* common sense, though not that of a Lockean Englishman.

Along the same line, his threat that the evil ruler's state "would undergo famine, even if flood or drought had not yet arrived," would "suffer sickness, even if heat or cold had not yet arrived," would have "misfortune, even if no uncanny phenomena had yet arrived," does not deny, but rather implies, that a slightly less evil administration might suffer famine as a result of flood, or misfortune as a result of uncanny phenomena. To read him otherwise would be to take him to be thinking our thoughts before us, rather than to mean what he most clearly appears to say, in terms of his logic rather than ours.

The Significance of "Tian Cannot"

A related problem is pointed out in the commentary, as to just how Xun understands the "cannot" in the apparent statement that "Tian cannot impoverish . . . send epidemics . . . chastise . . . ," and so forth. He apparently does not have a well-worked-out theory of possibility. The only place he attempts to distinguish "M cannot do x" from "M will never do x" is in *pian* XXIII, when discussing the proposition, "The man in the street can become a Yu." There he uses *bu koyi*, not *bu neng*, when he wants to say someone "is not capable" of doing x, and he uses *bu neng* to mean someone "cannot cause himself to do" x, that is, he "cannot bring himself to do" x.[2] He says specifically that "although he cannot (*bu neng*) become a Yu, that does not undercut 'he can (*koyi*) become a Yu.'" It is clear that here he uses *bu neng* to mean a *situational* or a *dispositional* impossibility and *bu koyi* to mean an inherent impossibility.

This is quite in line with his statement in *pian* XXIV that "Wu had Wu Zixu, but was not able (*bu neng*) to use him," when the inability was dispositional or situational (like an employer telling an applicant, "You're well qualified, but we can't use you"). In some texts of *Analects* 14.17 we find *bu neng* in "Guanzhong could not (bring himself to) die for Prince Jiu"; in 18.3 Duke Jing says of Confucius, "I am not able (*bu neng*) to use him"; other examples of such usage could be adduced. "Tian cannot" may well be a comment about the situation rather than about Tian *per se*; that would certainly fit the conditional construction better, and, as pointed out, would maintain Xun's consistency in not talking speculative theology.

It is worth noting that Gao Heng indicates an instance, in the *Tian lun*[3] (referred to in the commentary), where the graph for *neng* may be a graphic variant (simple form) for *tai*, "manner," equated by *Shuowen* with *yi*, "disposition, intention." This at least opens the door to such a reading here: not that Tian "cannot," but that it "is not disposed to." This is not so far from the reading of *neng* discussed above, nor from the use of *neng* in both the *Shi* and the *Shu* to mean "to help" or "to be well disposed toward."[4] There is thus more than a little justification for reading *Tian bu neng* as "Tian will have no inclination to" or "Tian would never."

A word here would be in place regarding the common observation that in Han Confucianism, and much more in neo-Confucianism, Tian can be referred to as "having no will." "Will," *zhi*, carries the idea of "aim" or "purpose," which is basic to our idea of personality. Yet in Chinese ethics, one may have a self-regarding will, and be evil; one may have a will directed toward a goal good for all, and be good; or one may need no will, because one has already achieved the character and position that best fits one into the total scheme of things. As Jiwei Ci puts it: "In the moral life as Confucius conceives it, the accent falls on obligations rather than rights, on self-sacrifice rather than fairness, on obedience rather than resistance, on harmony rather than progress through change."[5] If one already fulfills all obligations, yields oneself to the total process, shows no resistance, and exists in harmony, in what sense can one speak of will?

Thus, it is difficult to say just what denying Tian a "will" would mean, once one has given up any idea that Tian ever acts in an arbitrary or *ad hoc* fashion. In the same sense, the perfect sage, even a Confucian one, would also have no "will"—his mind is characterized by unity, emptiness, and stillness. In *pian* XXV Xun refers to the point where the sage-to-be finally "thinks down to essentials" so that his "spirit is perfected" in perfect unity, as the "end point of will." Where we hold "will" to be one of the perfections of a person, the Chinese idea would suggest that it is rather a mark of an imperfection, either in the person or in his or her situation, an imperfection that requires will or effort to deal with. Just as the perfect Confucian ruler does nothing, since his ministers, once he has established his perfect regime, take care of everything, so Tian, the highest in the cosmos just as the sage is in the human realm, need not "will" anything. As we interpreted the very beginning of the *Tian lun*, Tian's *xing* follows its Dao perfectly, *wu-wei*.

It is appropriate here for the philosopher to appeal to Leibniz's "identity of indiscernibles," and ask how such a perfectly constant "non-willing" entity differs from a completely nonpersonal, even a mechanical, process. In terms of a thoroughly antiseptic discursive description, it may not. Then is the difference merely one that could be called a "picture preference," a function of imagination? Not at all. Such a view assumes a theory of language that takes conceptual description to be the fundamental, and autonomous, functioning of language—a typical Enlightenment posture. However, the language of correlative thinking and that of fundamentally hierarchic thinking are not, without destructiveness or censorship, amenable to such analysis (as the fate of Augustinianism in Scotism and Ockhamism illustrates). So long as "Tian" functions for Xun in a way that is integrally moral, religious, and aesthetic as well as what we would want to separate off as "descriptive," our isolative categories can only hinder our ability to listen to him.

This is not the place to spend more time on theory of language. The issue has, however, been stated, and we believe it to be fundamental to comparative philosophy.

Omens

Another issue, somewhat similar to the first, arises out of Xun's discussion of omens. The question is raised about falling stars and tree noises. Xun refers such to various apparently minor disturbances among the things of nature, and says they are not to be dreaded.

He then speaks of quite different disturbances: eclipses, unseasonable wind and rain, strange stars appearing. These, he says, are not infrequent, but whether they accompany human evils depends on the quality of the government. Here he injects another conditional construction. How is it to be interpreted? When he says, "If government is stable because rulers are enlightened (read "follow LI"), in *that* case (*ze shi*) they [such omens] are without harm, even if all arise together," is he maintaining that what evil-accompanying force omens have may be rendered inoperative by good government? Is he implying that the omens may have a genuine involvement in evils that arise if that condition is not fulfilled? Conversely, he says, "If government is precarious because rulers are benighted, in that case things are without benefit, even if no omens arise." Clearly, lack of omens does nothing for order, which is the "benefit" government offers. In the former case, human well-being is apparently protected from disorderliness in nature by the benefits of good government; in the latter, even though one might expect human disorder to bring about correlative disorders in nature, if that does not happen, there is no lessening of human evil. He is not asserting there is no connection at all between omens and human welfare, for if he were, what is the point of the conditional construction?

In short, he seems to be saying: (1) Falling stars and tree noises have no relation to human welfare; they are disorders solely within Tian's province. (2) Eclipses and the like may have involvement with human affairs if government is unstable; otherwise not. He says that the former are not to be dreaded; he does not say that about the latter. As pointed out in the commentary, he is using an *a fortiori* argument: If the balefulness of important omens such as eclipses depends inversely on the government's harmoniousness with the order of things, how much less should one dread petty local oddities? One should concern oneself, rather, with the state of the government.

Though the petty events are but deviations in natural process, the more important events may not be solely within Tian's province; they may overlap humans'. He has already said that distinguishing between Tian's province and humans' is so difficult that only the "perfect man" can do it with clarity. Yet the key to any omen's significance is the state of civil society.

What are we to make of this? First, the reference to good and bad government clearly anticipates his upcoming discussion of "humanly precipitated omens," most of which involve governmental failures. In fact, their discussion is largely a spelling out of the "precarious government" that needs no omens to fail (as well as being a likely description of not-infrequent social conditions during the very late Zhou). Second, near the close of that section he quotes, "The books do not interpret strange things in nature"—but they do record them, in connection, apparently, with bad government: eclipses, unseasonable weather, and, no doubt, strange stars (but not falling stars[6] or tree noises). Xun had great respect for the books, and we should not expect him to doubt them. It would be typical of his concerns, however, to decry focusing on such omens rather than on the human disorders that may have precipitated them.

Eclipses and the like may then perhaps also be "humanly precipitated omens," but it is evident that Xun finds them of much less use for his argument than omens he can point to in the Zhanguo situation: fields devastated, hunger and death, government and households disrupted, and so forth. These are present and pressing. His emphasis on social disorder as correlative to cosmic disorder turns him away from allowing any real place for the reverse emphasis. If cosmic disorders have their own causes, they are irrelevant to us; if they have human causes, those causes demand our attention. In short, the *Tian lun* does not present us with enough evidence to establish that he "did not believe in" at least some omens; it does provide strong evidence that he believed in attending to human disorders, whether they involved omens or not, and some evidence that he believed they did. He does seem to distinguish eclipses and such, which "the books" record, and hence are taken to be important by scholars, from tree noises and falling stars, which disturb "the ordinary folk."

Sacrifice for Rain

Our disagreement with the usual interpretation of the rain sacrifice passage is evident from the commentary. One question not touched upon there is, "Just what is the misfortune that arises from taking the rain sacrifice to be a way of 'getting what you ask for?'" The good fortune that arises from treating it as Xun sees it is clear: a proper response to Tian in a difficult situation, affirming our place in the whole picture, and so fulfilling *wen*, "civilized culture," the counterpart in human affairs to the *li*, (the proper underlying structure of the cosmos). In short, it affirms order in a situation that could be pregnant with disorder. But what evil is threatened by the opposite? As we have repeatedly said, evil for Xun is basically disorder. What is disordered in popular religion that treats sacrifice as a *do ut des*? Xun has earlier said that Tian's proper functioning was "to bestow without being besought." Beseeching a superior in a way that grants his complete freedom to administer affairs his own way is appropriate, but attempting to manipulate him, "to obtain what you seek," is an effrontery that, even if not punished, nevertheless is a disruption of a proper relationship. Toward a god, it would be a violation of "showing reverence and maintaining a proper distance" (*Analects*, 6.22). For Tian to respond to that would be, as Wang Chong later suggests, a breach of Tian's Dao. In so violating the proprieties, it would be a disordering of one's self, and, if done as a public function, a disordering of society by violating the proper relation of humans to Tian.

That most rain sacrifices were not addressed directly to Tian (since only the emperor, in theory, could do that), but rather to mountains, rivers, and even more local gods, does not change the principle. The only model for the relationship between these more local deities and Tian that was available to a Confucian (whatever local plebeian ideas may have been) was that of ministers or lower underlings to a ruler. A petition to a minister by one lacking the status to address the ruler is still, in principle, addressed to the ruler, whose representative the minister is.

To adopt the sort of interpretation that takes *wen* here to mean "gloss over the matter" (Dubs) or "purely ornamental" (Unschuld), or to hold that the rituals are governmental moves to "keep the people quiet" (Li) either fails to do justice to Xun's deep commitment to governmental sincerity, or blinks either the importance of *wen* in his thought, or his commitment to traditional LI. LI was not merely instrumental; it defined and celebrated the relationships of people one to another, to institutions, and to deities. Xun, who never talks theology, has little interest in discussing the last of these, either affirmatively or negatively—unlike, for instance, the skeptical Wang Chong—but he constantly manifests a profound interest in the former two.

In setting the people's idea of *shen* over against his idea of *wen* it is his religion, not his lack of it, that he is setting over against their superstition. Consider two comments:

> Thus, superstitions manifest themselves as ways for their holders to maintain some semblance of control over the way things go in the world. . . Superstition is external to the life of the one holding it. . . [he] could be said to rely on the superstitious belief itself. . . . It appears that superstition has an external relation to the person. On the other hand, religious belief is internal to the life of the believer.[7]

Xun's whole discipline is aimed at internalizing *wen*, true human culture.

Just here in the essay *shen* clearly means "a way of manipulating spiritual things"—a competing with Tian—that would represent a lower level of Chinese worship than Xun would countenance. Compare Chan's

> The masses *pai*, that is, worship in the formal, orthodox, strictly religious sense, but the enlightened *chi*, that is, sacrifice or make offerings. . . . these offerings are oblations, not sacrifice in the ordinary Western sense of the term. The idea of propitiation or expiation is never present.[8]

He then quotes Legge, that the sacrifices "are the tribute of duty and gratitude, accompanied with petition and thanksgiving. They do not express a feeling of guilt, but a feeling of dependence."[9] Expressing dependence upon Tian surely differs from trying to manipulate it.

"Control Nature's Course?"

The last major problem arising out of the translation is covered in the notes, but may be reopened here. At the beginning of this book we emphasized Hu's translation of *zhi Tian ming er yong zhi* in the *Tian lun* poem as "control nature's course and use it," stressing the wide influence of his interpretation on twentieth-century understandings of Xunzi. Our translation, "make use of what occur naturally by organizing them" is not much different verbally, but rather far removed in spirit, since "organizing" (*zhi*) may be taken to imply a kind of already-present pattern, implicit in things as Tian produces them—"putting things into their proper places," so that they find their usefulness according to their (or the cosmos') *li*. It also suggests integrating things into institutions (Xun in fact uses *zhi* where we could use "institute" or "institution"). Institutions, for Xun, are established by and regulated by LI. Therefore the emphasis is not on *control* so much as on the bringing of things into the overall pattern of LI, which the mind of the sages has developed (*pian* XXIII) or discerned (IX) in their thinking or their "looking to Tian."

A second difference is our placing emphasis on particulars—"things that occur naturally"—rather than some overall "nature's course." This emerges from the problem of rhythm; the lines of the poem are perfectly regular, as is Xun's wont, except for the phrase *zhi Tian ming* and the later negation *wu shi* in the penultimate line. The latter, however, has excellent rhetorical justification, even if one counts the negative particle as more than an "empty word," poetically: the emphatic negative just before the final rhyme-word gains more forceful contrast with the preceding affirmations, receiving emphasis precisely by being an extra syllable, and assisting closure by being in the final line in that meter. It is followed by a summing-up couplet.

No such justification obtains for the second line. To maintain the parallelism, it should be two words, a verb and a noun. Were there any evidence at all that "*Tian ming*" was an expression so common it was pronounced as one word, the phrase might be left as it is. Nowhere else, however, does the phrase occur in the *Xunzi*, nor does it occur in the *Mencius* (except in a quote from the Odes), the *Guanzi* (except as *Tianzhe mingling*), or the *Zhuangzi*; and the three times it appears in the *Analects* it indicates "the Decree of Tian," something to be in awe of, a hardly viable use here. The line simply has one word too many.

The first word, *zhi*, supplies the verb; it cannot go. We must either delete *Tian* or *ming* to save the poem's pattern; in light of Xun's persistent references throughout the *Xunzi* to setting *things* in order or *things* gaining their proper places, and in light of the times he links Tian to the seasons, which he maintains are constant and need no ordering, there appears no alternative to assuming that it is *Tian* that was the clerical gloss, perhaps based on "the *ming* of a man lies with Tian" in the preceding paragraph. Xun, however, defines *ming* in *pian* XXII as *jie yu*, about which commentators differ.[10] Apparently, it may mean either "happenstances" or the opposite, "things that arrive regularly"—in either case, quite the opposite of the traditional "fate of a man" in what precedes. Thus, it is not Tian's "course" that requires "control," but "things" that "arrive regularly" or "occasionally" but are not "in their right place" (such as weeds in fields or horses lacking training) that need "making to accord with institutions"—that is, to be brought into the overall pattern of LI.

One further point: the moral that ends the poem warns against "losing what is really essential in things"; the alternative is "to assist what brings existing things to (their) completion." Things have an "essential" function that may be lost; what leads to actualizing that function needs "assistance." Here we have Xun's theory of education, his theory of government, his theory of music, his theory of LI, all encapsulated. Tian apparently gives both the things and their unfulfilled "essential"; Tian's order is not itself fulfilled until humans "assist" it (as its equal, "aligned" in the *can*, the "triad") "to attain its perfection." To that end, the sages appeared, who themselves were instances of "assisting" their Tian-produced selves to reach perfection.

"Transforming"

One last issue of translation, though minor, is worth mentioning: the connotations of *hua*, "to transform." Although the combination *bianhua* occurs four times in the *Xunzi*, the two words usually appear by themselves. If we ignore the special binome *jiaohua*, "moral training," we find 61 instances of *hua*. Setting aside the six that involve natural transformations of *yin* and *yang* or of the myriad things, we have 55 left. In 12 of these the transformation is associated, though sometimes only rhetorically, with *shen*, ("spirit"); in seven "the sage" or "sages" are the agent, in nine a sage-king, either so identified or named; in two, Confucius and "the Great Ru," who apparently is at least a near-sage; and in one, Tian. Thus, 56 percent of these instances involve an agent who clearly approximates in some way whatever Xun would take "the supernatural" to be.

Among the others, in seven instances the agent is identified directly or by context as the *ming jun*, often translated "the intelligent ruler," though there are grounds for holding that *ming* means "enlightened" in ways that go considerably beyond mere intelligence. One's judgment as to how far beyond would control whether these seven instances are to be classed along with the preceding 31 or not. In one puzzling passage in *pian* III *ming* is correlated to *shen* as *yi* is to *ren*, *li* is to *xing*, and *bian* is to *hua*.[11] In each pair, it is evident that the former stands for an external analogue of the much more inward latter term. *Ming* thus may have a more active meaning, as "exhibiting (inner) moral or spiritual power."[12]

To return to *hua*: in 10 of the instances where no agent is indicated, means are. In eight of these the means is LI-YI; in one, music; in another, DE or "virtuous inner power." Of the remaining instances, two are negative, three assert that it is at least possible to *hua* oneself, one is completely unspecified, and one likens flowing water to "skillful transformation."

It would seem to follow that when Xun uses the word *hua*, "to transform," as applied to humans, he intends something deep and fundamental, much closer to spiritual things than to ordinary manipulations. The fact that natural processes "transform" does not negate that fact; it only shows that his attitude toward nature was as Graham suggests: "There is also in Hsün-tzŭ a certain residual awe of the sacred in nature."[13] This awe was not restricted to nature; in a number of passages he exhibits great awe toward the sage, and that awe appears to be related to the sage's being "aligned with Tian-and-Earth." Whatever it is that demands this awe is what enables the sage to "transform." Thus, "transform" may simply denote a process, but it brings with it overtones of the deep, the subtle, the inscrutable, the wondrous—things associated with *shen*, "numinous."

9. The Two Hierarchies and the Sage

The Two Hierarchies

Central to our understanding of the *Tian lun* is Xun's vision of two fundamental hierarchies, which we shall distinguish as the cosmic and the cultural hierarchies. These are delineated in the *Xunzi* in several ways. In the *Tian lun* itself: "Tian has its seasons, Earth has its productiveness" indicates the one; "Humans have their 'setting-in-order'" the other. Similarly, "Tian and Earth are the source of production (life)" indicates one; "LI and YI are the source of order and the Junzi is the source of LI and YI" points to the other (*pian* IX).

The hierarchical character of the two parallel (but interacting) systems is here and there spelled out:

> Fire and water have *qi* (energy-stuff) but are without life. Grass and trees have life but no intelligence (*zhi*). Birds and beasts have intelligence but no YI (sense of duty? acceptance of roles?). Humans have *qi*, life, intelligence, and also YI. Hence, humans are to be deemed the noblest thing under Tian. (IX)

It is clear that here Xun is counting YI as part of our native endowment. (If YI is a virtue in itself, "rightness," as in Mencius, then humans may not be essentially disorderly, but how effective can an "acceptance of roles" be until roles have been defined by LI?)

Similarly, the cultural hierarchy is clearly represented in sequences such as the petty man/the scholar/the Junzi/the sage, or "the crowd"/"the people"/the "hundred surnames"/the knights/the ministers/the ruler/the true king, the former sequence representing the moral dimensions of the hierarchy, the latter the administrative.

An indistinct or overlapping middle ground is indicated: in *pian* XIX, the *LI lun*, we have, "the basis of life (production) is Tian-and-Earth" and "the basis of order is rulers-and-teachers"; this clearly distinguishes the two realms. In between, however, we find "the basis of kinship is ancestors." Ancestors are part of the realm of *sheng*, biological production, which is the way, according to Xun, one's *xing* or "nature" is produced by Tian. Through them we have our roots in the cosmic processes; but they are also part of the realm of the cultural hierarchy, things to whom moral duties are due. The duties are defined by LI, which is defined not through nature but through the sage (who, however, also received his *xing* from Tian by *sheng*, though he attained his sagehood by moral and cultural development). The way the family hierarchy bridges the biological and the cultural is evident.

Here we have a basic pattern: two parallel hierarchies, each extending down from its apex along one clear line distinct from the other, with an overlap in between that must be assigned in part to both. This overlap may be expected to contain unclarities and to raise problems.

There is also another basic pattern: each hierarchy, under conditions less than ideal, loses some of its orderliness as one progresses down it. In extreme cases—for instance, that of lands not yet brought under cultivation—Tian-and-Earth simply produce the myriad things in some kind of disorder, for "Heaven can give birth to creatures but it cannot order them" (*pian* XIX, W 103). Such a situation might be praised by an author of the *Zhuangzi*, with his "let it be, let it be," but would be considered far from ideal by Xun, who considered it a mark of good government when the ruler "opens up lands for cultivation" (*pian* IX, W 40).[1] Where things "grow wild" the cultural hierarchy does not yet impinge upon the myriad things, and they can go their own way untrammeled.

In that case, they may not yet fully cooperate with the cosmic LI. As Xun says at the very beginning of *pian* X, "What art is, is providing uses, for the sake of humans, of the myriad things with varied forms, which occupy the same world without being in their proper places." It is the business of the sage, or the quasi sage Junzi, to set them in their places. In *pian* VI, he says of the true Junzi that for him "everything. . . . fits into its proper place," and in VIII, IX, and X he speaks of "the myriad things attaining their proper places" under an administration that follows LI. Order at the bottom of the cosmic hierarchy is not only not by nature, but is attainable only through highly cultivated humans. It is not brought about by purely technological means, for Xun admits that the farmer knows more about farming than does the Junzi—any technologist knows more about his specialty than does the Junzi—but it is still the Junzi, following the sage, who sets things in order. This is because for Xun order is a moral matter, and requires moral resources, residing in humans, and at least quasi-moral responses from nature, for its achievement. This is crucial to grasping Xun's understanding of the workings of nature.

At the other extreme we have such a situation as the use of language, which Xun discusses extensively in *pian* XXII and exhibits concern for in many other places. Although any thoughtful definition of being human must be in terms of using language (if Neanderthal anatomy did not permit vocal articulation, they were not yet human[2]), Xun clearly took the artificial character of language to exclude it from the things Tian gives us, and hence from the cosmic hierarchy. Language belongs solely to the cultural hierarchy, where it must be made orderly from the top (though Xun admits usages must be accepted by the people), whereas at the bottom there are tendencies toward its disordering. Xun was aware of differences in language: "Barbarians . . . cry out the same when born, but when older follow different customs" (*pian* I, W 15), so that language is a matter of custom; but it is doubtful that he considered any language but Chinese able to order life in a truly cultured way. But even there, it was evident that there were disorderly tendencies in the human world that caused disordering in language—and vice versa, since disorderings are infectious.

If Tian "cannot" cause perfect order among the myriad things it brings to birth, it equally cannot bring, by its process of *sheng*, order among the many feelings and impulses it brings to birth in humans. Thus, "human nature is evil" (*pian* XXIII) is simply the parallel, in the beginnings of human development, of what holds true everywhere: what Tian produces at the lowest levels is neither sufficiently self-ordered nor adequately ordered by Tian (certainly not by "necessary laws!"). As befits hierarchy, wherein higher levels possess higher orderliness as well as higher worth, power, and dignity, Tian can and does order the seasons, and, with considerably less success, wind and rain.[3] Even in the higher echelons there is some possibility of deviation. Eclipses occur, "partisan" (subversive and self-serving) groups of stars may appear; and, in the lower echelons, there may be "deviant (rebellious) emergents among the myriad things." What infects the cosmos with such disorder is of no concern to Xun, as long as human agency has no part in it; nor does he believe it should be of any concern to any one else. "Thinking them weird is allowable; dreading them is an error."

Even when such natural deviations are destructive of human well-being, causing flood or drought, discomfort or epidemic, "understanding the decrees" that such things are "just the way Tian's Dao is" enables one to leave to Tian what lies with Tian, and to concentrate on what lies with us. We have no responsibility for "happenstances," because "the fate of a human lies with Tian." The individual human, as a product of and participant in Tian's realm of *sheng*, is, in isolation, no significant part of the main line of the cultural hierarchy, but that part of him or her is to be identified with the cloudy overlap between the hierarchies, with the shadowy ancestral line of production and its separate moral and ritual responsibilities.

The Mind

It is not as a biological being, part of a natural lineage, but as a mind, part of a moral lineage, that a human develops upward to higher levels of the cultural hierarchy. This mind is given to us by Tian, through the processes of *sheng*, to enable humans to participate in the cultural hierarchy—its job is to bring order (*zhi*) into the picture, in human character and eventually into the cosmic system also.

This latter point is important, and deserves a whole book in itself, since the order the mind brings to the cosmos is often spoken of by interpreters as if it were merely technological manipulation of nature. A few have caught something deeper. Thus, Metzger says,

> for Hsün-tzŭ the mind had a diffuse transnatural power interacting with the cosmos as a whole . . . the cosmos was not just a naturalistic, phenomenal entity impinged upon by people only in terms of instrumental knowledge and action. It was a normative order constituted by the complementary functions of heaven, earth, and the true gentleman. It also served as a normative standard, for instance by showing the naturalness of social hierarchy. Moreover, "heaven and earth produced" the ordering agent of the cosmos, i. e., the true gentleman . . . heaven and earth were inherently and diffusely amenable to the moral action of the true gentleman, and the latter had the power to control the former.[4]

"The true gentleman" is Metzger's translation of "Junzi," a word whose range of meaning we have already touched upon, and to which we shall return. Important here is his recognition that the developed human being is *Tian's* way of ordering things below the level of the seasons and Earth's productivity: "Tian-and-Earth produce the Junzi . . . (who) is the "general manager"[5] of the myriad things" (*pian* IX). The *telos* of the cosmos—what it does when it most perfectly does what it does—comes about because Tian produces not mere humans, but sages (and, sages being absent, Junzi), who "*assist*[6] that by which things are brought to completion."

The mind, generated by Tian in the course of cosmic processes, has the ability to select; does it have by nature the ability to order, and, above all, to order itself? Of its gifts at birth, Xun names only rulership over the senses and the ability to decide which things not of its own species nurture its species; but, Xun says, "the sage" *purifies* his mind, *rectifies* his senses, cherishes his nurturance, accords with the government-by-nature, and *completes* the work of Tian by becoming a sage. He is explicit that it is the work of *Tian* that the sage completes, not some creation of his own. Thus, the ordering of things is Tian's aim, even if Tian cannot, without the sage's help, accomplish it. Yet, without being born and equipped by Tian, there would be no sage. Alternately, one might say that the sage is Tian's way of ruling nature. But what Xun does not tell us is whether the mind, just by "deciding about things not its species," can really "transform its own nature" so as to become sagely of itself. Yet neither can we demand of him conformity to our Western dictum of *ex nihilo nihil fit*.

How does a sage become a sage? Xun gives more than one account. We have already presented the *Tian lun* account. In *pian* XXI we find (remembering that one may *follow* Dao without *understanding* it, may be a Junzi but not a sage):

> How does a man understand the Dao? I maintain, by his mind. By what does the mind understand it? By its emptiness, unity, and stillness. It has what may be called emptiness, despite its constant storing new things up. It has what may be called unity, despite always having diverse contents. It has what may be called stillness, despite constantly being in motion. . . . With emptiness, he who would abide by Dao may enter it; with unity, he who would practice Dao may do so completely; with stillness, he who would meditate on Dao may discover it. . . . Emptiness, unity, and stillness—this may be called the greatest, most pellucid enlightenment (or manifestation).

Then follows a paragraph describing and praising the sage, ending with, "As for the mind, it may be host to such a divine manifestation because it is the ruler of the body."[7] As a natural ruler, it is already a candidate for a much higher office, the achievement of sagehood.

Thus, it is not by virtue of its technological cleverness that the mind may rule in nature, but by reason of its transcendent emptiness, unity, and stillness. These are there, somehow, underneath, despite the presence of its more usual functionings. Xun does not seem to include these three traits of the mind as part of humans' *xing* or "nature," as given to us by birth, but the sage must either develop them or gain them from outside himself in some way.

Xun does not give any clear statement on this. In *pian* XXII we do find a puzzling passage, which may be translated,

> Shun dwelt in unity and raised it to the heights; he attained its flowering fully and more. When he had nurtured the subtleties and flowering of unity, no one could understand (him? the process? the result?). . . Hence the *Daojing* says, "How elevated the mind of The Man! How subtle the Dao-permeated mind!"

Perhaps he was confessing his own uncertainty as to how the sage's self-developmental efforts and his final wondrous transformation were connected.

What relation this account of the mind in Xunzi has to Daoist ideas or the proto-Daoism of the *Nei ye* tractate of the *Guanzi*[8]—whether it approaches such ideas or is a reaction against them, whether such talk is characteristic of Daoism or was much more generally used and adopted by both Xun and Daoists—we simply do not have the data to determine. That Xun associates such sagehood with establishing LI and governing in close accordance with Confucian standards would seem to militate against too close an identification with Daoism. That the cultivation of emptiness, unity, and stillness is stressed in Hindu, Buddhist, Christian, Jewish, and Muslim spirituality would suggest that the need for such development might be discovered in any human society (even a Confucian one) seeking to develop more of the mind than just its conceptual and practical resources, its "natural endowment." (And it would appear that a culture satisfied with its conceptual and practical mental resources might not make such a discovery.)

The Supremacy of Tian

Tian, as the top of the cosmic hierarchy, as perfect *yang* and as the preeminent *shen*, is, of course, the embodiment of order, as manifested in the constant *xing* of the heavenly bodies and seasons. Earth's order, apart from its perfect *yin* and its "constant dimensions," is its response to Tian's seasons. As the ultimate source of all motion and creativity, of light and life, Tian (with Earth) is that upon which we have, in Schleiermacher's phrase, "absolute dependence." Hence it transcends all lesser beings by its essential priority—yet it has no "absolutely independent being," it is not *a se*, since there is no Chinese concept of being except as dynamic reciprocity. Tian gives birth to things, and without giving birth to things, Tian would not be Tian. Without the whole cosmos to contain Tian-and-Earth, they could not contain the myriad things (yet nothing lies *outside* of Tian-and-Earth). Thus Tian, Earth, things (and humans) make up together a mutually defining cosmos—with, however, Tian as the leader, the originator of all productiveness, and in that sense the focus. Unfortunately, the cosmos shows itself to be unable of itself to manifest in its lower reaches the glorious order of Tian's immediate *xing*, except insofar as it is a cosmos that can produce a sage.

Xun never admits the question, "What was the beginning of Tian-and-Earth?" Dao may in some way *include* Tian-and-Earth, but Xun never suggests it is prior thereto. The question of the beginning of human culture had, however, long been raised, and the accepted history showed that human life, having sometimes peaked, had by the Zhanguo period lost order progressively for centuries. How was human order brought about? The tradition already ascribed its origin to sages. But the sage-kings were "sons of Tian," and Tian raised them up—"Tian-and-Earth produce the Junzi" (*pian* IX), not just humans, but the Junzi—to establish that order "between Tian and Earth" that would harmonize with the cosmic order. The order of Tian was thus mediated to the world of disorder through the sages. How was their ability to mediate that order mediated to them? Clearly, not by the processes of *sheng*, which could not even guarantee order among the myriad things, among which humans (including sages) were, in their origin, numbered.

Here, again, we have Xun's break with Mencius. Mencius relied far too much on the ability of the processes of *sheng* to produce the sort of human the cosmos needed for its own orderliness. How could something whose products were disorderly bring about order? There must be some other channel through which Tian's order could be mediated to the human mind. Since it was through the classics and the teachers who reflected them—through poetry, history, music, and ritual—that the *wen*, the elegant order, of the past was transmitted to us, and through which we enter onto the path of developing order within ourselves; and since these point to the sages, the key must be there. Tian mediates the beginnings of cosmic order through the natural processes of production; it mediates the completion of order through the sage-mind.

This was Xun's fundamental point of difference with Mencius and the *Zhongyong*; in their routing all mediation from Tian to men through the processes submerged in nature, they were much more "naturalistic" than was Xun—something for which subsequent generations of Chinese, unwilling to have their nature myth fractured by Xun's insights, never forgave him. His own myth of Tian-mediation supervening upon human history, albeit a somewhat supernaturalized human history of sages, could not survive the political realities of Qin and Han, when rulers who were clearly no sages had to be legitimated by Tian through nature.

The Sage-Mind

However, the mind produced by natural process itself needs ordering. Order comes by response to order, not to disorder, as Xun insists in *pian* III: one puts chaos into order by "reaching over" to what is well ordered, so as to "transform" chaos. It is not "making chaos orderly," but "leaving chaos behind."

One wonders whether Xun's principle that "Whatever a man lacks in himself he will seek outside" (*pian* XXIII) applies here. The sage, he insists, is by birth just like any other man,[9] and any man without LI will have disorderly behavior and be wild and irresponsible.[10] He must first have a model and follow LI-YI. After the first sage, later candidates would have a model, and after its first promulgation, later generations would have LI.

Xun need not, for his practical purposes, delve into the problem of the first sage, since there already have been sages, but he does seem to imply that, were he forced to give an answer, he would hold that the first sage had Tian for a model and the LI of the cosmos to follow, since only there could he find "outside himself" what, on his showing, human development requires.[11]

The order that is LI thus has its roots in Tian rather than in nature (except insofar as Tian's order is visible in its heavenly *xing*). Of the sage Xun says, "Above, he has contact with Tian"[12] (*pian* IX). Yet he also says, "The sage concentrates his meditation and contemplation, repeatedly puts them into action, so that by producing LI and its flexible application (YI) he gives rise to standards and apportionments" (*pian* XXIII).

Just what kind of mental activity on the part of the sage is involved in forming LI is not made clear; apparently, it is not some normal, common-sense ratiocination, since "The sage, transforming his nature, initiates special action," as if the "special action" (which Watson calls merely "conscious activity") is something only one with a "transformed nature" can do.[13]

It is entirely consistent with Xun's treatment of the sage as beyond the ordinary human's understanding that he does not lay out just what this "special action" of the sage is. (He does use the same word in non-sage contexts, a few times in its common meaning of "fake" or "put-up," and once [*pian* XVIII] he claims the sage-kings caused the incompetent to "improve their nature by 'special action,'" presumably striving guided by the sages themselves).

At times the difference between sage and ordinary man is treated as a matter of intensity: the sage "accumulates" or "concentrates" (*ji*) his action or striving. Elsewhere he uses this word to call for "piling up" skillful ("good") acts as the way to attain full human development. The whole problem is complicated by the real possibility that Xun himself used originally, for the word translated "special action," the common parent word "to make" or "represent," hence "do" and eventually "act as" or "is". It would appear there are a number of kinds or degrees of "conscious activity." It is reasonable to suppose that any action that would lead to sagehood becomes, along the way, an unusual type of action, and actions done by one already a sage would certainly be unusual.

We have, to this point, largely laid out the relation of Tian to nature (as the realm in which *sheng* as "natural production" operates) as participation in a hierarchical system in which Tian is both the apex and the ultimate source of change, a system that shades down from the constancy of Tian's heavenly bodies to the possible deviations that occur farther down, especially by infection from disorganized humans. In doing so, we have traced the completion of the ordering of nature, the "completing Tian's work" that attains Tian's ends in nature, to the ordering influence of the sage. The emergence of the sage has posed the problem of the mind, which, as produced in nature, is disordered by the things of nature unless ordered by standards from outside nature, which are nevertheless the standards of Tian. Tian is thus distinguishable from nature both by its primacy and by its functions, whatever they be, by which Tian enables the sage to transcend the disordering tendencies in nature to become instead the orderer of nature.

The sage, and the sage's "mind," is thus a crux to understanding Xunzi. Sagehood, as outlined, is unnatural, artificial, and, indeed, supernatural. All three of these contraries to what is "natural," need attention, since they are aspects of sagehood.

The sage is unnatural in the sense that he is not produced by the process of production *sheng*, but rather by his own "transforming" of his "nature," his *xing* given to him "by Tian" through such productive activity. The sage, however, is natural in the sense that he becomes one of the basic triad, the alignment of Tian, Earth and (the) Man that fulfills all three and the rest of the cosmos. Thus, he is in no way foreign to the cosmos as an outcome, nor is he foreign in his first origin, his raw material, even though as outcome he so transcends his origin that he might be thought "foreign" to it. (This is a problem only insofar as we cling to our Enlightenment assumptions of uniformitarianism.)

Nor is his process of becoming a sage unnatural, though it is not "by nature." He becomes a sage by the activity of his mind, which itself is naturally given, but completes itself by a path outside ordinary natural processes. Though his original motive may only have been a sense of lack, of "what he did not have within himself," the standards he demands of himself and the goal he seeks are not provided by nature's productive process, but must apparently be "read off" in some way from Tian's following of its Dao.

Here we have Tian functioning through nature to produce a possible sage by *sheng*, but, as Xun says, it "is unable" to "order" him into being an actual sage. Tian gives him a mind, but only by his own effort does that mind grasp the idea of order that Tian presents in the heavens, the cosmic LI, in order to invent for human life the LI of mankind. Since it is only humanity living in accord with LI that produces no disorder among the myriad things, human LI, though artificial, is also a completion of the ordering of the cosmos, the "completion of Tian's work."

Tian, then, as presiding over nature, seems to have no more than a limited prescriptive function (except perhaps in producing things having their *li*, or potentiality for fitting into the harmonious whole); but Tian, as exhibiting the cosmic LI that is the prototype of the earthly LI which establishes all human values, is the origin, though indirectly, of those values, and may be called their sponsor. But since they are evaluated, at least partly, in terms of the satisfaction of needs that humans have by nature, and the satisfaction of those needs is collateral with and dependent on satisfaction of nonnatural needs developed by the culture of human's minds, and that culture is a response to Tian's value aspects—its order, brilliance, dignity, height, harmony, purity—its *cheng*, in fact, its *shen*—we must conclude that Tian is the source of value, and, implicitly, the ultimate criterion of value (since Xun does not try to measure human happiness empirically; its occurrence is postulated as a necessary consequence of the harmonizing of human life with Tian-Earth).

To the extent, then, that earthly values depend upon the sage, and the sage's conduct is "following Tian" and "responding to Tian," we cannot say that Tian is "value-free Nature." The sage "reads off" values from Tian that nonhuman lower levels of the cosmos cannot actualize without the sage's mind. Thus, there are values of Tian that can be actualized in nature only through the sage; besides the pathway of *sheng* by which Tian actualizes things, there is also the pathway via the sage through which Tian actualizes higher values. Tian is the apex of the cultural hierarchy as well as of the natural one.

The Supernatural

Is the sage, then, supernatural? That predicate itself must be examined before we can answer the question. One of the limits that Western thought has set to nature is this "supernatural," although the word itself goes back only to the Middle Ages. Thomas Aquinas followed Aristotle in holding that each thing had a "nature," but went beyond him in asserting that created things could be perfected beyond their natural perfections by the addition of "supernatural" attributes. Thus, a good woman, full of courage, temperance, wisdom, and justice, could, by the grace of God, be given the even greater moral perfections of faith, hope, and charity. Though these are not "natural," they would "complete" her nature in ways that she herself could not have done "naturally." This, of course, required "supernatural" powers, and was a "supernatural" event.[14] The "supernatural," on this showing, was not contrary to nature, but coordinate and superordinate.

Later, as every modern knows, the word was expanded to include anything thought to be miraculous, weird, spooky, diabolical, or inexplicable by common sense or science. This was but the counterpart of the development of the modern belief that nothing "natural" could be miraculous, weird, spooky, diabolical, or inexplicable—that such would be "contrary to nature." Insofar as Xun insisted there are inexplicables, that it is appropriate to take some things to be weird, and that the transformation a sage can induce in the people is miraculous, "as if by a god," we might say he did not in this respect have a concept of "nature" as opposed to "the supernatural," as we do. In that case, claiming that Xun "rejected everything supernatural" is at best misleading, and possibly hardly relevant.

This, however, is only part of the story. Our view of nature as made up of separate "bits" (the analogy with the "computer view" of knowledge is not accidental) connected only by external relations that can be conceptually clearly defined, measured by those machines we call "instruments," and mathematically expressed—what some call the "real world"—has much less in common with Xun Qing's view of the world than we like to imagine. Our view, if rigidly accepted, gives us, with regard to occurrences that are qualitative in ways we cannot reduce to quantity, only the options of denying their existence or ignoring them as epiphenomena of no importance. Otherwise, we would have to postulate a realm of things beyond "common sense" and beyond scientific investigation—a transcendent realm.

This problem arises for us because the Israelites came out of Egypt. Out of that event, or at least the many adversions to it in the centuries following, emerged the conviction that Yahweh, the Israelite's god, *used* nature and history, not just this or that natural or historical event, and hence was free of, and prior to, both. Nature and history were connected to him only as he chose, which implied his realm transcended any particular empirical process or event. A corollary to this was that nothing in nature itself could be divine or "supernatural," since "beside Him there is none other." This "desacralization of nature," the "destruction of nature-myth," was crucial to the difference between the ways Western and Chinese thought developed.[15]

A sense of transcendence also arose, eventually, in Greece, in a different guise: the transcendence of thought over things and events (or the transcendence of language over the things talked about). Begun in Plato and Pythagoras, it was completed in Plotinus, and also in the Church Fathers, who combined the two ideas of transcendence. The subsequent articulation in Scotist and Occamite philosophy was an important precursor of modern science and of the way the problem of transcendence emerged in Western thought.

"The problem of transcendence" thus became a problem for Western philosophy in a way it never did for the Chinese. There are interpreters of Chinese thought who have made much of this difference. We find Hall and Ames saying,

> The ubiquity of the concept of transcendence in the Western tradition has introduced into our conceptual inventory a host of disjunctive concepts . . . which, although wholly inappropriate to the treatment of classical Chinese philosophy, nonetheless have seriously infected the language we have been forced to employ to articulate that philosophy. The mutual immanence of the primary elements of the Confucian cosmos—heaven, earth, and man—precludes the use of the language of transcendence and therefore renders any sort of dualistic contrast pernicious.[16]

This is in large part true, but neglects the issue that is most important in dealing intelligently with any idea of the supernatural as more than an emotive category. As theologians are more acutely aware than many of us philosophers seem to be, the problem of transcendence is complementary to the problem of mediation. "The transcendent without the relevant is empty; the relevant without the transcendent is blind," to paraphrase Kant.

Islam, Judaism, and Christianity pretty much agree on God's transcendence; they disagree on the question of mediation. Further, there can be degrees of transcendence and degrees of immanence, and these degrees closely involve issues of mediation. Consequently, the question of transcendence with respect to problems such as "the supernatural" cannot be properly discussed without discussion of relevant structures or processes of mediation, and vice versa.

Thus, it may be futile to discuss Xun and "the supernatural" apart from questions not only of the invisible, inscrutable, subtle, ominous, and unpredictably influential—the traditional Chinese notes of *shen*, "spirit"—but also of *how* and *through what media* their influence appears in human consciousness or affairs.

The Sage and the Supernatural

When we address questions of this sort to the *Xunzi*, we find what seem to be mixed answers. In the *Tian lun*, as we have translated it, we find that the unseen powers of natural creativity are "properly called *shen*" in their productive response to Tian, but this dimension ceases being significant once biological humans are produced. Thereafter mind, *xin*, becomes important. However, Xun speaks a number of times of the strange dimension of *shenming* as characterizing some minds, most probably limited to the sages' minds, even though some of the occasions of the phrase do not explicitly say so.

Shenming

We have several times adverted to the term *shenming*, sometimes translating it "divine enhancement." It is time to give a fuller exposition of Xun's use of the term.[17] The phrase does not occur at all in the *Odes*, the *Chunqiu*, the *Analects*, *Mencius*, the *Zhong Yong*, or the *Da xue*; nor does it appear in that compendium of philosophic viewpoints contemporary with Xun, the *LSCQ*. In pre-Han Confucian works (outside of the *Xunzi*), it appears in the *Documents* (once), the *Zuochuan*, and, if it be pre-Han, the *Xiaojing*.

In all of these *shenming* refers to "the gods" (with one ambiguous instance in the *Zuo*), as it also does in most of the occurrences in the

Zhuangzi. This use is still current—images in Buddhist and Daoist temples are referred to as *shenming*. Xun uses it in this way in *pian* XVI. Three other times (*pian* VIII, XV, XXIII) he uses the phrase *tong yu shenming*, "to be in communication with the gods,"[18] and commentators interpret one other occasion (in *pian* I) as being equivalent.[19] That *shenming*'s primary meaning is "the gods" is acknowledged by Knoblock in his excellent glossary note on *shenming* at the end of his first volume (253).[20]

However, he also notes another use, one that "suggests a 'divine' or 'magical' clarity and sharpness of awareness, unmediated by conscious effort or thought, which enables those who possess it to discern subtle and minute distinctions that others miss" (255). In three cases Xun seems to use *shenming* in this way, and, in fact, he is the only clearly Confucian pre-Qin author to use it so[21] (though it occurs thus in the *Chuci* and the *Guanzi*). No matter how interpreted, it must be assumed not to indicate a mere psychological enhancement, but to carry overtones that are strongly of the supernatural.

The problem of interpretation arises when one asks what the connection is between the two uses, particularly since there are cases that could be taken either way.[22] Since the first meaning appears earlier and more frequently, and has continued for well over two thousand years, the other can hardly not be derivative; hence there seems good reason for maintaining as much continuity between the uses as is consistent with the actual instances of use. The "mental enhancement" cannot be read to exclude overtones of "the divine."

The subjects to which Xun attributes *shenming* as a state already achieved include (*pian* VIII) one who "is aligned with Tian and Earth"—elsewhere a characterization of the sage; (*pian* XV) one who is "a true world-class general"—in a context where his examples are Tang and Wu, both sages; and (*pian* IX), "the sage-king." As a goal rather than a possession, he promises it twice (*pian* I and XXIII) to those who "pile up good actions" until they attain "the mind of a sage." Thus, he uses the phrase only in contexts where he is speaking of sagehood, either as achieved or as a goal. Since the sage is for him the highest of all beings except for Tian itself (and perhaps Earth), Xun may be said not to conform to the quasi-Daoist uses of the phrase (possibly present in the *Guanzi* and the *Chuci*), which indicate a more private achievement of no cosmic significance. The evidence would thus suggest that one ought not to read such relatively private overtones into Xun's uses. In fact, it would be incompatible with his sense of hierarchy to democratize *shenming* by assuming that the highest kind of human situation would be an entire citizenry imbued with it. The sage, having received (or achieved) *shenming*, must be a rare individual.

Shenming, in the *Xunzi*, refers to something that will "come of itself" as the end of a process of "piling up skillful goodness (*shan*) to perfect your virtuous inner power (*DE*)" so that "the sagely mind finds its completion in it" (*pian* I). Earlier, the same *pian* has said that "nothing is more divine than to be transformed according to Dao." Or, again, in *pian* XXV, "When what is essential (*qing*) in one and divinity (*shen*) blend one with the other, when they become unified and inseparable, one will have become a sage."[23] These suggest that the "coming" or "transforming" may have an external source; however, such an idea is never made explicit.

One may compare *Mencius*, 7A25:

> The desirable is called "good" (*shan*). To have it in oneself is called "true." To possess it fully in oneself is called "beautiful," but to shine forth with this full possession is called "great." To be great and be transformed by this greatness is called "sage"; to be sage and to transcend the understanding is called "divine."[24]

Xunzi might largely agree with this characterization, though he would not agree with the implication of Mencius' account that it is the "greatness" of the sage-to-be that is itself the transforming agent. He indicates that the process toward sagehood has less continuity than that: for him *shenming* arrives "of itself" (as it does in the *Nei ye* of the *Guanzi*, 16:49 3a [SBBY]), although he does not tell us how discontinuous he takes the process to be.

In *pian* XXI, Xun characterizes the "great and pure enlightenment":

> Not one of the myriad visible things is unperceived, none perceived without its natural relationships, none seen as related that misses its proper place. Sitting in his room, he perceives the four seas; residing in the present he can enter into and discuss the distant past. Having a penetrating view of the myriad things, he knows their deepest nature; he investigates order and disorder and penetrates to their basic pattern. Perceiving the warp and woof of Tian-and-Earth, he makes use of all things by causing them not to misfunction; analyzing the Great Principle, he ties the universe together. Great! Great! Vast! Vast! Who knows his limits? Ample! Ample! Broad! Broad! Who knows his

> virtuous power? Effervescent and many-sided! Who knows his pattern? Brilliant as the sun and moon, his greatness reaches the eight extremes—he is to be called the Great Man.

He goes on immediately to say, "The mind can be host to such divine manifestation (*shenming*) because it is the ruler of the body." In short, the mind, which, as produced by *sheng*, is only "the ruler of the senses," has immense capabilities beyond that, being potentially all the wondrous things Xun has just gloried in.

After a similar eulogy of the sage in *pian* VIII Xun stresses his unity, his steadfast clinging to *shen*, which is "perfectly good and thoroughly ordered," and which cannot be swayed by "things." In his discussion of human nature, it is the nature of humans to be swayed, and hence disordered, by things. Clearly, the sage has radically transcended ("transformed") his human nature, his *xing* given to him by Tian through the processes of *sheng*, to become "equal to Tian-and-Earth."

The sage, then, besides being in a sense "unnatural" and "artificial," has achieved a status that is, except perhaps for Tian itself, the most "supernatural" of beings. As Xun says more than once, he is "in communication with the gods." If we only knew what Xun really thought about "the gods" we would have a much better idea of what he meant. Lacking that, it is hardly a justifiable hermeneutic to interpret him as conforming to our modern assumptions and preferences (or even neo-Confucian ones), as we have been tempted to do.

The sage, then, embodies the highest possibilities for human life—not just his own, but corporate human life as well. The basic moral standard for humans is to do the things that lead to sagehood (though few will attain it), to conform to the sage's organization of human life, and to "honor such men." The Dao of humans is thus to conform to the sages, who are the "pitchpipe" (the standard) of the Dao; indeed, "The pitchpipe for the Dao of all under Tian is this; it is the unity of the Dao of the Hundred Kings" (*pian* VIII). Thus, the *shen ming* of the sages is the incursion of the divine into human life, giving standards for life (Dao) to the world, and causing the world to follow Dao. This Dao is formulated and promulgated by the sages, but its ultimate source is Tian. Its result is "alignment" with Tian and Earth. The sages are therefore, for Xun, the mediators of Tian's ultimate intent, nisus, or (at least) tendency; its *energeia* is directed toward that *telos*—the perfect harmony of both human and natural life to Tian-and-Earth. The sages may thus justly be considered gods—and greater gods than most, since a sage is "equal to Tian and Earth."

Such an apotheosis of humans into godhead is, of course, no great problem for Chinese culture. In the third century A.D. Guan Gong was a man; for a thousand years he has been declared a god; as late as 1915 president Yuan Shi-kai officially declared a recently dead young man to have become a city god.[25] No clear line was drawn between the divinity (*shen*) of one's ancestors and *shen* that were gods of some other sort, nor is it clear that the images of Confucius, Mencius and Yen Yuan in Confucian temples (and, for a time [c. 1084–c. 1530] Xunzi himself)[26] do not represent gods. They are at least the objects of ritual attentions (though Confucian literati would no doubt resist their being thought parallel to Buddhist and Daoist gods). That *shenming* was "divine enhancement" was thus as natural for Xun Qing, in his cultural situation, as his limiting it to sages was distinctively Confucian.

As for Tian, since it is both the source of order and production among natural things, the source of the human mind in both its biological origins (through *sheng*) and its ability (its unity, emptiness, and stillness, of unspecified source) to "respond to Tian" in ways that override its biological tendencies and lead to *shenming*, "divine manifestation," it cannot be identified simply with the realm of *sheng*, or natural process. As the sage, Tian's product, transcends his biological inheritance, transforms his relation to the cosmos, and becomes "a god" (even though his is a relative, not absolute, transcendence), and the sage "looks up to Tian," which is always the first of the triad of alignment, it is clear that, for Xun, affirming that Tian is "a god" is more defensible than denying it, whatever the inadequacies of either characterization.

If Tian is both continuous with nature and distinguishable from it; if fulfillment of Tian's order requires that it produce the sage to be both its subordinate and its equal, and to be the "orderer" of natural things; if the sage reflects aspects of Tian that the things of nature do not; if the human mind in its origin is a product of Tian's *sheng*, but in its perfection it transcends radically its natural origins by becoming a "divine manifestation," what model do we have with which to describe Tian? Perhaps there is no set of terms that can function unequivocally to do that; some would hold this to be normal for a "prime religious term," and much in the history of religions would support their contention. In that case, it might be better to seek what metaphor Xun might suggest to describe the whole system of processes that make up the cosmic whole, and understand Tian functionally in those terms. This we will attempt, but will first draw together some conclusions from the discussion so far.

10. Conclusion

Our original point of departure was well put by Eno:

> Modern scholars have focused on the "Treatise" to find Hsün Tzŭ's implicit answer to a question central to their interpretive frameworks: was T'ien, for Hsün Tzŭ, a god or a natural force? A consensus has emerged which characterizes Hsün Tzŭ's position on T'ien by stressing that he saw T'ien not as anthropomorphic god, but as an impersonal force of Nature, or as natural or universal law. (Eno, 131)

In chapter 1 we set out six theses involved in this consensus, indicating our doubts as to their defensibility. We did not, in so doing, embrace the alternatives that Eno mentions; it does not appear that denying that Tian is either "universal law" or "a force of nature" commits one to taking it to be an "anthropomorphic god," unless one takes the vague term "anthropomorphic" so broadly as to make "anthropomorphic god" redundant. The question is not, "Which of our alternatives did Xun Qing pick?" but, "What do his writings indicate he understood by 'Tian'?"

Eno's response is that interpreters have made the mistake of assuming that "the *Hsün Tzŭ*'s theories about T'ien reflect an abstract philosophical interest in T'ien," rather than recognizing that Xun was interested primarily in "rationalizing" his "commitment to ritual and self-realization."[1] As we indicated very early, Eno takes this last interest to indicate that we must not expect coherence in Xun's idea of Tian, and he claims to find in the *Tian lun* three "theories of T'ien" that are "in many respects mutually contradictory."

As the first of these, he accepts the "consensus view," holding it not to be original with Xun, but to be "derivative, reflecting what were probably the dominant trends of late Warring States metaphysical speculation"; thus, he agrees with the usual exegeses of the best-known passages. We expressed in the first chapter (and expanded in the notes) some of our grounds for questioning such an interpretation of late Zhou philosophy, and explained in the commentary our grounds for questioning the exegeses.

Eno's "second theory" is that Tian is Nature, but as having "ethical significance" in picturing "man's ritual-making ability" as a "manifestation of a normative natural endowment possessed innately by man," with LI as "an extension of natural patterns." This includes, he says, an account of "human psychology endowed with normatively described 'T'ien-like' qualities." Our translation gives only partial acknowledgment to this picture; where he reads "T'ien-like" we find "in the unordered condition in which Tian gives them," a reading that takes the descriptions not to be normative, but rather to require the imposition of norms. This undercuts Eno's claim of an implicit assertion, at that point, of the continuity between natural production and moral order.

Eno rightly recognizes the parallel between LI in the human order and *li* in the natural order, but takes there to be more direct continuity in terms of biological transmission than we grant. We hold, in short, that the "Tian-like" qualities of the sage are mediated not by the natural process of production, but through some Tian-to-human channels Xun implies, but was saved from having to identify by the fact that there had already been sages, and hence their cultural functional equivalents had already been opened. Without this, his opposition to Mencius is much less understandable. (It was, in fact, misunderstood generally.)

Eno's "third theory" includes references to Tian "as a normative term without any direct reference to Nature at all." We take little exception to this observation in itself,[2] though we consider his continuation, that "In these instances, T'ien, as god, as ethical prescript, or as fate, is employed in conventional Ru fashion to legitimize Ruist ritual interests"[3] to be far too narrow an interpretation of Xun's aims or his language use, though not in itself false. (Part of the problem here is Eno's apparently applying too strictly a Western idea of "Nature" to the interpretation of Tian.)

Eno's claimed "mutual contradictions" evaporate under such an analysis. Instead, there remains a complex but reasonably unified view, vague because Xun is not trying to do theology, to delineate carefully for us what he believes about Tian, but to address the need of his hearers (readers) for guidance in a rather desperate political climate, and at the same time to celebrate the vision of the cosmos that he has found exciting. In so doing, he has provided for us significant clues as to how the ideas of the whole *Xunzi* may be put together. Before summarizing our understanding of Tian and nature, let us return to the six theses mentioned in the long introductory chapter (theses we there indicated we rejected), and deal with them in order. Our answers to them have already been grasped by the reader, no doubt, but a review may nevertheless be useful.

First is the assertion that Xun Qing was "skeptical regarding the supernaturalism of his times." As already indicated, the concept of "supernaturalism" is not itself clear or even univocal, and is better treated retail than wholesale. Xun did reject physiognomy, but there is nothing supernatural about that, nor would one's attitude toward it imply any particular attitude toward the supernatural, however understood. He does specifically reject one popular superstition, that of "beating a drum and offering a pig" to cure a cold. This would seem to imply two things: that he expects his audience to have rejected it already, for otherwise his argument would not go; and that such a ritual was vulgar and not a part of LI, or he would have had specifically to claim it was not. It is difficult to say to what extent his remarks can be generalized—although they have often been extended, pretty much at the will of the interpreter. Making fun of the crude ideas of *hoi polloi* has been an elitist sport in every age. What is clear is that, unlike Wang Chong, attacking such superstitions is not his aim, since he uses them only to illustrate other sorts of points.

The same may be said of his story of the man who died of fright from thinking he saw an ogre (*mei*) and a ghost (*gui*), where Xun assumes his audience shares his belief that the man's mind was distraught. *Gui*, after all, are by definition *wu xing*, invisible, unless incorporated in a human or (at least at the plebeian level) an animal. Whether we are entitled to hold, on the basis of this one passage, that he denied the reality of *gui* is not at all clear.[4]

It is true that whereas the *Analects*, the *Mozi*, the *Zhong Yong*, the *Zhuangzi*, the *Guanzi*, and Shen Dao all use the phrase *gui shen*, the *Daxue*, *Mencius*, and the *Xunzi* do not (except in quotations). Xun uses *shen* 37 times, *gui* only four; for Mencius the figures are three and zero; for the *Zhong Yong*, five and three (*gui* only with *shen*). This suggests two things: (1) that there was a trend in Confucianism away from correlating *shen* with *gui*, and (2) this tended largely to eliminate *gui* from the vocabulary. This trend is also evident in those parts of the *Zhuangzi* that Graham labels "syncretist" (which are also the parts least distant from Xun's thinking, as compared to the rest of that collection).[5]

Releasing *shen* from its double harness with *gui* encourages broadening its use. *Gui* is nearly always a noun, sometimes quite particularized; *shen*, in the *Xunzi*, is often more adjectival in force (eight times) or part of an adjectival or adverbial phrase (eight times); twice, as a noun, it refers to one's vital functionings. The rest of the time it clearly indicates "supernatural" beings or forces, which Xun may refer to rhetorically, but never denies or denigrates. As pointed out, in his use of the binome *shenming* he sometimes shares with other Confucian writers the usual reference to "the gods," but at other times his use is unique among Zhou Confucian writers.[6] In every case, however, he treats it as referring to something both elevated and important. He was certainly no skeptic regarding the clearly supernatural term *shen*, though it is difficult to estimate its full range or its principal focus in his usage.

Thus, though in *pian* XIX, speaking of funeral sacrifices, he contrasts the Junzi's understanding of them as a fulfillment of humans' Dao with the common folk's deeming them to be dealings with *gui*, he himself speaks of them approvingly as "reverently serving the departed's *shen*." And when he ends the *pian* with "When we serve the dead as if serving the living, and serve the lost as if serving the surviving, thus ascribing a form to an invisible (*wu xing*) shadow, we complete humane culture," he is hardly denying that the "invisible shadow" exists. He is celebrating the expressiveness of the rite, not discussing existents and nonexistents. If anything, he is implying that there is an "invisible shadow" involved, for the other three times he uses *wu xing* he clearly intends something real but invisible, and the four times he uses the verbal negative with *xing*, as *bu xing*, he indicates something that may well be real but is not manifested. From these and other references to *shen* it would appear that whatever doubts Xun may have had about *gui* did not extend to *shen*.

Twice he gives characterizations (not definitions) of particular uses of *shen*. In *pian* VIII he says the unity that the sage enjoys is to be understood in terms of the steadfastness arising from his *shen*, and "That which is utterly good (skillful) and fully ordered is what is called *shen*." In *pian* XVII we find, "It is to be called *shen* because though we do not see its workings, we see its effectiveness." In one of these he is speaking of the sage, who is by title a "holy man" (*sheng ren*) and "the equal of Tian and Earth," both of which latter were acknowledged as deities by solemn sacrifices, and whose cosmic importance justified such rank[7]; in the other he is speaking of the invisible productive forces in the world that stem from Tian's DE, its "virtuous inner power," which "transforms and changes in their turns" (*pian* III). That he gives each of these characterizations in a particular context bars us from taking them to be in any way exhaustive of what he means by the term, though taken together, they illustrate something of its range of use.

Thus, the evidence would seem to indicate that Xun's skepticism regarding certain popular superstitions cannot be taken to show any overall skepticism regarding the numinous dimension of those matters he took with the utmost seriousness.

Second, we contested the claim that, for Xun, Tian, as "equivalent to Nature" was "impersonal and devoid of moral significance." Nowhere does Xun say this, and nowhere does he deny it. Both the claim and our demurrer can only be based on indirect evidence, although Xun's Confucianism and his cultural conservatism would seem to lay the burden of proof on those who would affirm such a claim. We quoted in chapter 2 Taylor's notice of the "deeply and profoundly religious" element in Confucianism that revolves around "the Confucian understanding of *T'ien*," whose core is "the relationship of humankind to Heaven," which "functions as a religious authority." As Thomas Berry says, "Ultimately the supreme reality in the Chinese world-view and its supreme spiritual attainment is the comprehensive, loving communion of heaven, earth, and man."[8] It is not enough to label Xun a maverick Confucian; it must be established that he was a maverick *on this point*, and that by better evidence than merely the assumption that if he did not see the relation between Tian and man as Mencius saw it, he saw none at all, and then interpreting his utterances on that basis.

We may note that two of Eno's three "theories of T'ien" affirmed moral significance, and one implied personal characteristics. In the commentary, we have pointed out that the familiar "Tian cannot" may be read "Tian will not be disposed to"; such passages do not, then, decide the issue. His remark that "Tian does not stop winter because men hate cold" occurs as parallel to the Junzi's steadfast willing to follow his Dao despite the petty man's complaints, which would affirm Tian as having a steadfast will rather than none at all. Xun (on our reading) does not use the phrase *Tian ming* (Mencius uses it only once), which might be read "the will of Tian," but arguments from silence are notoriously misleading.

As noted in the commentary, Xun refers *xing* 行, as a noun, exclusively to moral agents, unless Tian be made an exception. Even though *Tian xing* may refer just to the motions of the heavenly bodies, we have no indication at all whether Xun thought them to be moral beings, or Tian's guidance of them to be willed or unwilled.[9] Whether "competing with Tian" implies an effort on Tian's part is debatable. Since Xun uses *Dao* in the moral ways typical of Confucianism, and does not speak of *things* having a Dao, but "proper places" (though he does say "each sort of thing presents only part of the Dao"), the fact that for him Tian has a Dao and follows it may indicate an attribution of moral agency and commitment on Tian's part, or it may not. One's choice on that depends on one's prior decision as to the degree to which Xun's usage is on all fours with Daoists' usage. Where he does adopt terms used by Daoists, he reinterprets them to his own Confucian use, and we cannot with any confidence assume he simply adopts any Daoist use or idea.

Xun speaks of Tian having a *chang* Dao in a context where *chang* appears as a moral quality. In *pian* XXVI he assures his students that "Tian will not forget." In XXVII we find, "Thus, if he who acts as king is first benevolent (*ren*) and afterwards follows ritual (LI), Tian will act generously." In *pian* IX, apropos of graded ranks (which for Xun always implied moral qualifications), we read, "In Tian-and-Earth's existing we have the distinction between higher and lower (ruler and subject?)," and also, "Above, (the sage) has intercourse with Tian," or, "Above, he examines Tian," depending on the textual reading; the two verbs are graphic variants. The latter is the received reading, but even there, "examine" refers primarily to examining persons, and has sacrificial or divinatory antecedents.

Finally, as already remarked, since Tian is the apex of a hierarchy that has some ideological relation to bureaucracy, there is nothing incongruous in the expectation that Tian ignore matters that should be handled at lower levels, or that its behavior is *impersonal*, like that of any thorough bureaucrat, without being *nonpersonal.* As pointed out in the commentary, the idea that the Junzi ought not to be swayed from following Dao just because the petty man complains is a *moral* idea, appropriate only to a person; so the parallel claim that Tian does not shorten winter just because humans dislike cold is an affirmation of Tian's moral character, not its denial. "That's the way Tian's Dao is." Muslims, Jews, or Christians have never denied either God's person, His concern for humans, or His moral supremacy just because winters were cold; it seems strange that interpreters of Xunzi would expect a Chinese to do so regarding Tian.

On this point a saying attributed to Shen Dao, who could still have been at the Jixia academy when Xun studied there, is interesting:

> Heaven possesses light; it is not distressed by the darkness in which men live. Earth possesses riches: it is not distressed by the poverty in which men live. The sage possesses power, but is not distressed by the peril in which men live. Though Heaven is not distressed by the darkness in which men live, yet, by opening doors and parting windows, men may unfailingly draw from it their own light. It follows that Heaven has no tasks to attend to.[10]

Shen goes on to point out that humans may draw wealth from the earth and may get security by obedience to the sage, so that neither Earth nor the sage has "tasks to attend to." He is certainly not denying personality to the sage, merely asserting that the tasks of Tian, Earth, and sage have their appropriate stopping points, beyond which the responsibilities are ordinary humans'. We take Xun to be saying much the same thing when he says that "Tian's official responsibilities have been established"; so that when fully discharged, Tian "has no (further) tasks to attend to." Such a claim makes no statement at all as to whether the sage, or Tian, or Earth are or are not "devoid of moral significance."

Third, we questioned to what extent Xun understood nature (equated to "Tian") to be regular, law-abiding, and predictable. Both the translation and the commentary have expanded on those doubts. That the courses of the heavenly bodies and the seasons were regular was their (and Tian's) glory; Xun assumed this and argued from it. That responses to that regularity might be deviant among lower-level things, just as among humans, Xun seems to take for granted. Only when a sage is "equal to Tian-and-Earth" do the myriad things completely "function as obedient servants." Tian produces things, but it "cannot" (= "does not") "order" them; without the sage, they are not "ordered." Even if government is "enlightened" there may be eclipses (which no ancient Chinese held to be predictable), "strange self-serving groups of stars," "unseasonable wind and rain," and "deviants among the myriad things." Floods, droughts, and baneful visitations may occur with moral reason or at times without it. One must conclude that Xun saw the universe to be neither chaotic and totally unpredictable nor regular, law-abiding, and predictable, but one whose seasons were reliable although many other things were not, and wherein moral causations made some sense. It was a world wherein Tian did not "specially act," but wherein there were "happenstances" that "resided with Tian" and which one should live with by "understanding the decrees" (*ming*) and not "resenting Tian." Never does he even suggest any idea of causal determination across nature, or anything remotely resembling "natural laws." Order, indeed, is the kind of order reflected in LI, which involves consistent responses rather than predetermined reactions.

The fourth thesis claimed that Xun held nature to be available to arbitrary human exploitation. Such a conclusion flies in the face of his sense of the primacy of order, especially traditional or prepatterned order; his sense of the cosmos functioning according to its own LI, apparently congruent to the *li* inherent in things; his remarks about things "finding" or "receiving" their "proper places"; his recognition that improper "responding to Tian" may cause the loss of "what is essential in things." Most specially, it is contrary to Xun's clear enunciation of the idea that it is not humans as an empirically found species, but The Man, the sage, who "orders things," and that he does so only after he has achieved his "alignment with Tian and Earth," which is a special metaphysical, even supernatural, status, and the summit of moral achievement.

Xun labels one of his most rhetorical descriptions of a properly done human "arranging" of "things" the *Da shen*, or "the greatest spirituality." In the past we have resisted the commentators' equation of *shen* here with *zhi*, "to set in order"; we now think it appropriate if read both ways: for Xun, the "great" or complete "setting in order" would indeed be the acme of spirit activity, since for him, all activities of *shen* are directed toward the achievement or maintenance of cosmic order.

The fifth thesis has already been sidestepped: that Xun holds nature (or Tian) to have a negative value, since it produces humans' "nature," *xing* 性, and he holds that to be "evil." Tian's *zhi*, its "official duty," as far as the production of humans goes, is to act through the natural processes of *sheng*, and *sheng* simply *cannot* order its productions. Some of its productions among "things" influence human senses and desires to produce chaos within and without. This might be called a deficiency in *nature*, but not in Tian, for "that is its Dao." To produce an already-ordered human nature, Tian would have to violate its Dao, which its elevated status (and its following LI) prohibits (quite apart from any question as to in what sense it "could not" do so). Mencius' error was not that he attributed the good in humans to Tian, but that he mistook the channels through which Tian mediates moral value to them: not through *sheng*, production and growth, which Xun saw to be impossible, but through the mind *xin*, education *xue*, LI, music, cultivation of unity, emptiness, and stillness, and finally, the divine enhancement, *shenming*—that is, through sagehood.

The sixth thesis parallels the fourth to a degree: that culture is not just an artifact, but an imposition upon nature. In Tucci's words, it is not merely *artificiale*, but *artificiosa*. If Xun had adopted the Daoist's premises, he could hardly have avoided this consequence; however, he strongly rejected them. If the "*Da shen*," the "highest achievement of order," is characterized by the most developed of human institutions, the thesis obviously cannot hold. The function of the sage is to "complete fully the work of Tian," not to "compete with Tian." Hence, Xun's view of nature must be read off his understanding of the fulfillment or completion of the cosmos.[11] By making the cosmic process itself dependent on humans for its completion, he overcame the split between the moral incompetence of *sheng* and the moral demands of the cosmic LI.[12] That this leaves us puzzling about the "proper place" for yak's tails (*pian* IX), whether they should be on yaks or be dyed for ritual purposes, we must simply accept. There is no indication it was a problem for Xun Qing. No institution that accords with LI, apparently, is a violation of nature. Rather, such are fulfillments.

What, then, is "nature" in the *Xunzi*, and what is Tian? We have not been aware of any difficulty in using "nature" and "natural" to apply to every nonhuman thing except Tian (and possibly Earth in some contexts), even to *shen*, for Xun does not share our inherited prejudice against including "things miraculous, weird, spooky, diabolical, or inexplicable by common sense or science" in "nature." He was very concerned about the social results of how people deemed them important, and indicated clearly instances of no importance as well as instances of importance. The myriad things, and *yin* and *yang* as functioning through them, surely may be included in "nature." Human beings, as "things" produced by natural processes, are "nature." With these things we have no trouble until we try to demand a clear-cut, conceptual criterion by which to delimit the set of things to which "nature" is to apply. That, however, is to make an impossible demand. The logic of Archaic Chinese is not violated by vague boundaries that require context to precide them.[13] So "nature" can be a useful term in interpreting Xunzi, but "Nature" can not; for, as a proper name, it begs for a denotable referent, which in turn begs for just the kind of conceptual demand—one for a uniformitarian system—that our arguments have held to be improper.

Insofar as "Nature" implies for us a uniformitarian system, bound together by univocally expressible causal laws, operating unrelated to any moral, aesthetic, or spiritual dimensions, the word is systematically misleading as a reading for "Tian." Uniformitarianism denies the significance of Xun's basic model of hierarchy; and causation independent of moral, aesthetic, and spiritual involvements violates his sense of how things relate to one another. It may have an appearance of usability only because it also brings echoes of Wordsworth, John Muir, and perhaps, Longfellow's *Hiawatha* along with it. These are echoes, however, that are foreign to the main tendencies of the word, at least as used in philosophy and the sciences.

But what if by "Nature" we mean "the Chinese view of Nature," a "system," in some sense, not devoid of moral, aesthetic, or spiritual dimensions? Then we are confronted with the fact that the early Zhou view, the Daoist views, the "five-processes" view, and Dong Zhong-shu's view differ from one another, yet all are certainly Chinese. Each, in its way, has a place for Tian. Where shall we locate Xun Qing in such company?

What is "Tian" for Xun? Is Tian part of nature? Tian is, of course, naturally there. It is not artificial, it is not unnatural. It is supernatural, but that does not debar it from being, for a Chinese thinker, natural, since our line between the natural and the supernatural has little meaning for him, except perhaps in terms of the kinds of ritual response that each might require. As the apex of the cosmic hierarchy, Tian is unique; it is "above nature," or, as Xun says, it is "the extreme of height," and the polarity of high/low indicates political power and moral status quite as much as physical relationship, in accord with human perceptions everywhere. (Is there any natural language wherein a ruler is "below" his subjects? Isn't the phenomenology of dominance and submission everywhere high/low? Is the good man ever the "low" character and the bad man the "high?") As the giver of light and rain, Tian is the "provider." As the source, through the seasons, of order for the world of things, and, through the sage, of order in the human realm, how could Tian not be unique, as compared to all things natural and human that are so dependent upon it?

Is Tian, then, in terms of Eno's posed alternative, an "anthropomorphic god?" Or is it rather, in Creel's words, "an impersonal moral force?"[14] Must it be either one or the other? Anthropomorphism in art or poetry may be easy to identify, especially as over against one of its classic opposites, theriomorphism. In terms of implicit, basic images it is much more elusive. In any conceptual application, it is completely dependent on one's connotations for *anthropos*, "human," and on which of those connotations one is metaphorically trading at the moment. In the language of the Bible, anthropomorphism is significantly ruled out: "To what will ye liken Me?" "There is none like God"; yet God has "thoughts" and "loves," but, as Aquinas held, these are only applicable by analogy. (The Bible and Aquinas both used hierarchical and correlative thinking.) If one holds that humans are the only "moral forces" in the universe, and that this is a singular trait of humans, Creel's "impersonal moral force" is either an anthropomorphism or it is conceptually incoherent (probably both). The demand that for Tian to be a god it must be anthropomorphic in some determinate way is not, as it stands, a philosophically viable demand, and where hierarchical and correlative thinking are involved, it is unclear just what is being asked for.

Insofar as Tian was sacrificed to (which Xun acknowledges and does not criticize), and could be sacrificed to with sincerity (which Xun valued highly) only if approached as something that can be meaningfully addressed, Xun thought of Tian as an entity it was appropriate, at least for the king, to address. Clearly, then, Tian is a god, in the appropriate ritual sense. Tian possessed DE, "inner moral power"; since Xun attributed DE on every other occasion only to moral beings, it would appear that Tian is a moral being (unless one insists that our criteria for understanding Xun's language must be derived from the usage of the Daoists [whom he clearly did not admire] rather than from his Confucian training and own usage).

Since Xun spoke of LI as of the most significant kind of structuring standard in the universe, and as if it is basically made up of the kinds of offers and responses that characterize moral persons; since he took "response" to Tian to be of fundamental significance, and spoke of Tian as the apex of not only the cosmic hierarchy but, through the sage, the cultural (moral) hierarchy, we are constrained to characterize Tian as addressable, responsive, LI-following (or Dao-following, remembering that the Confucian Dao always has moral significance), and, indeed, more sagely than the sage, who "follows Tian."

Some writers seem to assume that if Tian does not arbitrarily reward and punish, cannot be manipulated by rituals or special virtues, does no "special acts" other than follow its proper "office," or is not spoken of in clearly anthropomorphic terms, it cannot be divine, or in any proper sense "a god." But if one contemplates sufficiently Xun's ideal ruler, who rules "without acting"; his ideal of the sage, who, like Shen Dao's, "has no tasks to attend to"; or even his ideal bureaucrat, who "has no aims of his own," but simply performs (perfectly) what is his job description, not being "turned aside by offers of reward"; and notes the high sensitivity and responsiveness he demands of each, they may recognize that the function of a god, as representing "the highest" or "the ultimate concern," is well filled by Tian. This is true even if the latter is also the sky and the background for the sun, moon, and stars, whose motions are its vehicle for the DE by which it makes itself that upon which Xun and all Chinese were "absolutely dependent." Whether Tian, in the *Xunzi*, is or is not a god thus would seem to depend on what one demands of a god.

Part of the problem is that there are no narrative myths about Tian correlative to the rituals worshipping it. Even the attribution to Tian of determination of a human's fortunes or life span carries no narrative myth of judgment. We in the West are much affected by the Hebraic myth of God's freedom, that God has no roles except those He has freely defined for Himself, in the creation story, for instance. "Let us create" is a narrative myth; without it God has no role as Creator. Such myths also define God as having a "will." These affect our idea of what "a god" must be.

Deism broke with the tradition of God's self-definition by limiting God's roles to only two abstractly defined functions—creation and last judgment—but still allowed both to be presented as narrative myths.

Buddhist gods also have narrative myths—they were Bodhisattvas, and achieved their various heavens or Buddha-worlds in storied ways, but however much this fact may have influenced neo-Confucian ideas about gods, Chinese religious imagination in Xun's day had hardly to wait for Buddhism. There is evidence that the Shang mythology included Yao as a god, with mythical birth and so forth—exactly the sort of mythology the literate elite euhemerized into "history." It would not be surprising if part of the Confucian restriction of religion to ritual was not based on resistance to such stories, which dealt with "unique events" not easily assimilated into the kind of rationalizing of morality that characterized the Confucian discipline. Just as earlier ancestors became completely defined by their ritual roles, unless personified by clan stories, so any higher deities should be absorbed into their roles as defined by ritual without myth.

It is evident that Tian's roles are those of "eternal return," and Tian, as far as its relation to nature is concerned, is completely absorbed into its perfect performance of those roles. Xun's criticism of the popular interpretation of rain sacrifices can be understood as a refusal to qualify in any way Tian's resolute following of its Dao. "That's the way its Dao is"—and a morally resolute deity, like a perfect bureaucrat, is to be understood in terms of its roles.

In Xun's view of administration, the sage-king attracts the people into orderliness by his DE, the winsome power of his moral perfection, but the administration of the state is in the hands of his ministers. This is the functioning of the human hierarchy. But the sage has been attracted into *his* orderliness by the DE of Tian, and, in the administration of the cosmic hierarchy, is put by Xun into the role of the minister of Tian's order, "completing Tian's work." Once LI has been formulated for humans, both Tian and the sage-king have been absorbed into their roles, *as far as their religious function is concerned*. The sage has a human narrative, not a mythical one—that of the discipline that led to his sagehood—but having arrived, in his superhumanity he is just a sage; whatever stories there may be about him are stories about his humanity, not his sagehood.

Thus, Tian performs the functions of a god, but has no anthropomorphizing stories. Those who would demand the latter, whether consciously or unconsciously, will naturally refuse Tian godhood. Those who acknowledge Tian's ritual and ideal roles will not.

Having said all this, we immediately return to what we said at the beginning: "God" is a thoroughly inappropriate translation for "Tian," but so is "Nature." The "metaphysical compliments" that Western theologians have bestowed upon God are inapplicable to Tian, but so are many of the predicates that Western philosophers have bestowed upon "Nature." Tian has no independence of the things of nature, but they are more precariously dependent on Tian than it on them. Tian may not be able to order the things of nature or human life, but their order is, at bottom, more dependent upon Tian than Tian upon it. Even the "Greatest Divinity," the *Da shen*, Tian confers upon itself and the rest of the universe only by achieving, through things and the sage, an alignment with Earth and "The Man." Yet the ultimate origin of this alignment is Tian.

Tian, then, is correlative to natural things, correlative to the sage, to LI, to order, and to morality, but hierarchically above them. To adapt a favorite locution of a colleague whose specialty was medieval philosophy, "Natural things are somewhat like Tian, but Tian is not at all like natural things; other humans are somewhat like the sage, but the sage is not at all like other humans." Our modern Western tradition of insisting that the relation of "being like" must be reciprocal, even symmetrical, and univocal, is one of the things that makes it difficult for us to understand both hierarchical and correlative thinking.

Thus, the processes at work producing the myriad things may properly be called *Tian*, because they are *shen*, and *shen* are "somewhat like" Tian in a way that surpasses whatever way the myriad things themselves might be taken to be; but Tian as the *fons et origo* of those likenesses is "not anything like" the myriad things. The gap between Tian and the sage is apparently not nearly as wide, although "the greatest wisdom lies" where the latter does not think and "the greatest skill lies" where "he does not act." Yet the gulf between the sage, "The Man," and ordinary humans, even the Junzi, who do not "have intercourse with the numinous" (*tong yu shen ming*), seems analogous to that between Tian and things. If we insist that Tian is "Nature," we must use "Nature" in so different a sense from any of our other uses that the word itself becomes an anomaly.

Nietzsche upbraided the English for being "a nation of shopkeepers." Bertrand Russell said of Plotinus' philosophy that it had the great philosophic virtue of being beautiful, even if not true. Xun had a magnificent vision of the universe; whether true or not, it has its beauty. Reducing his "Tian" to the bloodless abstractions implied by equating it to "the concept of nature," with the dead, uniformitarian, mechanical, utilitarian connotations intended by such a phrase, would seem to justify Nietzsche's adding at least some philosophers and sinologists to his "Englishmen" set.

The same might be said of those Chinese who would equate it to *ziran*, when the latter is intended as the equivalent of our Western scientistic "Nature"; those who intend the phrase as Guo Xiang or even Wang Chong used it may escape being "shopkeepers," even though their concept, as compared to Xun's, still misses the hierarchical distance Tian has above the rest of nature, and has had much of its moral life blood squeezed out.

Let the untranslatable remain untranslated; let Xun speak to us rather than we conform him to ill-fitting concepts we find useful. The result may be as lacking in precision as are our conclusions, but there may well be times that truth is not felicitously served by precision. As Aristotle remarked, we should not demand greater precision than the subject matter calls for.

11. The Cosmic Dance

A number of authors have called attention to the fact that to understand anyone's metaphysics or her idea of nature, it is helpful to identify her "root metaphor," "model," or "paradigm."[1] Just as the model for premodern cosmology in the West was the biological organism[2] (probably because muscle power ran the economy), and the Enlightenment model was that of a machine (probably since it arose with the "machine age"), a model may be presumed for early Chinese thought. Keightley has suggested a model implicit in Shang divination; Schwartz, at times, seems to suggest one rooted in family relationships.[3] It would appear that Chinese thinking did not follow the same sharp, conceptual manner as was the pattern in the West, and, with regard to the most basic questions, there was enough general agreement, in a vague way, that the really fundamental issues, though present, were not sharpened until long after Xun's day. (The issues between Zhou Daoisms and Zhou Confucianisms seem much more to be reflections of current political involvements or disinvolvements than acute formulations of metaphysical answers. Although deep questions were raised in the *Zhuangzi* and the *DDJ*, their answers were hardly worked out until much later, if then.) If the question of describing nature as a whole was not clearly posed, it is doubtful whether any particular metaphor was pressed into use to meet the problem. The political and the cosmic hierarchies may have given each other some mutual support, but the relation was hardly worked out clearly.

Models and metaphors, however, operate also at levels somewhat less profound. Kant pointed out acutely the incompatibility of the Enlightenment view of nature and of the knowledge of nature with the Enlightenment view of the moral dignity and freedom of humans. His own model, however, was itself the Enlightenment view of humans, carefully analyzed but dehistoricized, so that Fichte, Schelling, and Hegel led to

Kierkegaard, Ritschl, and Nietzsche. We may ask whether Xun had a distinctive model that guided his own understanding of nature, even though that was itself a subtype under the general Zhou Chinese understanding (just as the various "Naturalist" schools were also subtypes). Because it is common for thinkers to be unaware of their own deep metaphors, it is likely that Xun was himself so unaware, so that any attempt to attribute one to him cannot claim to be based on explicit affirmations on his part, but can only be a construction of the interpreter. Interpretations of the last three centuries have worked primarily with either a neo-Confucian paradigm or an Enlightenment one; some more recent ones have celebrated a claimed Daoist version with resemblance to process philosophy. We would suggest another possibility.

Two of Xun's essays have a special place in understanding him, though they are often discussed more briefly than some others. I refer to the *Li lun* and the *Yue lun*, the *Discussion of LI* and the *Discussion of Music (joy)*. In them he makes some of his most revealing statements. When we ignore the short separate essay that has been tacked on irrelevantly at the end, we find the *Discussion of Music* to have a climactic closing, translated by Watson as

> the spirit of the dance joins with the Way of Heaven. The drum is surely the lord of music, is it not? Hence, it resembles Heaven, while the bells resemble earth, the sounding stones resemble water, the mouth organs and lutes resemble the sun, and the scrapers resemble the myriad beings of creation. How can one understand the spirit (*yi*) [意] of the dance? The eyes cannot see it; the ears cannot hear it. And yet, when all the posturings and movements, all the steps and changes of pace, are ordered and none are lacking in the proper restraint, when all the powers of muscle and bone are brought into play, when all is matched exactly to the rhythm of the drums and bells and there is not the slightest awkwardness or discord—there is the spirit of the dance in all its manifold fullness and intensity! (W 118)

This kind of elevated rhetoric is characteristic of Xun when he is dealing with something of extreme importance to him.[4] Eno takes it to exhibit the kind of ecstasy he believes Confucians felt when they lost themselves in the dance.[5] That may be. But the intellectual content of Xun's rhetoric deserves careful attention, for, as indicated above, in correlative thinking a metaphor works both ways. In characterizing the dance as he does, he is also characterizing Tian and Earth, the waters, the heavenly bodies (Watson omits the stars, moon, and the not-clearly-identified *chen*), and the myriad things—the entire cosmic hierarchy.

Xun has already said that "music unites what is the same, LI distinguishes what is different." LI separates each level of the cosmos into its "proper place," just as it creates the appropriate distinctions (*fen*) among grades of people, and between Tian and the sage. What unifies them is music, which includes dance. We may, therefore, at least hypothesize that dance provides an underlying metaphor for Xun's perception of the cosmos as a whole, just as LI is his metaphor for the cosmos as a functioning hierarchic structure. LI is correlative to dance; both are the embodiment of that order or harmony which in natural things follows *li* and in human affairs appears as *wen*.

Ancient classical Chinese dances involved careful choreography, leadership, proper response to that leadership, harmonizing of individual styles to the total pattern, and unifying music.[6] These parallel closely Xun's idea of the state embodying the right pattern, involving careful assignment of roles by the leader, proper fulfillment of those roles in response to the leader, adjustment to particular emergents, and an overall harmony. Skillful (*shan*) dancers (ministers) do not cause each other to dance (administer), they simply dance the dance (fulfill their roles), but in doing so they fulfill themselves as dancers (administrators) and fulfill the overall choreography, which is the implicit pattern that the dance (governing), properly performed, will accomplish (*wen* in its fullest sense).

Similarly, the cosmos involves an implicit pattern, a Dao, carried out under the leadership of Tian (like the drum). Earth (like the bells) and the other instruments respond (*ying*) to the rhythmic leadership of the drum, and, if they play well, the harmony is perfect. If they play poorly, the result is a disgrace.

It is difficult to decide just how much we should make of the fact that when Xun speaks of the meaning of the dance (*wu yi*) he speaks chiefly of the instruments, but little of the dancers, the singers, or the songs). Is it because he begins the paragraph by speaking of the "symbolism of music" in representing the cosmos, and prefers to let the dancers, as humans, be subordinate to the "meaning" or "intention" (*yi*) in its largest context? One is tempted to say that just as the music exists that the dancers might dance, but the dance is the expression of the music as a whole, not primarily of the dancers, nature exists that humans might be well and secure, but that would be the expression of the whole harmonious reality, not just of human needs. How well the music is played affects how the dancers dance, but how the dancers dance also affects how the music is played, since the dance is a whole, without "the slightest awkwardness or discord."

How this fits our discussion of Xun's two hierarchies is evident. Humans need to learn the dance (LI), to internalize it to the extent that rituals are "perfected in elegant culture (*wen*) and end in gladness." Just as Tian corresponds to the drum, which sets the rhythm, so the sage parallels the dance leader, who assigns the roles that the others follow. If the leader has done his job well, "there was nothing for him to do but to hold himself in a respectful posture and to face due south," as Confucius said of Shun in *An.*, 15.5 (Lau translation). The sage, however, must be fully attuned to the other hierarchy, so that the Tian-Earth-human alignment is perfect.

Such a picture implies that LI are not arbitrary. Xun admits that other cultures ("barbarians") have their own institutions (*zhi*), but never grants they have their own LI (XVIII). In XXIII he says that the sages produced LI *after* they had "transformed their natures," which apparently means they had conformed themselves perfectly to Tian's Dao. Thus, the inherited LI are, as it were, the echoes of the cosmic music, transcribed by the sages to be the choreography of humans' part in the cosmic dance. Xun calls LI "the ultimate of the Dao of humans." This must be maintained as a balance to those interpretations of the *pian* on LI which stress Xun's accounts of the practical benefits of LI, or which take the Sage's "ordering" of nature, there and elsewhere, to be "control."

Further, he insists that, although the Junzi is one who "does nothing not in accord with LI," "only a sage can fully understand them"[7] (or "it"; whether for Xun LI is a single basic reality, which may be "divided down" into particular functions, or whether LI is a collection of 'rules of proper conduct,' as Dubs prefers, is a real question. We prefer the former, as embodying the Chinese "dividing down" principle.). He further distinguishes the Junzi from the sage by referring to LI: to the Junzi, abiding in LI in all his ways is "his altar, his canopy-of-heaven, his mansion, his court"; the sage, in addition to so abiding, "wanders widely and masters all its corners and gradations" (W 96), and so is "the acme of Dao."

The cosmic dance is formal, in contrast to another dance version of the cosmos, the dance of Shiva in Hinduism. Shiva's dance is *lila*, play; it is entirely his own extemporization, as befits the deep motif in Hindu thought of the ultimate value of freedom from all restraints (even if that freedom is complete isolation "like a stone," as Śankara characterized the Vaiśeṣikas' *apavarga*).

Karl Potter remarks,

> Indian philosophy does in fact elevate power, control or freedom to a supereminent position . . . the ultimate value recognized by classical Hinduism in its most sophisticated sources is not morality but freedom . . . complete control over one's environment.[8]

A profound difference between the Chinese and Indian worlds is here evident. Xun's cosmic dance is the celebration of order, of harmony, of perfect teamwork, wherein all is "aligned" and each thing "has its place"; wherein LI "distinguishes what is different" and "joy" (music) "unites what is the same." And as "the drum is the lord of music," so is Tian the "lord of the dance," the heavenly maestro who "has no will" of its own, for to *be* is not to assert individuality, but to have one's "own proper place" in the dance. The perfect lead dancers, Tian, Earth, and the sage, maintain the perfection of the dance by their "virtuous inner power," to which all the rest respond according to their ability. No "special acts" are required of the leaders, for, ideally, only those rewards and punishments are appropriate which are themselves part of the dance.

When Tian-and-Earth and the sage are "perfectly aligned," then "as Tian and Earth perform their functions the myriad things act as their servants; their courses are completely ordered, the nourishment they provide is completely apt, their emergence causes no injury." Under the sage's influence, "the people are transformed as by a god." The dance is the *Da shen*, the "Great Order," the "maximum of divineness," the fulfillment of the Dao of Tian and the Dao of humans. Just as "man must have his joy" and "joy must find expression" (*pian* XX), so the universe can dance, for the macrocosmos has its joy, too.

Though one may doubt that such a state really was achieved under Yao, Shun, Yu, Tang, and Wu, it is a sublime vision, one that would justify Xun's occasional elevated, poetic prose. We may not have delineated it aright, but this account is surely closer to his perception of the world than the dead, overconceptual, quasi-mechanical, utilitarian accounts found in the received interpretive tradition.

Epilogue

Odile Kaltenmark, in his review of Chinese literature, said of Xunzi:

> He was nonetheless an original thinker, perhaps the only one of the Confucian school. Although less highly esteemed by his compatriots than Mencius—perhaps because he was less orthodox—he was also less brilliant, but certainly more profound.[1]

One aspect of Xun's greater profundity is seen in his willingness to tackle the question that neither Mencius nor the other schools of philosophy faced squarely: (1) moral distinctions exist only by virtue of institutions; (2) institutions do not arise by nature; (3) institutions change nonhuman nature; (4) institutions change human nature; (5) the moral person must be in harmony with nature to be truly moral. How is the normative demand of (5) to be met in a world where the other four are true?

Mencius' theory of human nature did not face up to (1), so it bypassed (2), (3), and (4) to embrace (5), assuming somehow that nature's processes could beget moral institutions. Zhuangzi and those like him emphasized (3), treated (4) only negatively, waffled on (1) and (2), saying that some moral distinctions are natural, and that it is natural for humans to plow and weave, but more advanced institutions are artificial; and took (5) to be something that could happen spontaneously. Legalists simply discarded (5) entirely, and ignored the moral character of institutions. Only Xunzi wrestled with the five together.

Xun saw the only answer must be in institutions that harmonize with nature, and change humans and nature in harmonious ways. He did not ignore the serious problems such an answer entailed: Such institutions can only be defined by someone already in tune with nature and knowledgeable about the effects such institutions would have upon nature and humans. Luckily, he believed he had historical cases of such harmony, and records of the institutions that then obtained. What was needed was to follow such institutions, and let them produce leaders who would understand how to adjust them to changing conditions. Their knowledge of nature would see to it that the changes that institutions brought about in nature would not be disruptive. Nature would then respond by functioning happily; as he says in his poem, things will "manifest their potential" and "conform to their underlying rationale," since human leadership has "assisted what brings existing things to full completion."

We see his naivete readily, because our own situation, so well describable in terms of the same problem, is so much more complex. Our heritage from the Hebrews leads us to look to the future rather than the past, especially as our most promising institutions have a checkered past history. Capitalism ignored (3), (4), and (5), only to produce men unable to face the problems they so produced. Marxism naively assumed (5) and overstressed (4), with an even worse track record. And some of our contemporary enthusiasts for (5) ignore all of the first four.

If we consider carefully the problem he posed, rather than his solution, it becomes apparent that, of all the classical Chinese philosophers, Xun had the profoundest grasp of the problem, a continuing, perhaps eternal human problem. With good reason, we have jettisoned our past sages, since none of them presided over a truly golden age. We know too much critical history to accept any such guides. Like Xunzi, we have neither sages nor true kings. But we are also left without the institutions that might produce future ones. Worse, we are addicted to institutions almost guaranteed to move the world farther from sagehood, while allowing them to corrupt the institutions that might be of use. *Mutatis mutandis*, Xun's criticisms of his day could be of our own.

He had faith that Tian, above the processes of the world yet immersed in them, the active ground both of the world of nature and the world of culture, could be so understood by the sagely mind, the mind that had devoted itself to the perfecting of its own deep humanity, that the underlying order so little apparent in the empirical world could be educed by the "inner power" of that mind. Then Tian, Earth, and humans could be in harmony together.

Xun's world collapsed (as he anticipated), and new situations gravitated to different answers. His insights could not legitimate the powers that came to be, so the naturalists and then Mencius won the day, whether for good or ill, and the human problem was cast in different terms.

His problem, though, is still very much with us. We cannot accept his cosmology, nor do we know what to do with ours. We don't have his faith in history—the Hebrews may have taught us to look ahead rather than back, but they had hope in resources we are not at all sure are available. His assurance that the answer lay with a deeper grasp of human possibilities and the effort that might imply, rather than the study of nature, commends itself to those disappointed with the results of piling up vast mountains of data that produce no sages.

What answer do we have to Xun's problem? Just where do we catch even a whisper of his invitation to the dance?

Notes

Preface

1. This claim appeared earlier in Machle (1976).
2. Most recently, Eno, but earlier in Schwartz (1985) and Metzger (1977). Eno refers (131) to Japanese authors Ikeda (1965), Itano (1968) and Matsuda (1975), unavailable to us.
3. The third volume of Knoblock, to contain the *Tian lun*, has not yet appeared at the time of writing.
4. Belpaire, successful as a translator of poetry, does not seem so successful with Xunzi. There was no problem for which we found him helpful.
5. Welch (1957), 182.

Introduction

1. Though *li* became so important in neo-Confucian philosophy that Leibniz, trying for accord between Christianity and Confucianism, came close to identifying it with "God the Son," in Zhou philosophy it had somewhat less importance. In the *Xunzi* in particular, it appears to refer to a basic structure in things, which, however, is reflected in their usefulness, but only the usefulness they should have in a completely harmonious cosmos, as established by a sage. *Li* does not appear quantified, so we do not know whether it should be treated as singular or plural. (On Leibniz, see Mungello, *Leibniz and Confucianism*, 75ff.; on *li*, W-T. Chan, "The evolution of the neo Confucian concept *li* as principle," *Tsing Hua Journal of Chinese Studies*, V, 2, (1964), 132–49.
2. *Shenming* is discussed in chapter 9.

Chapter 1. "Nature" and "Heaven"

1. The title of Dubs' 1927 book.
2. Liu (1955), 91.
3. Walter B. Veazie (1892–1962).

4. See Cua (1985), Hansen (1983), and Eno (1990).
5. Watson 79; Knoblock, I, 11.
6. Cited by Randall, "Epilogue," in Krikorian, 354.
7. Tu Wei-ming, "Yen Yuan," 511.
8. Suzuki, 101–11, 179–80.
9. Hu, 152.
10. Shanghai, Oriental Book Co.
11. Hu, "A Note," in *The development of the logical method*.
12. Dewey's figure still loomed large during my own graduate student days at Columbia (1944–47), and my officemate for 14 of my first years of teaching had been a student of Dewey.
13. Dubs (1927), 62–63.
14. *Ziran* early meant "functions of itself" or "spontaneously," which is the only use found in the *Xunzi*. In the earliest chapters of the *Zhuangzi* it means "the way things are." In *DDJ*, 25 it is said, "Tian follows Dao, Dao follows *ziran*," but that is often taken to mean "Dao follows its own ways" (Wu) or "that which is naturally so" (Lau), though Chan does translate it "nature." It does not appear that it became a term for "nature" until the Han.
15. The *DDJ* is considered a prime work of Zhou "naturalism," one whose writing (or collecting) very likely was contemporary with Xun Qing. Though the word *Tian* occurs therein 17 times (apart from *Tiandi* and *Tianzi*), in 10 different translations of the *DDJ* in my library, "nature" occurs as a reading for it only once—in Medhurst's rendition of canto 7, where, instead of something like Wu's "Heaven lasts long, Earth abides," he has only "Nature continues long" for *Tian zhang di jiu*. Here, "nature" clearly stands for the inclusive "Tian and Earth," not "Tian." Similarly, the *Zhuangzi* is considered a prime early document of incipient naturalism. In the uncontested early *pian* (the first six), *Tian* occurs (apart from *Tian di*) 48 times. Two are place names, seven surely mean "sky"; the other 39 are ambiguous, and could be translated "the deity Tian" or "fate" or "nature." Watson, hardly an antinaturalist translator, treats none of them as "nature," all as "Heaven."
16. *Sourcebook*, 122.
17. Knoblock, I, 67.
18. Mathews (but see next paragraph in text) lists "nature"; Fenn, Schuessler, Karlgren (*GSR*), and *Han-ying shi-shi yong-yu cihui*, do not.
19. *Donghua Dacidian* and *Cihai* do; the *Kangxi*, quoting many uses for *Tian* (including one attributed to Xunzi but not in the *Xunzi*), associates it with *ziran* only in a quote from the neo-Confucian Shao Yong (1011–77); whether this is intended to illustrate a "first use" or not is not clear.
20. Shau-wing Chan, 175.
21. *Han-ying shi-shi yong-yu cihui*, 175.
22. Note, for example, the ambiguity of "natural child" as opposed to "legitimate offspring."
23. *Contra* Eno's claim to find at least three (in one locus he implies six) "theories of Tian" that are, "to a large degree, mutually contradictory." To demand the

kind of logical coherence of a Chinese idea that Western techniques for isolating "different uses" expect is to misunderstand the way correlative thinking tends to merge the various universes of discourse.

24. For a useful summary of some theories, see Eno, 181–89.
25. Chen Ta-tsi, "Kaotze's view of righteousness being external and the spirit of the natural sciences," *Tsing Hua Journal of Chinese Studies*, n.s. I, 2 (Apr 1957), 1–16.
26. Li De-yong, "Xunzidi sixiang," reprinted in *Zhongguo Gudai Zhexue Luncong*, 72–96, and his *Xunzi*, 18.
27. We translate *Tian* in these quotations as "nature" in accordance with the clear intention of the authors.
28. Li Di-sheng, *Xunzi jishi*. Taibei, 1975.
29. Our comments about Enlightenment thought reflect a long and sometimes painful trek out of the philosophic orthodoxies in which we were trained and that were so strongly supported by the academic environment.
30. The various winds of doctrine that have blown across mainland China's philosophical scene may be noted by scanning the files of any appropriate Chinese journal, or, for the English reader, those of *Chinese Studies in Philosophy*.
31. Eno, 131.
32. Some dissents may be found in Metzger, Schwartz, Graham, and others, and perhaps in Hughes' reference to Xun's "spiritual philosophy."
33. Creel, *Confucius and the Chinese Way*, 115, n. 4.
34. Wang Zhong (1745–1794) may have been the first serious interpretive commentator since Yang Liang. See Liang C-C., xxxvii.
35. Xie Yong (1719–1795); Liang C-C., xxxv.
36. Creel, "Confucius and Hsün tzŭ," 30f.
37. Dubs, *Works*, 320ff.
38. Creel, in the article just referred to, criticizes Dubs' vast overemphasis on Xun's influence. Knoblock's chap. 3 in vol. I covers a considerable amount of evidence that seems insufficient to support his claims. Eno (267) separates any influence Xun Qing might have had from "the enormous influence that the *Xunzi* exerted during the early Han," attributing to multiple authorship what we would suggest was due to diverse half-understandings and varied new uses, in response to the significant differences between the Han situation and Xun's milieu. Despite references to a few pupils of Xun, there is little evidence of anything that could be called a continuing "Xun Qing school" in the Han.
39. Forke, *Lun heng*, introduction.
40. Wang Chong, *Lun heng*, 15, 45 (*ming yu*).
41. Dubs, *Moulder*, 44.
42. Fung, *History*, II, 410.
43. The introduction of Sanskrit learning undoubtedly stretched the language patterns of Buddhist scholars, but there is little evidence it had any effect on Confucian understandings.

44. The idea of "nature myth," though not the term itself, is well explicated in Frankfort, chap. 8.
45. The Kangxi dictionary "early use" quote relating Tian to *ziran* is from Shao Yong (1011–1077): "There is no Tian outside of *ziran*."
46. See Mungello, *Curious land*, passim.
47. Dubs, *Moulder*, 64, 65, 72.
48. Knoblock, I, 170.
49. Graham, *Disputers*, 239.
50. Shryock, review of Dubs' *Moulder*, *JAOS*, 89.
51. Li Di-Sheng, 361.
52. Li Du, 531.
53. Fung, *History*, I, 286.
54. Li Di-sheng, *loc. cit.*
55. Dubs, *Moulder*, 62.
56. A number of years ago I read an explicit laying out of this argument in a Chinese history of philosophy, which I remembered to be that of Xie Wuliang. Returning to it, I have been unable to find it there. Either my search was inadequate, or the reference must be elsewhere.
57. Shryock, review of Dubs, *JAOS* 50, 90.
58. *Cihai*, article on *Xunzi*, 2449.
59. G. Tucci, *Storia*, passim.
60. In a 1975 article in *The Iliff Review* we acknowledged that Xun "accepts the artificiality of institutions as Chuang tzŭ taught. He agrees that they do not spring from nature, but are imposed on it by human conventions" (25). We now hold that Xun's idea of the artificiality of institutions was different from, and not influenced by, that of Zhuangzi.

Chapter 2. Some Recent Work

1. Both London: Probsthain.
2. Fung Yu-lan, *A history of Chinese philosophy*, trans. Derk Bodde. 2 vols. Princeton University Press, 1952, 53; *A short history of Chinese philosophy*. New York, 1948.
3. Burton Watson, *Hsün Tzŭ, basic writings*. New York, 1957.
4. Honolulu, University of Hawaii Press.
5. Stanford Univ. Press. Vol. III was first announced for June, 1992, but has been postponed until 1995.
6. Albany: SUNY Press, 1990.
7. Eno, 173.
8. Eno, 174.
9. It is less than self-evident that Han Fei and Li Si sought Xun Qing's tutelage to learn to sing and dance, though it may well be that singing and dancing were a part of Xun's curriculum that put them off. It is difficult to believe that Xun's political writings do not echo much that he taught his pupils, or that

some sections of *pian* III, V, VII, and others do not represent copybook paragraphs for pupils hoping to enter public life. Likewise, few experienced city officials will believe that Xun's office as "magistrate of Lanling" was a sinecure (despite Eno's pleading on 135).

Eno's other conclusion, that we cannot attain any real understanding of what Xun (or any Ruist) thought about Tian, apart from participating in their long training in ritual skills, seems to rest on an insufficiently nuanced understanding of three issues familiar to philosophers of religion. Eno appears to hold that (1) an understanding which is inseparable from participation in certain practices and skills (as is true, for instance, of any genuine theology) is to no significant degree communicable in words outside such a practicing community; (2) such a community has no concern for the intellectual integrity of its language; and (3) if language can be understood to legitimate certain activities, its significant functions are all adequately accounted for. All three of these are in some measure true, but only partially so. That makes it important that any discussion of a community involved in such skill activities (analogous to playing music or exercising laboratory skills) be sensitive to the question of degree: to what extent is each of these three true regarding a particular language and skill practices in such a community? (See also notes 10, 14, 15, 18, and 19.)

10. On "prime religious term," see Slater, 91ff. on "ultimate religious term." We use "prime" because Chinese religious terms had not, during the Zhou, developed intellectually to the point where the question of ultimacy might emerge. Not until the Daoist discussions of *wu*, and the arrival of Buddhism, did the problem arise. Nevertheless, there was no religious term *beyond Tian* during the Zhou. Eno, if we understand his language aright, seems to come close to our perspective when he acknowledges, "What *was* T'ien . . . In many ways, it makes little difference. Perhaps T'ien really 'was not.' Perhaps even in its most concrete sense T'ien was a vanishing point, representing the apex rather than the object of reverence" (188–89)." But if so, we would have expected somewhat different judgments in his main arguments, unless his idea of religious ultimacy is quite different from ours.
11. Eno, 21f.
12. Eno, 23, 24.
13. Eno, 27.
14. Though popular wisdom speaks of Copernicus as robbing mankind of a familiar, comfortable Earth-home, the actual literature of the day reflected more the kind of reaction Luther showed in criticizing Copernican astronomy because it elevated the Earth—this sinful Earth—to the same level as the heavenly bodies. The Enlightenment's moral optimism about the universe, coupled with its uniformitarianism, led educated folk to identify God's wisdom with the reason apparent "in Nature and in the heart of man," leading to demands that God can only be "good" in terms that fit human understanding (an issue still characteristic of much Western philosophy of religion). Thus arose a typical set of expectations for deities in the West, expectations based on the exaltation of human moral reason and empirical knowledge that the late-Renaissance gentry needed to combat the traditional "reason" of feudal structures. The Lisbon earthquake, in fact, produced so many atheists be-

cause Enlightenment theologians had bought into Enlightenment ideas of goodness and applied them to God. Eno is apparently unaware of his application of these standards, a rather recent Western development, to ancient Chinese history.

15. Clear instances of delegitimization, as in the case of the god of one Mesopotamian city "conquering" the god of another city, are not relevant here. Tian had no rivals, and we have no evidence of any mythological materials that could have provided such. Eno is correct in perceiving a serious tension between legitimacy and the social situation, but we doubt his apparent assumption that all significant dimensions of a deity are sociological.
16. R. Otto, *Das Heilige*. Eng. trans., *The idea of the holy*, Oxford, 1923. Reprinted by Harper Torchbooks.
17. Schwartz, 39, 32.
18. See Mencius, V, B 9; VII, A 13, 14; IV, A 9, etc., and Xun, *pian* IX, "If the world is not unified and the feudal lords desire to rebel, the man who holds the title is not a king appointed by Heaven" (Knoblock, II, 108). That the self-styled "kings" of the Warring States period sacrificed to Tian (which Eno admits, 26) in attempts to affirm their own legitimacy, and perhaps as invitations to Tian to grant them its mandate, hardly tells against Tian's moral importance for the competing late Zhou rulers, or affirms its identity with the house of Zhou. It does manifest a certain arrogance on their part, as Tian was so elevated that only a universal king, a "Son of Tian" could, according to tradition, appropriately sacrifice to it.
19. The inscriptions on ritual bronzes that Eno quotes do not unambiguously support his interpretation. In any case, such inscriptions cannot be taken at face value. Any student of rituals would want to know, before resting a case on such inscriptions, much more about the ritual language conventions of the time, and the involved rituals themselves, than is available to us. Affirmations of royal innocence, complaints and even accusations against deities can be quite conventional ritual forms. One has only to read the Old Testament Psalms to run into this phenomenon. To rest an argument in cultural history upon such evidence is to place it on a very shaky foundation.

    In this connection one might consider Ode 191 (Mao), containing lines such as these:

    Heaven is continually redoubling its afflictions;
    Deaths and disorder increase and multiply . . .

    O unpitying great Heaven . . .

    Great Heaven, unjust, is sending down these exhausting disorders.
    Great Heaven, unkind, is sending down these great miseries . . .

    O unpitying, great Heaven, there is no end to disorder . . .

    From Heaven is the injustice . . .

    In a poem blaming the problems on the king and his chief minister:

    Yet you will not correct nor bemoan yourself!
    It is not right he should reduce us all to such misery!

[Yet] he will not correct his heart,
And goes on to resent endeavours to rectify him.
I, Kea-foo, have made this song,
To lay bare the king's disorders.

That it is the king, through his chief minister, who is to blame for Tian's chastisement does not make the poet refrain from calling Tian "unjust . . . unkind . . . unpitying." Tian's ways are obviously not his ways, nor Tian's thoughts his thoughts. Tian is not bound by either the king's sacrifices nor by men's ideas of justice, kindness, or pity. Yet the punishment is seen as deserved, in terms of the people having their identity before Tian not only through the king as "Son of Tian," but also through their own exposure to "death and disorder." The picture is much more complex than Eno sees, and much less useful to his argument.

20. Schwartz, 31.
21. Taylor, *The religious dimensions of Confucianism*, 2.
22. Taylor, 21, 29; 79, 144.
23. See the end of *pian* VI, the middle part of *pian* VIII, and, in *pian* I, "If you are first of all unable to love such men and secondly are incapable of honoring ritual, then you will only be learning a mass of jumbled facts, blindly following the *Odes* and *Documents*, and nothing more. In such a case you may study to the end of your days and you will never be anything but a vulgar pedant." (W 21)
24. Ch'en Shou-yi, Chinese literature, 105.
25. Yang, 245.
26. For discussions of the sage and *shenming* as religious, see my articles in *Philosophy East and West* (1976) and *Journal of Chinese Philosophy*, 19 (1992) 361–386.
27. Xun does in one locus in *pian* I criticize Ru who concentrate too exclusively and pedantically on the *Odes* and *Documents*.
28. When Han Fei (*pian* 50) speaks of schools of learning, he names three schools of Mohists and eight schools of Confucians; he names no others. Apparently he did not consider other trends of thought to be "schools," or did not consider them to be "learning." This would seem to imply they either had no recognized cohesion, or had no body of literature to refer to.
29. Rickett, 375.
30. See Nathan Sivin, "On the word 'Taoist' as a source of perplexity." *History of Religions*, 17, 3–4, (May 1978), 303–30. Cf. Fung, *History*, *I*, 284; Knoblock, I, 71ff.; Eno (with reservations), 138ff.; but cf. Creel, *Chinese Thought*, 112, "Although Hsün Tzŭ was aware of Taoism, he was not greatly influenced by it."

Chapter 3. Some Philosophical Issues

1. See Tu Wei-ming, "The continuity of being: Chinese visions of Nature"; Allan, Sarah, *The shape of the turtle*; Mitukuni Yoshida, "The Chinese concept of nature."

2. Wheatley, 421, 425.
3. Analects, 2.1.
4. Wallaker, *Chinese walled cities*, passim.
5. Wheatley, 421, 425.
6. This highly speculative hypothesis is my own.
7. Watson, 49, 103.
8. Compare the *Guanzi*, with 119 occurrences, many of them referring to the physical world; there are 44 in the *Zhuangzi*, with similar reference. The word is also frequent in *LSCQ*.
9. Knoblock spends two pages explicating qi in preparation for interpreting one use of the word (in *pian* II) as "vital breath." It seems more reasonable, especially in context, to take it as *xueqi*, "animal vitality," rather than bring in a tendentious reference to ideas of the naturalists that elsewhere Xun either rejects or ignores.
10. Despite Waley's interpretation in his *Three ways*, appendix 2, 204f. (followed by Knoblock), it seems more reasonable to take *pian* VI as it most probably reads (and as others have translated it), and grant that Xun did know something about Zisi and Mencius dabbling in five-processes theory, even though we have no further evidence this was the case. Mencius' use of *qi* and his reliance on natural processes of production surely lead him in that direction, and incompatibilities between five-processes thinking and Confucianism may have been as rarely noticed during the Zhou as during the Han. See Liang in loc.
11. Watson, 120.
12. Merchant, *The death of nature*, chapters 4, 7, 8, and 10 especially.
13. *Pian* XXI and XXII.
14. *Pian* XXI, H-Y 80/21/43.
15. Allan, *The Shape of the turtle*, 29.
16. Granet, *The religion of the Chinese people*, 76f.
17. The Canaanite Baal was a storm, rain, fertility, and mountain god, but also a god of war; the Sumerian En-lil was a storm and war god who had to have "mountains" built for him. China, with monsoon rather than merely thunderstorm precipitation, does not seem to have connected rain with warfare.
18. "Peak" as a top-level rain god appears only in the Shang; later, mountains were sacrificed to for rain, but none had the status of Tian. See Allan, 99f.
19. Wilhelm, *I Ching*, 10.
20. *Pian* I, reading *gui* 貴 for *jian* 見, with Yu.
21. Granet, chap. 1.
22. The reason for omitting his third category will become evident later on.
23. Allan, chap. 5; Keightley, *Sources of Shang History*, *passim*.
24. *Xunzi*, *pian* XXIX, refers to some of these.
25. Mencius, 2A2.
26. See n. 10 of chapter 2.
27. Rosen, "Changing conceptions of the hegemon," 114.
28. Schwartz, *The world of thought in ancient China*, 11.

29. See, e.g., Achtemeier, 3–9, and his bibliographies.
30. Graham, *Disputers of the Tao*, 228.
31. Shiji, 85.10. We do not know how many of the books in the imperial library listed by Liu Xin over 200 years after Xun's death were actually written before the Han. Many Han works claimed to be pre-Qin, but were not.
32. See Graham, "*Studies in Chinese philosophy*, 322–59 and *Disputers*, 262, 286, 389ff.; and also Hansen.
33. John B. Henderson, *Chinese cosmology*, 1.
34. Keightley, "Late Shang divination," 22f.
35. Chung-ying Cheng, "Model of causality," *Philosophy East and West* xxvi, 1: "Heaven is the source of all forms of life. Heaven is also that order and pattern according to which things are created and conformed to in their becoming," so that any two things seen to be causally related are to be understood by "correlative thinking," and the natural and social, the physical and mental "are to be understood in terms of the same orders and patterns" (7, 8 and 13, 14).
36. Keightley, *ibid.*, 23.
37. Munro, *The concept of man in early China*.
38. Cf. Cheng, "A generative unity," 98: "This contextual dependence of the part on the whole is so strong that without this one cannot make correct and real subtle distinctions and unifications (by way of resemblance) of philosophical schools such as Confucianism of Hsün Tzŭ and *Ta Hsüeh* from Confucianism of Mencius and *Chung Yung*."
39. See Victor Mair, review of Jullien, *PEW* 41, 3 (July 91), 373ff.
40. Keightley, "The religious commitment," 223: "The form that political authority, and the civil theology supporting it, eventually took . . . continued to manifest a commitment to hierarchical, authoritarian, quasi-magical, bureaucratic features whose presence may be discovered in . . . Shang ancestor worship."
41. Schwartz, *The world of thought in ancient China*, 22.
42. Allan, *Shape*, 99–101.
43. Shi, *Da ming*, Legge, II, iii. 1. 2, 432ff.
44. Allan, *Heir*, 4, 5; see also *Shape*, 64.
45. Aquinas' well-known "fourth way" of proving God's existence relies on the inescapability, for a hierarchic thinker, of there existing a "top" item in any series of gradations, such that nothing could be higher. For Chinese thinkers, the all-inclusive "whole" was of course higher than anything it contained, but until such an inclusive matrix was finally named, the highest *thing* was Tian, and even after such naming, Tian was always the only candidate for absorbing the attributes of such a matrix into itself.
46. Eno, 22.
47. The graph *ling*, 靈, a rain shaman or her power of divining for rain, used in *DDJ*, 39 for the power behind all spirits, does not appear, except in proper names, in *Analects*, *Mencius* or *Xunzi*. Apparently, Zhou Ruism did not connect the powers of *shen* with the powers of shamans (though the *Guanzi* does).

48. This distinction was developed by Filmer S. C. Northrop, particularly in *The meeting of East and West*. It is conveniently summarized in his essay in Moore, *Essays in East-West philosophy*, 151–60. The distinction has been so modified by later criticism that his terminology is no longer used, but as a rough generalization, it points to some significant issues.
49. *Zheng* 政, does occur 76 times in the *Xunzi*, but nearly always means "the government," or "governmental."
50. Although it is true that order, hierarchy, and leadership were important in Mussolini's version of fascist theory, there is little similarity between Xunzi's ideas and those of the Italian dictator. The connotations of these terms are very different in the two cases.

Chapter 4. The Text of the Tian Lun

1. Shiji, 74. 5a.
2. Knoblock, I, 3–35.
3. Dubs, *Moulder*, 28, 29, n. 4.
4. Graham, *Disputers*, 237.
5. Dubs, *Moulder*, 44.
6. *Ibid.*, 46.
7. Fang Xiaobo, *Xunzi Xuanzhu*, 83.
8. Eno, 136.
9. Guo Mo-ro, *Shi pipan shu*, chap. 6.
10. The word *lun*, "discussion" or "treatise," does not occur anywhere among the titles of the 55 *pian* of the *Hanfeizi* or the 86 *pian* of the *Guanzi*; though it appears three times in the 159 two-word titles in the *LSCQ*, only once is it the second word. We conclude that "*x lun*" was not at all typical of third-century titling patterns.

Chapter 5. The Occasion and Argument of the Essay

1. Allan, *The heir and the sage*.
2. Kirby, *A geography of Han China*, 90–116.
3. Knoblock, I, 11f.
4. *Pian* X; see Knoblock, II, 135.
5. We take *de* 得 here to be a loan for its cognate *de* 德, in the sense of "bestowing kindnesses." Cf. *Shi*, Mao 294 (Legge, 326), Mao 202 (Legge, 352), Mao 247 (Legge, 475); *Mencius*, 3 A 4.

Chapter 6. On the Translation

1. Hermann Köster, *Hsün-tzŭ ins Deutsch Uebertragen*. Kaldenkirchen, 1967.
2. Bruno Belpaire, *Les plus belles pages du philosophe Chinois Suen-tse*. Brussels: Editions de l'Occident, 1960.

3. Ch'u Chai and Winberg Chai, *The humanist way in ancient China*, New York: Bantam (1965), 226–32; E. R. Hughes, *Chinese philosophy in classical times*. London: Dent (1942), 226–31.
4. Especially Bodde's translations in Fung, *History*; and Graham's various works. We also refer to translations found in Unschuld, but primarily as instances of tendentious treatment.
5. See B. Karlgren, *Authenticity*, 30–31; 63–64.
6. Christoph Harbsmeier, *Aspects*, 1981.
7. Graham, *Studies*, 359.
8. Richards, in Wright, *Studies*, 250.
9. On dynamic vs. formal translating, see Nida, *Toward a science of translating*, 159–77.

Chapter 7. Translation and Commentary

1. Xun's references in *pian* IV and XVIII to the "*xing* of birds and beasts" do not constitute exceptions, since he is in every case making a moral judgment on human behavior, just as he is in *pian* II when he speaks of the petty man "acting like the birds and beasts."
2. Shu (Legge), 342; Shi (Legge), 320; Guanzi, 11.10, 21.4, 21.7.
3. Graham, *Disputers*, 239. Also, Watson, 79, Eno, 198.
4. Graham, *ibid.*
5. In *pian* XXIV, Xun says, "The state of Wu had Wu Zixu, but would not employ (*bu neng yong*) him." Not unrelated instances of such a use of neng can be found in *Analects*, 7.3, 14.7; *Mencius*, 5B6 and 6A6; and possibly *An.*, 7.34, 9.11, 11.12, 13.13, and 14.30, depending on how one reads the construction.
6. (1) The use of *neng* discussed in note 5; (2) Xun does not say, "Tian cannot impoverish" simply; or that it has nothing to do with becoming poor. He merely says that when responded to perfectly Tian "cannot" make you poor, and under the extreme opposite conditions Tian "cannot" make you rich. Tian can make you rich (through Earth's productivity), but not under conditions of neglect. Nowhere does he say Tian cannot make you poor or rich under other conditions, other ways of responding; nor that there are no cases intermediate between his two extreme examples (one ought not to take his dramatic rhetorical opposition here to indicate he had no common sense). In fact, when he later says, "the fate of a man lies with Tian" his hearers [readers] would normally understand that to refer to Tian's recognized function of allotting success or failure—things that he says are to be left to Tian. He would, then, seem here to be contrasting his extreme cases with the normal cases wherein such success or failure does "lie with Tian." (3) *Ze*, the "then" of the "if. . . then" clause, tends to indicate a consequence involving *temporal succession*, not a gnomic or timeless implicate (see Harbsmeier, 245–49 on this). And (4) in the light of his strictures against "investigating Tian," it would be inconsistent for Xun here to discuss what Tian can or cannot do, but perfectly fitting to point out what Tian will not, under appropriate circumstances, do.

7. Watson, Köster, Eno, and Dubs omit gu. Chai and Chai give "under such circumstances." Hughes has "the fact is that"; only Chan comes out for the obvious "therefore."
8. Chung-ying Cheng, "On implication . . . ," 231: *gu* "generates an argument which asserts a proposition with justification based on another. . . . The sentence prior to *ku* can be regarded as a reason-giving assertion and the sentence following it as a reason-receiving assertion."
9. *Lun heng*, in Knoblock, II, 309, n. 12.
10. Unless one follows Hughes' translation, which questionably treats *gu* as separating: "The fact is . . . ."
11. Knoblock, I, 158.
12. Following Yu in Liu Shi-pei, *in loc.*
13. Hughes, 227. Köster has: "That other ages which hold to social order, experience good times, and unhappiness and ill remain strange to them—that no one ought to ascribe to Heaven, for it is only their firm commitment to the right way (Dao) that is responsible for it." ("Dass jene Generationen die die soziale Ordnung hochhalten gute Zeite erleben und ihnen Ungluck und Unheil fremd bleiben das dürf man nicht dem Himmel zuschreiben denn nur ihr treues Erhalten des rechtes Wegen (Tao) ist dafür verantwortlich.")
14. "Used in this meaning, the common convention is to translate *de* as "kindness" . . . such acts of kindness created goodwill . . . The opposite of the goodwill created by *de* acts of kindness was *yuan*." Knoblock, I, 89.
15. Watson, *Chuang tzŭ*, 362.
16. Cua, *Ethical argumentation*, 121ff.
17. Allan, *Shape*, 118.
18. Tsa-lin Mei, "Sino-Tibetan 'year,' 'month,' 'foot,' 'vulva.'" *Chinghua Xuebao* n.s. XII 1, 2 (Dec 79) 117–32.
19. Graham, *Disputers*, 239.
20. Knoblock, II, 305, n. 52.
21. On compliance as part of the Chinese idea of the moral self, see Jiwei Ci, "Freedom and realms of living," *Philosophy East and West* 41, 3 (Jul 91) 303–26.
22. Karlgren, *Grammata Serica Recensa*, 647.
23. Cua, 121, 127.
24. *Zhongyong*, xvi, 1, 2.
25. The balanced parallel between *shen* and *Tian*, both in rhythm and in meaning, is too typical of Xun's style. The existing *gong* ("effects") parallels *cheng* ("completion"), and clearly refers to *sheng* ("which produces it") in the preceding sentence.
26. Graham, *Disputers*, 241.
27. Harbsmeier, 132, concludes that *wei* in such positions is "a copula in subordinate position," requiring "Only if one is a sage does he act, not seek, to know Tian." However, his examples elsewhere would suggest the reading "It is only that the sage acts . . ." In light of instances of initial *wei* much weaker than these, it seems justifiable to leave it untranslated.

28. See Machle, "The mind and *shen-ming* in the *Xunzi*," *The Journal of Chinese Philosophy*, 19 (1992) 361–386.

29. Metzger, *Escape from predicament*, note, 264–65.

30. See Gao, 113.

31. Knoblock surely claims too much when he says of Xun, "His stay in Qin. . . required *Xunzi* to reexamine his whole philosophy. The visit to Qin. . . shattered the world that. . . still permitted the comfortable Ru confidence that moral suasion alone could transform the age" (I, 22). Warring States Ru might believe that moral suasion could *start* the process leading to transformation, but would any intelligent man in those times be as naive as Knoblock suggests? Our narrower theories of causality make it hard to appreciate the dimensions of what seems to us to be merely "the power of persuasion and example."

32. Hughes has "with Heaven and Earth discharging their responsibilities the myriad creatures are at man's command," splitting the logical subject. Dubs and Watson do the same, with Köster adding the touch "alle Dingen dienen ihm wie Kulis." Chai and Chai have the sage "function with Heaven and Earth." The referential syntax seems to fit ill with our ideological expectations.

33. Chan's sort of reading may appeal to other passages using *yi* (which we have translated "serve-as-servants" here): "The Junzi enslaves things, the petty man is enslaved by things" (*pian* II) and "this is what it means to value the self and make other things work for you" (*pian* XXII, W 156). These are not very apt. When Xun speaks elsewhere of the sage managing things, he uses *cai* (five times) or *cai guan* (once), *li* "establishes" (once), or he speaks of things "finding their places" *de qi yi* (four times). In one place where he uses *cai guan* of the myriad things, Yang indicates it means that the sage uses things so they do not miss their proper functions (*bu shi qi ren*), an interpretation he also gives at the one other place where *guan* is used as a verb in connection with the myriad things. We conclude there is little support in Xun's diction for taking the sage to be the subject of *yi* here. But since the alignment of the sage with Tian-Earth makes them a unity, it may make little difference what relative ranks Xun may seem to assign them by his choice of words; the perfect outcome is the same, as the "order" that is achieved is a fulfillment of all three. However, it is the sage as *harmonious* with Tian-Earth, not (as in a technological ideology) *man* as *conquering* nature, that is the underlying motif.

34. Eno, 133, 136–38.

35. Knoblock, II, 135 and n. 23, 309.

36. The *pian* XXVIII story includes: "When Confucius traveled south to Chu, he was in trouble with Chen Li, and suffered a week with no one to cook for him. He ate broth made of weeds, not cakes of rice and meat. His disciples were all passionately hungry. Zilu approached him and asked him, "I, Yu, have heard that Tian requites acting with goodness by sending good fortune, and not acting with goodness by sending misfortune. Now, Master, you have multiplied your virtues, piled up righteous deeds, cherished excellence, and practiced these things daily for a long time. Why, then, are you living in such poverty?"

Confucius said, "Yu, you don't remember. I'll remind you. Do you think knowledgeable men are always employed by states? Then Prince Bigan wouldn't have been disemboweled! Do you think loyal men always are employed? Then Guang Lung-fang wouldn't have been punished! Do you think men who reprove always get employed? Then Wu Zixu would not have been torn apart by chariots outside the east gate of Gusu!

"Whether something occurs or not is just a matter of the occasion, but whether one meets it worthily or unworthily is a matter of one's (inner) resources. Since the superior man, studying extensively and thinking deeply, does not often meet with many times like these, he can therefore go on studying and thinking. Many such men have not met up with ages like this one. Alas, how is it that I, Qiu, alone has!"

"Now, consider the fragrant iris and the epidendron. They live in the deep woods, and even if no one is there to smell them, they are fragrant. The gentleman's studying may not have an attractive appearance. He may be considered to be poor, but he doesn't act accordingly; when sad, his thinking is not enfeebled; knowing both good and bad fortune and their ends and beginnings, his heart is not filled with unease. But as for whether he is worthy or unworthy, that is a matter of his (inner) resources. How he acts or does not act is up to the man! But what happens or does not happen is a matter of the times. And whether he lives or dies is decreed."

"Now, here is this man: his time has not arrived. Even though he is worthy, are his abilities doing anything? If his time arrives, what difficulties does he have? Therefore the gentleman studies widely and thinks deeply, develops his character and corrects his behavior, so as to await his time."

This bit of Xunzi tradition may be the best commentary on our passage in the *Tian lun*.

37. Graham, *Disputers*, 417.

38. Are stars Tian? When one falls, is that a transformation or just a change? It appears Xun considers those stars which constitute the "reference points" for calendar setting to be part of Tian's "seasons"; it also appears that such stars as might "fall" are to be counted under *yin* and *yang* mutations, or even less; they are not Tian in any significant sense. The KX dictionary quotes the *Li Yao pian* of the *Liji*: "Tian upholds Yang and hangs down the sun and stars. Xunzi says that Tian is without substantial form; the entire emptiness above Earth is all Tian"—a saying not present in the *Xunzi*, but which, taken with the rest of the comment, clearly distinguishes Tian from the stars.

39. This *wei* occurs 26 times in the first 26 *pian*. In 14 of these, "to be in awe of" on "to overawe" is an appropriate translation; in 8 cases, "dread" or "to dread" would be.

40. At the conjunction (of the sun and moon) in the tenth month,
On the first day of the moon, which was *sin-miao*,
The sun was eclipsed,
A thing of very evil omen. . . .

The sun and moon announce evil,
Not keeping to their proper paths . . .
For the moon to be eclipsed
Is but an ordinary matter.

Now that the sun has been eclipsed,
How bad it is!
Mao 193; Legge, 320f.

41. Though Liang claims that anciently 嘗 (*QSZY*) and 常 (Yang) were equivalent, one could take the former as an indicator of past tense. However, the principle of *lectio difficilior* would support Yang's text.
42. Sivin, "Cosmos and computation," in *T'oung Pao*, 55.
43. Quoted in *Zhonghua Dazidian*, 1893.
44. Eno, 297, following Ikai.
45. Legge, *Shi* 91; cf. Waley, *Ode* 46.
46. Forke, *Lun heng*, 330; Wang Chong, *Lun heng*, 15 (*ming yu*).
47. On rain sacrifices, see Cohen, in *History of Religions*, 17, 3/4, 244–65.
48. Allan, *Shape*, 123.
49. *Ibid.*, 118.
50. Dubs, *in loc.*; Unschuld, 65.
51. See further discussion in chapters 8 and 10.
52. The passage runs: "Fire and water have *qi* ('energy'? 'vital breath'?) but are without *sheng* (life). Herbs and trees have life but no *zhi* ('intelligence'? 'awareness'?). Birds and beasts have *zhi* but no *yi* ('sense of duty'? 'moral sense'?). Humans possess as *qi*, *sheng*, *zhi* and *yi* as well. Thus they may act as the very highest of the valuable things beneath Tian."

    In the subsequent passage Xun claims that human supremacy is based on the ability "to set up hierarchical divisions" as a result of *yi*. Since divisions are defined by LI, and it is the sage who develops LI, is Xun making a statement about humans generally, or just about the possibilities of the sage? Or does he mean there is, latent in humans, a sense of the appropriateness of one's place? The continuing context, when looked at closely, does not answer the question as well as at first sight it appears to do.
53. Gao, 118, citing Wang Nian-sun and several *Xunzi* loci, points out the rather frequent apparent interchangeability of 財, 材, and 裁, all pronounced *cai*.
54. Ancient meanings of the graph 制 (*zhi*) include "to cut (clothes) to a pattern" and "to cut up a sacrificial animal in the proper ritual way," both implying an already-established pattern to conform to. In *pian* IX (*wang zhi*), Xun details "the (true) king's *zhi*," saying "they do not seek to pattern themselves on anything earlier than the three dynasties, they do not reject the model of the later kings . . . This is what is called reviving the old" (W 42). This hardly implies untrammeled technological freedom. *Zhi* might be translated "regularize," if that would retain its connection with *regula*, "rule"; or "institutionalize" might do, against the background of Xun's use of *zhi* and his belief that all true institutions should be grounded in LI. Besides the passage referred to, Xun says in *pian* XVIII,"if the soil, appearance, and institutions (*zhi*) of people are different, their tools and decorations cannot but differ . . . ," and also "The Mang, Yi, Rong, and Di are alike in dress, but differ in their institutions (*zhi*)." Where *zhi* functions as a verb, it often is better translated "to institute" than "to regulate."
55. This is discussed in chapter 9. Here we only point out that *Tian* makes one

word too many in the line, without the justification that the emphatic negative *wu* has three lines later; that no other word is as good a candidate for omission; that it would have been a good candidate for some scribe's insertion; and that whatever change in meaning its excision brings about causes no inconsistency with the rest of the poem.

56. T'ang Chun-I, "The T'ien Ming [Heavenly Ordinance]," says: "Men will always encounter something, so there will always be something for them to manage or arrange. Therefore, men are always in a situation to control and utilize the Heavenly *ming*. What Hsün Tzŭ meant by 'controlling the Heavenly *ming*' is something like the modern idea of controlling circumstances or destiny. Hsün Tzŭ's view of *ming*, therefore, is completely different from the other views discussed above." Even if *Tian* be not treated here as a gloss (as we take it to be), the phrase need not indicate such a gap between Xun and his predecessors, unless one has already accepted the view of Xun as having a strong technological interest. But as we take it, it merely presents another use of *ming*, not of *Tianming*.
57. Reading *you*, 有 "to have," as *you*, 友 "friend" = "to assist."
58. Cf. the passage in *pian* XXXI: "Confucius answered, 'He may be called a great sage who knows exhaustively the Great Dao, who does not lack resources when responding to changing conditions, but discriminates the inner natures of the myriad things. The 'Great Dao' is that by which changes and transformations lead to the completion of the myriad things; the 'inner nature' is that by which their true structure functions or ceases to function, is brought out or inactivated. Thus, it is his proper business to enlarge the whole range of Heaven and Earth; he clearly investigates days and months and sees to what is necessary for the myriad things in matters of wind and rain. Wonderful! Wonderful! Profound! Profound! His activities cannot be matched. His works cannot be understood, just as if he were Heaven's successor! The lesser nobility are so simple, they don't understand the things closest to them. If a man is as I have just said, he may indeed be called a great sage!'" This passage contains many of the motifs regarding the sage that run through the *Xunzi*.
59. Thompson, 183–90.
60. Thompson, 512–13.
61. Watson, *Chuang tzu*, 370.
62. On Lao Dan as traditional author of the *DDJ*, see Graham, "The origin of the legend of Lao Tan," in his *Studies in Chinese Philosophy*, 111–24.
63. Watson, *Chuang tzu*, 369.
64. John Dewey, *The quest for certainty*, chap. 10, quoted in Morton White, *The age of analysis*, 184.
65. Legge, III, 331.
66. See Watson, 43–44; Knoblock, II, 102f.

Chapter 8. Some Interpretive Issues

1. See Knoblock, II, 135, and especially n. 123, p. 309.
2. See an early formulation of this in my "Hsün Tzŭ as a religious philosopher,"

Philosophy East and West 26, 4 (Oct 1976) 443–61.

3. Gao, 118.
4. *Shi*, III, 2. ix. 1 (Legge, 495); *Shu*, V. 22. 8 (Legge, 548); 28. 4. (Legge, 619).
5. Jiwei Ci, *PEW* 41:3, 317.
6. But not falling stars or tree noises—with the exception of impressive meteor displays, as in *Chunqiu*, 3, 7, 2.
7. Ray, R. J., "Crossed fingers and praying hands," 476, 478.
8. W-T. Chan, *Religious trends*, 143.
9. James Legge, *The religions of China*, 53, quoted in Chan.
10. Compare Liang and Yang, for instance.
11. Knoblock, II, 169f., acknowledges that in this passage "*Xunzi* makes use of ritual language that addresses . . . matters of the spirits," but feels compelled to go on, "But *Xunzi* discounted the magical qualities of ritual and disbelieved entirely in the spirit realm." This is reasonable only if one reduces the religious functions of rituals to their "magical qualities" and limits "the spirit realm" to those elements that Xun clearly dismisses. A more sophisticated view of both ritual and "spirits" could escape so reductionist a treatment of this passage.

    Knoblock translates the passage (177–78) thus:

    > If with truthfulness of mind he upholds the principle of humanity, it will be given form. Having been given form, it becomes intelligible (*shen*). Having become intelligible, it can produce transmutation. If with truthfulness of mind he behaves with justice, it will accord with natural order. According with natural order, it will become clear. Having become clear, it can produce transformation. To cause transmutation and transformation to flourish in succession is called the "Power of Nature."

    The passage might also be translated:

    > If with a mind characterized by authenticity one fosters genuine humaneness, it will become embodied; so embodied, it will become divine (*shen*); divine, it can transform (things [especially folk] into what they ought to be). If with an authentic mind one fosters correct responses to situations, one will then order things in their harmonious usefulness. Doing that, then one will manifest outwardly (the inner spiritual powers); doing so, one is then competent to change things (into their "proper places"). Causing such transformation and change to originate in their proper succession is to be called (= is the same as) the "beneficence of Tian."

12. At the beginning of the *Daxue* we have, twice, *ming ming de*, which Legge translates "to illustrate illustrious virtue"; Chan, "manifesting the clear character"; Lin Yu-tang, "preserving man's clear character"; and Hughes, "shining with the illustrious power of moral personality." In light of the oft-suggested relationship between the *Daxue* and the school of *Xunzi*, we may question whether any of these is satisfactory. *Ming ming de* may well have had deeper religious overtones than any of these translations suggest—overtones that would have been unlikely to commend themselves to Zhuxi when he was editing the *Daxue*.
13. Graham, *Disputers*, 241.

Chapter 9. The Two Hierarchies and the Sage

1. The comparison with the *Zhuangzi* is confused by the claim, in 23/9/7 of the latter, that both farming and weaving are by nature (*xing*).
2. See Philip E. Ross, "Hard Words," *Scientific American* 264, 4 (Apr 1991), 147, and letters of response in subsequent issues.
3. Allan (*Shape*, 30, 37, 43–44, *et passim*) shows that in early myths (still recounted in Han time), whereas drought was from "above," the sky realm, floods were not so much associated with rain as with the welling up of the subterranean waters from "the below," the opposite of the sky. Thus, floods were an incursion of forces diametrically opposed to those of the sky. There is no evidence at all that such ideas had currency in the elite circles in which Xun moved, since they did not emerge in literature until later (or obliquely, as in the *Chuci*, which Xun no doubt would spurn).
4. Metzger, 264.
5. Following Liang. "Leader" (*ling*, with Yang) is possible. Knoblock reads it "the organizing principle" (K, II, 103). If read thus as *cong*, perhaps it should be "the one who puts together" or "unites."
6. "Are friends to," taking *you*, ordinarily "have," as a loanword for *you*, "be a friend, assist," as above.
7. For further argument on behalf of this reading, see Machle in *Jour. of Chin. Phil.*, 19 (1992) 361–386.
8. See Graham, *Disputers*, 100–105, for one interpretation.
9. *Pian* VIII and XXIII have a number of instances of this claim.
10. This is explicit in *pian* IV and XXIII; suggested in I, II, VIII, XIX, XX, and elsewhere.
11. Xun's indications that the sage "follows Tian" are indirect. Thus, in *pian* IX: "Without the true ruler [Junzi as quasi sage] Tian and Earth will not exhibit their order and LI will lack cohesion . . . The proper relationships of ruler and subject, father and son, elder brother and younger, husband and wife . . . share with Tian a common inherent pattern . . . are to be called the great fundamental." Later,"Above, he [the sage-king] has intercourse with Tian ('examines Tian'?) and below he arranges Earth." But his whole case for sagely government is that such "responds to Tian."
12. In *pian* IX, where we translate the sage "has intercourse with Tian," the received text has *shang cha yu Tian*. Watson gives"He looks up to examine Heaven," and other translators have equivalents. In *pian* XVII, however, Xun says the sage does not examine Tian's doings, with *sui jing bu cha yen*—which we translated, "no matter how subtle his research, he does not extend it into (Tian's work)." In the three cases of *cha* followed by *yu* (or the allegro *yen*) in the *Analects* and *Mencius*, it clearly means "examine carefully into"; mere observation or superficial examination is expressed by an object without *yu*. The same appears true of the three occasions with *yu* or *yen* (out of 58) in the *Xunzi*.

    Liang notes, apparently favorably, Gao's solution: that the correct reading is not *cha* 察 but *ji* 際, with the same basic, and meaning "connection" or "intercourse." We follow Liang in this. (An alternative might be the basic by itself, *ji*, "to sacrifice"; but that does not seem as good a candidate for scribal alteration.)

13. On *er* as indicating consecution, see Boltz, "Etymology," 396.
14. Paul Tillich always used "supranatural" for "supernatural," justifying it to us students on the ground that "super" would imply "even more natural," whereas "supra" implied "above the natural." He, of course, knew full well that on Thomas' Aristotelian idea of "nature," "supernatural" was perfectly sound; it was our change in the meaning of "natural" that raised a problem. Tillich's point was largely lost on a culture where literates did not attend a German *Gymnasium*. We are quite content to use "supernatural."
15. Our use of "nature-myth" is well prefigured in Frankfort, et al., *Before philosophy*, chap. 8, though he does not use the phrase itself.
16. Hall and Ames, 17.
17. See the discussions in Knoblock, I, 252–55; Graham, *Disputers*, 102–5; Machle, "The mind and *shen-ming* in the *Xunzi*."
18. An alternate reading of *tong yu shen ming*, as "attains (a status of some sort) equal to that of the gods," as in Dubs' "he will become as wise as the gods" (115) or Watson's "He partakes of a godlike intelligence" (67) seems to be undercut by instances of the parallel phrase *tong yu gui shen*, as in Thompson's *Shen Tao fragments*, no. 16. Would any Chinese aspire to "attaining to equality with a *gui*" (a "ghost" or "devil")?
19. Wang, *in loc.*; Knoblock attributes this interpretation to Wang Nian-sun.
20. The converse phrase, *ming-shen*, occurs in the *Zuochuan*, where Legge translates it "intelligent spirits"; we take it rather to imply "spirits manifesting themselves," in the way that *ming* is used of ritual objects that "manifest" numinous presence.
21. Since the instance in *Zuochuan*, *zhao* 7, deals with attainment of the status of *shen ming* after death, when as ancestor one can become *shen* (if properly ritually buried), its relevance here is disputable.
22. See note 18.
23. Malmqvist, 71, canto 20.
24. Lau, *Mencius*, 19.
25. From a lecture by H. H. Dubs at Columbia University, March 20, 1945.
26. Creel, "Confucius and Hsün-tzŭ," 30.

Chapter 10. Conclusion

1. Eno, 1. Eno speaks of Xunzi as "legitimating" his practices, and also as "rationalizing" them. The former would seem to indicate a concern for external opinion, the latter a concern either for internal consistency or the avoidance of some sort of dissonance, moral or intellectual. Eno never makes it clear in just what forum, or how, these processes were supposed to take place, or how they differed from any Chinese philosopher's attempts to organize his thoughts and commend them to others. In any case, his account does not seem adequate to support his contention of conceptual incoherence. Surely both aims would have been better served by consistency and continuity of

ideas ("conceptual" may not be a suitable word to apply neat to Chinese thought) than by the kind of philosophical "devil-may-care" he seems to ascribe to the Ru.

2. Eno seems so deeply committed to the Western linguistic convenience of separating "normative" from "descriptive" discourse that he feels it must be imposed upon Chinese philosophical language, where it is confusing or misleading rather than clarifying.
3. Eno, 133.
4. This point was also discussed in Machle, "Hsün tzŭ as a religious philosopher," *Phil. East and West* 26, 4 (Oct 1976). A further note on the point Xun is making in the passage would be in place here. He says *fan ren zhi you gui ye*, which Dubs (275), followed by Needham (83), translates, "Whoever says that there are demons," thus taking Xun to be making a general statement about the existence of spooks; the context shows, however, that Xun is emphasizing the particular situation involved: "Whoever says there is a ghost *present*." Watson catches this by translating (135), "Always when people see ghosts." This is consistent with the understanding of *you* as implying not so much independent, abstract *existing* as *being contained in a context*, so that what follows in the text is not "thinking that things that do not exist do exist," but "thinking that something that is not present in that situation is present." Graham, in *Studies*, 322–51, argues strongly against equating *you* with the Western "exist."
5. *Gui shen* occurs just once, 29/12/6, in the "syncretist" sections (as identified by Graham, "how much?"); *gui* by itself occurs once, 34/13/16. *Shen* occurs alone nine times. In the rest of the *Zhuangzi*, *shen* occurs 56 times, *gui* 11, and *shen gui* once.
6. See E. J. Machle, "The mind and *shenming* in the *Xunzi*."
7. Cf. *Zhuangzi*, 34/13/29, "Heaven is honorable, earth lowly—such are their ranks as gods," and *Xunzi*, XIX, "The Son of Heaven alone performs the suburban sacrifice to Heaven . . . but sacrifices such as the *t'an* may be carried out by the officials. . . . In this way rites distinguish and make clear that the exalted should serve the exalted and the humble serve the humble." (W 91)
8. Thomas Berry, review of Streng, et al., *Phil. East and West* 24, 1 (Jan 1974), 104.
9. Needham's search for some parallel between *Tianming, li, ze*, and the like in China and the Western idea expressed in the 1796 hymn:

   Praise the Lord, for He hath spoken,
   Worlds his mighty voice obeyed
   Laws which never shall be broken
   For their guidance he hath made.

   largely drew a blank. Do we know quite what we are asking when we ask, for instance, "Does Tian *will* the *xing* of the stars?" if they have always followed it?
10. Thompson, 512.
11. Schwartz, "On the absence of reductionism," 38, on Xunzi:

"The dissonance between man and heaven is only provisional. . . the human intellect which brings order into chaos is itself an incarnation of the powers of Heaven. Heaven's working in the non-human sphere is described in a language which can almost be described as mystical. Once the normative human culture is realized, man is aligned with the harmonies of the universe."

12. This uniting of the fulfillment of man and the fulfillment of nature is in sharp contrast to the implicit enmity between humans and nature that is evident in a number of ways in Western culture—in the Greek chthonic myths and in their fear of the chthonic gods, in the Fall story in Genesis, in the Enlightenment myth of "conquering Nature" (see Merchant, *The death of nature*). When the goal of unification did appear in the West, it was often eschatological, as in St. Paul's "The universe is waiting with eager expectation . . . up to the present [it] groans as if in . . . childbirth . . . while we look forward eagerly to our . . . liberation" (Rom. 8:19–23, *Revised English Bible*). Whereas we have separated them (except eschatologically), *Xunzi* identified the perfection of mankind with the perfection of nature, and vice versa.
13. Peirce's "to precide" is preferable to Copi's "to precise," as having a slightly better claim to ancestry in the Latin *praecido*.
14. Creel, *Confucius and the Chinese way*, 117.

Chapter 11. The Cosmic Dance

1. See the discussion of paradigms and models in Barbour, chap. 2.
2. See Merchant, chap. 4.
3. Keightley stresses the bureaucratic patterns implicit in Shang religion (*Sources of Shang history*, 214 ff.). Schwartz refers to the family (including ancestors) (*The world of thought*, 31). Allan suggests the turtle plastron as a model for the universe (*The Shape of the turtle*, 103ff.).
4. Cf. the rhetoric in *pian* VIII (Knoblock, II, 76), IX (W 47 and n. 22), or XXI (W 128–29) regarding the sage.
5. See Eno, esp. 30–33, 176–80, and Appendix B.
6. Eno's suggestion (in his Appendix B) of a connection between the origins of Ru philosophy and shamanic dancing seems to fit ill with the central Chinese states' apparent reservations about the place the Chu and the barbarians gave to shamanism. See, e. g., Major. Xun, in *pian* IX, gives shamans the tasks of exorcism and divining, but makes no mention of dancing in their connection. It is difficult to find any shamanic traits in his reference to the dance in *pian* XX, unless one would want to label any evidence of enthusiasm to be shamanic. Even if *Ru* philosophers rejected any reference to such a past, surely their critics would have made much of it—unless the connection was so distant that recognition of its significance would have been negligible. However, since Eno admits that his basic suggestion has to do with the origins of the word *ru*, and is not even strong enough to function "as a supporting argument" for his main thesis; that it is "speculative," and that links in his chain of argument are "weak," it would be unfair to suggest he claims to present more than another hypothesis regarding a word whose origins remain a puzzle. Even if Ru dancing did develop, over many centuries, out of early shamanic dances, it would

hardly follow that the shamanic elements carried through to Confucius, or that we can lay any weight upon such an origin of the word *ru* in our interpretation of Confucianism.

7. Watson, *Hsün Tzŭ*, 110.
8. Potter, *Presuppositions*, 3.

Epilogue

1. Kaltenmark, 33.

Bibliography

Standard Sinological reference works used, whether specifically cited or not, are not included in this bibliography.

Texts and Commentaries

Xunzi, SBBY ed.

Chang Shi-tong, *Xunzi jianshu*. Shanghai, 1974

Daodejing, many translations. Text as found in Wu, Carus, Man-ran Cheng, and Gia-fu Feng, and SBBY ed.

Fang Xiao-bo, *Xunzi xuanzhu*. Hong Kong 1974.

Gao Heng, "Xunzi xinjian," in *Zhongguo gudai zhexue luncong*. Beijing, 1957.

Guanzi, SBBY ed. 2 vols.

Legge, James, *The Chinese Classics*, 5 vols. in 4. Taibei reprint, 1971.

Li Di-sheng, *Xunzi jishi*. Taibei, 1975.

Liang Qi-xiung, *Xunzi jianshi*. Taibei reprint, 1973.

Liu Shipei, *Xunzi bushi*. Taibei reprint, 1950.

Lu Bu-wei, *Lüshi chunqiu*. SBBY ed.

Ruan Ting-zhuo, *Xunzi jiaozheng*. Taibei reprint, 1959.

Wang Chong, *Lun heng*. Shanghai: Ren min, 1974.

Wang Xian-qian, *Xunzi jijie*. Taibei reprint, 1967.

Wei Ri-chun, *Xunzi xueshu*. Taibei, 1973.

(The *Zhuangzi* text used is that of the HY concordance.)

Other Works

Achtemeier, Paul L., "Omne verbum sonat: The New Testament and the oral environment of late Western antiquity", *Journal of Biblical Literature*, 109, 1, (Spr 90), 3–27.

Allan, Sarah, *The heir and the Sage: dynastic legend in early China*. Asian Library Series No. 24, San Francisco: Chinese Materials Center, 1981.

———. *The shape of the turtle: myth, art and cosmos in early China*. Albany, NY: SUNY Press, 1991.

Ames, Roger T., and David L. Hall, *Thinking through Confucius*. Albany, NY: SUNY Press, 1987.

———, and J. Baird Callicott, *Nature in Asian traditions of thought*. Albany, NY: SUNY Press, 1989.

Barbour, Ian. *Religion in an age of science*. San Francisco Harper, 1990.

Bauer, Wolfgang, *China und die Hoffnung auf Glück*. München, 1971; paperback reprint, 1974.

Belpaire, Bruno. *Les plus belles pages du philosophe chinois Suen-tse*. Brussels: Editions de l'Occident 1960.

Berry, Thomas, review of "The religious life of man" series, F. J. Streng, ed., in *Philosophy East and West*, 24, 1 (Jan 74) 99–110.

Bishop, John L., ed., *Studies in Chinese Literature*. Harvard-Yenching Institute Studies XXI. Cambridge, Harvard Univ. Press, 1966.

Bodde, Derk, *Essays in Chinese Civilization*. Princeton, NJ: Princeton Univ. Press, 1981.

———. *Chinese thought, society, and science*. Honolulu: Univ. of Hawaii Press, 1991.

Boltz, William G., "The etymology of the old Chinese numeral 'two': Grammatical and semantic considerations". *Journal of the American Oriental Society* 107.3 (1987) 395–399.

Carus, Paul. *The Canon of Reason and Virtue*. Chicago: Open Court, 1945.

Chai, Ch'u and Winberg Chai. *The humanist way in ancient China*. New York: Bantam, 1965.

Chan, Shau Wing (Ch'en Shou-jung). *A Concise English-Chinese dictionary*. Stanford: Univ. Press, 1946.

Chan, Wing-tsit. *Religious trends in modern China*. New York: Columbia Univ. Press, 1953.

———. *Sourcebook in Chinese Philosophy*. Princeton, NJ: Princeton Univ. Press, 1963.

———. "The evolution of the Neo-Confucian concept of *li* as principle". *Tsing Hua Journal of Chinese Studies* V, 2 (1964), 132–149.

Ch'en Shou-yi. *Chinese Literature, a historical introduction*. New York: Ronald, 1961.

Chen Ta-tsi. "Kaotze's view of righteousness being external and the spirit of the natural sciences". *Tsing hua journal of Chinese studies* n.s. I, 2 (Apr 57), 1–16.

Chen Yuan-te, *Zhongguo gudai chexue shi*. Taibei, 1962.

Cheng, Chung-ying, "A generative unity: Chinese language and Chinese Philosophy". *Ch'ing Hua xuebao*, n.s. X, 1, (Jun '73), 90–104.

———. "On implication (*tse*) and inference (*ku*) in Chinese grammar and Chinese logic". *Journal of Chinese Philosophy*. 2, 3 (Jun 75), 225–243.

———. "Model of causality in Chinese philosophy: a comparative study". *Phil. East and West* xxvi, 1 (Jan 76) 3–20.

Ci, Jiwei. "Freedom and the realms of living," *Phil. E. and W.* 41, 3 (Jul 1991), 303–326.

Cheng, Man-jan. Lao-tzŭ: "*My words are very easy to understand*", translated by Tam C. Gibbs, Richmond, CA., 1981.

Cohen, Alvin, "Coercing the Rain Deities in ancient China", *History of Religions* 17: 3,4 (Feb–May 1978), 244–265.

Creel, Herrlee G. *Chinese thought from Confucius to Mao*. Chicago: University of Chicago Press, 1953.

———. "Confucius and Hsün-tzŭ", *JAOS* 51 (1931) 23–32.

———. "Was Confucius agnostic?", *T'oung Pao* 29 (1932) 55–99.

———. "I 彝 as equivalent to Tao 道". *JAOS* 52 (1932) 22–34.

———. *Confucius and the Chinese Way*. New York: Harper Torchbook, 1960 (reprint of *Confucius, the man and the myth*, first published 1949)

———, *Shen Pu-Hai, a Chinese political philosopher of the Fourth Century B.C.* Chicago: Univ. of Chicago Press, 1974.

———, *What is Taoism? and other studies in Chinese cultural history*. Chicago: Univ. of Chicago Press, 1970.

Cua, Antonio. *Ethical argumentation, a study in Hsün tzŭ's moral epistemology*. Honolulu: Univ. of Hawaii Press, 1985.

DeBary, Theodore, *The unfolding of neo-Confucianism*. New York: Columbia Univ. Press, 1975.

Dewey, John, *The quest for Certainty*. New York: Minton, 1929. Extracted in White, *The Age of Analysis*, New York: Mentor, 1951.

Du Guo-xiang. *Xian Qin zhuzi sixiang gaiyao*. Beijing, 1949.

———. *Xian Qin chuzidi ruogan yenjiu*. Beijing, 1955.

Dubs, Homer H., *Hsüntse Works, from the Chinese*. Probsthain's Oriental Series, No. 15. London: Probsthain, 1928.

———. *Hsüntse, the moulder of ancient Confucianism*. Probsthain's Oriental Series, No. 16. London: Probsthain, 1927.

Duyvendak, J. J. L. "Notes on Dubs' translation of *Hsün Tzŭ*". *T'oung Pao* 29 (1932), 1–42.

———. "The Chronology of Hsün-tzŭ". *T'oung Pao* 26 (1929), 73–95.

Edwards, Richard, "The artist and the landscape—changing views of nature in Chinese painting". In *The translation of art: Essays on Chinese painting and poetry*. Edited by Watt. Seattle: Univ. of Washington Press, 1976.

Eno, Robert. *The Confucian creation of Heaven*. Albany NY: SUNY Press, 1990.

Fang, Thome H. *Chinese Philosophy, its spirit and development*. Taibei, 1981.

Fehl, Noah E. *Rites and propriety in literature and life*. Hong Kong: Chinese University Press, 1971.

Feng, Gia-Fu. *Lao Tsu, Tao Te Ching*. New York: Random House, 1972.

Forke, Albert. *The world-conception of the Chinese*. London, 1925.

———. translator, *Lun heng*. 2 vols., Leipzig, 1907.

Frankfort, Henri, et. al. *Before philosophy*. Pelican, 1959 (First published Chicago: Univ. of Chicago Press, 1946, as *The intellectual adventure of ancient man*).

Fung Yu-lan. *A history of Chinese Philosophy*. translated by Derk Bodde. 2 vols. Second ed., Princeton, NJ: Princeton Univ. Press, 1952, 53.

———, *A Short History of Chinese Philosophy*. New York: Macmillan, 1948.

Graham, A(ngus) C. *Later Mohist logic, ethics and science*. Hong Kong: Chinese University Press, 1978.

———. *Studies in Chinese philosophy and philosophical literature*. Albany NY: SUNY Press, 1986.

———. *Disputers of the Tao*. LaSalle, IL: Open Court, 1989.

Granet, Marcel. *The religion of the Chinese People*. translated by Maurice Freedman. New York: Harper, 1975 (first published as *La religion des Chinois*, Paris, 1922).

Hall, David L., and Roger T. Ames. *Thinking through Confucius*. Albany NY: SUNY Press, 1987.

Hall, Douglas John. *Thinking the faith*. Minneapolis: Augsburg, 1989.

Han-ying shishi yongyu cihui. Hongkong, 1972.

Hansen, Chad, *Language and logic in ancient China*. Ann Arbor: Univ. of Michigan Press, 1983.

Harbsmeier, Christoph, *Aspects of Classical Chinese syntax*. Scandinavian Institute of Asian Studies No. 45. London: Curzon Press, 1981.

Henderson, John B., *The development and decline of Chinese cosmology*. New York: Columbia Univ. Press, 1984.

Hightower, James. R. "Some characteristics of parallel prose", in *Studies in Chinese literature*. Edited by Bishop (Cambridge, 1966). 108–139. [Reprinted from *Studia serica Bernhard Karlgren dedicata*.]

Hu Shih. *The development of the logical method in ancient China*. Shanghai, 1928.

Hughes, Ernest R. *Chinese philosophy in Classical times*. London: Dent, 1942.

Jiang Shang-xian. *Xunzi sixiang tixi*. Tainan, 1966.

Kaltenmark, Odile. *Chinese literature*, translated by Anne-Marie Geohagen. New York; Walker Sun, 1964.

Karlgren, Bernhard. *On the authenticity and nature of the Tso chuan*. Göteborgs Hogskolas Arsskrift XXXII. Taibei reprint 1968.

———. "On the script of the Chou dynasty". *Bulletin of the Museum of Far Eastern Antiquities* 8 (1936) 157–78. 178.

———. *Grammata Serica Recensa*. Museum of Far Eastern Antiquities, no. 29. Stockholm, 1972.

Keightley, David N. *Sources of Shang history*. Berkeley, CA: Univ. of California Press, 1978.

———. "The religious commitment: Shang theology and the genesis of Chinese political culture." *History of Religions* 17: 3, 4, (Feb–May 1978). 211–25.

———. "Late Shang divination: the magico-religious legacy", in *Explorations in early Chinese cosmology*. Edited by Henry Rosemont, 1–34.

———. "The Shang state as seen in the oracle-bone inscriptions". *Early China* 5, 25–34.

Kirby, John L., *A geography of Han China according to the Shi chi, the Han shu, and related texts*. Ph.D. thesis, University of Washington, 1964. (University Microprints #65-8519)

Knoblock, John. *Xunzi, a translation and study of the complete works*. 3 vols. Stanford: University Press. 1988–. 1990; vol. III, forthcoming.

Köster, Herrmann, *Hsün-tzŭ, ins Deutsch uebertragen*. Kaldenkirchen: Steyler Verlag, 1967.

Krikorian, Yervant H.. *Naturalism and the human spirit*. (Columbia Studies in Philosophy, no. 8). New York: Columbia Univ. Press, 1944.

Lau, D. C. *Confucius, the Analects*. New York: Penguin Classic, 1979.

———. *Mencius*. New York: Penguin Classic, 1970.

Li De-yong, "Xunzidi sixiang", in *Zhonguo gudai zhexue luncong*, (Beijing, 1957), 72–96 (First published in *Wenshizhe* 1957, 1).

———. *Xunzi, gongyuan jiansanshiji zhongguo weiwuzhuyi zhexuejia*. Shanghai, 1959.

Li Du. "Xunzidi Tian, Dao yu Tiandao". *Zhexue yu Wenhua Yuekan*, 5, 9.

Liang Ch'i-ch'ao, *Intellectual trends in the Ch'ing period*, translated I. C. Y. Hsu. Cambridge MA: Harvard Univ. Press, 1959.

Lin Yutang. *The Wisdom of Confucius*. New York, 1943; The Illustrated Modern Library edition, New York: Barnes, n. d.

Lindbeck, George A. *The nature of doctrine: religion and theology in a postliberal age*. Philadelphia: Westminster, 1984.

Liu Wu-chi. *A short history of Confucian philosophy*. New York: Penguin, 1955.

Machle, Edward J., "Hsün tzŭ: a revisionist view". *Iliff Review* XXXII, 3 (Fall 1975). 19–31.

———. "Hsün tzŭ as a religious philosopher", *Phil. East and West*, 26, 4 (Oct 76) 444–461.

———. "The mind and the *shen-ming* in the *Xunzi*", *Jour. of Chin. Phil.*, 19 (1992) 361–386.

Mair, Victor H. "The Language of Chinese Thought" (review of Francois Jullien, *Proces ou Creation*). *Phil. E. and W.*, XLI, 3 (July 1991), 373–386.

Major, John S. "Research priorities in the study of Ch'u religion". *History of Religions*, 17, 3–4, (Feb–May 1978), pp. 226–243.

Malmqvist, Göran. "The Cherng Shianq Ballad of the Shyun Tzyy". *Bulletin of the Museum of Far Eastern Antiquities* No. 45. Stockholm, 1973, 63–89.

Medhurst, C. Spurgeon. *The Tao-teh-king: sayings of Lao-tzu*. Wheaton, IL, 1972 (orig. publ. 1905).

Mei, Tsa-lin, "Sino-Tibetan 'year', 'month',' 'foot', 'vulva'". *Chinghua Xuebao*, n. s. XII, 1, 2 (Dec '79) 117–132.

Mei, Yi-pao, "Man and nature in Chinese Philosophy" (Mahlon Powell Lectures for 1954, I), *Indiana University conference on oriental-western literary relations*. Bloomington, IN: Indiana University Press, 1954, 1–10.

Merchant, Carolyn. *The death of nature*. San Francisco: Harper, 1980.

Metzger, Thomas A. *Escape from predicament, neo-Confucianism and China's evolving political culture*. New York: Columbia University Press, 1977.

Moore, Charles A. *Essays in East-West Philosophy; an attempt at a world Philosophical synthesis*. Honolulu: Univ. of Hawaii Press, 1951.

Mungello, David E. *Leibniz and Confucianism: the search for accord*. Honolulu: Univ. of Hawaii Press, 1977.

———. *Curious Land. Jesuit accommodation and the origins of Sinology*. Honolulu: University of Hawaii Press, 1989.

Munro, Donald. *The concept of man in early China*. Stanford: University Press, 1969.

Needham, Joseph. *The shorter science and civilization in China*. Abridged by Colin A. Ronin. Cambridge: University Press, 1978.

Nida, Eugene A. *Toward a science of translating*. Leiden: Associated Bible Societies, 1964.

Nida, Eugene A., and Charles R. Taber. *The theory and practice of translation*. Leiden: Assoc. Bib. Soc., 1982.

Northrop, F. S. C. *The meeting of East and West*. New York: Macmillan, 1946.

———. "Methodology and epistemology, oriental and occidental", in *Essays in East-West Philosophy*. Edited by Chas. A. Moore. Honolulu: Univ. of Hawaii Press, 1951, 131–160.

Potter, Karl. *Presuppositions of Indian philosophies*. Englewood Cliffs NJ: Prentice-Hall, 1963.

Pulleyblank, Edwin G. "Emphatic negatives in classical Chinese", in Roy and Tsien, *Ancient China*. pp. 115–35.

Randall, J. H. Jr., "Epilogue: the nature of naturalism", in *Naturalism and the human spirit*. Edited by Y.H. Krikorian. New York: Columbia Univ. Press, 1944.

Ray, R. J. "Crossed fingers and praying hands: remarks on religious belief and superstition", *Religious Studies*, 26, 4 (December 1990), 471–482.

Ren Zhuo xuan, "Xunzi zhexue tixi". *Zhexue niankan*, 62–92.

Ronan, Colin A. *The shorter Science and Civilization in China, an abridgement of Joseph Needham's original text*. Cambridge: Univ. Press, 1978.

Rickett, W. Allyn. translator, *Kuan-tzŭ*. vol. 1, Princeton NJ: Princeton University Press, 1985.

Richards, I. A. "Toward a theory of translating", in *Studies in Chinese thought*. Edited by Arthur F. Wright. Chicago, 1953.

Rosemont, Henry, Jr. "State and society in the *Hsün tzŭ*: a philosophical commentary". *Monumenta Serica* xxix (1970–71) 38–79.

———, ed. *Explorations in early Chinese cosmology*. JAAR Thematic Studies L/2. Chico CA: American Academy of Religion, 1984.

Rosen, Sydney, "Changing conceptions of the hegemon in pre-Ch'in China", in *Ancient China: studies in early civilization*. Edited by Roy and Tsien, 99–114.

Ross, Philip, "Hard words". *Scientific American*, 264, 4 (Apr 1991), 147.

Roy, David, and Tsuen-Hsuin Tsien. *Ancient China: studies in early civilization*. Hong Kong: Chinese University Press, 1978.

Schneider, Herbert W., "The Unnatural", in *Naturalism and the human spirit*. Edited by Y. H. Krikorian. New York: Columbia University Press, 1944.

Schuessler, Axel. *A dictionary of early Zhou Chinese*. Honolulu; Univ. of Hawaii Press, 1987.

Schwartz, Benjamin. "On the absence of reductionism in Chinese thought". *Jour. Chin. Phil.* 1. 1, (Dec 73). 27–43.

———. *The world of thought in ancient China*. Cambridge: Harvard University Press, 1985.

Serruys, Paul L-M, C. I. C. M. *The Chinese dialects of Han time according to the Fang Yen*. Berkeley CA: Univ. of California Press, 1959.

Shryock, J. K. review of Dubs, *Hsüntze, the moulder of ancient Confucianism*. *JAOS* 49, 88–91.

Sivin, N(athan). "Cosmos and computation in Early Chinese Mathematical Astronomy". *T'oung Pao* 55 (1969), 6ff.

———. "On the word 'Taoist' as a source of perplexity. With special reference to the relations of science with religion in China". *History of religions* 17: 3, 4 (Feb–May 1978), 303–330.

Sivin, Nathan, and Mitukuni Yoshida, *Chinese Science: explorations of an ancient tradition*. East Asian Science Series. Cambridge MA: MIT Press, 1973.

Slater, Robert Lawson, *Paradox and Nirvana*. Chicago: Univ. of Chicago Press, 1951.

Suzuki, Daisetz T. *A history of early Chinese philosophy*. London: Trubner, 1914.

Tang Chün-i, "The T'ien Ming [Heavenly ordinance] in pre-Ch'in China". *Phil. E. and W.* XI, 4 (Jan 1962), 195–217 and XII, 2 (April 1962), 29–47.

Taylor, Rodney. *The religious dimensions of Confucianism*. Albany NY: SUNY Press, 1990.

Thompson, Paul Milligan. *The Shen Tao fragments*. Ph.D. thesis, Univ. of Washington. Ann Arbor: University Microfilms, 1971.

Tregear, T. R. *A geography of China*. Chicago: Aldine, 1965.

Tu Wei-ming, "Yen Yüan: from inner experience to lived concreteness", in *The unfolding of Neo-Confucianism*. Edited by Theodore de Bary. NY: Columbia Univ. Press, 1975, pp. 511–541.

———. "The continuity of being: Chinese visions of Nature", in *Nature in Asian traditions of thought*. Edited by J. Baird Callicot and Roger T. Ames. Albany: SUNY Press, 1989, pp. 67–78.

Tucci, Giuseppe. *Storia della Filosofia Cinese Antica*. Bologna: Zanichelli, n. d.

Unschuld, Paul U. *Medicine in China, a history of ideas*. Berkeley: University of California Press, 1985.

Waley, Arthur. *The book of Songs*. New York, 1960 (first published 1937).

———. *Three ways of thought in ancient China*. New York: Doubleday Anchor, 1960 (first published 1939).

Wallaker, Benjamin E., et. al., editors. *Chinese walled cities; a collection of maps from Shina Jokaku no Gaigyo*. Hongkong, 1979.

Watson, Burton, *Early Chinese literature*. New York: Columbia Univ. Press, 1962.

———. *Hsün tzŭ, basic writings*. New York: Columbia Univ. Press, 1963.

———. *The complete works of Chuang tzŭ*. New York: Columbia Univ. Press, 1968.

Watt, James C. Y., editor. *The translation of art: essays on Chinese painting and poetry*. Renditions No. 6. Hong Kong and Seattle: University of Washington Press, 1976.

Welch, Holmes. *Taoism, the parting of the Way*. Boston: Beacon Press, 1957.

Wheatley, Paul. *Pivot of the four quarters*. Chicago: Univ. of Chicago Press, 1971.

White, Morton. *The Age of Analysis*. New York: Mentor Books, 1951.

Wilhelm, Richard. *The I Ching or Book of Changes*. translated by Cary F. Baynes. Bollingen series XIX. Princeton NJ: Princeton University Press, 3rd ed., 1967.

Wright, Arthur F., ed., *Studies in Chinese thought*. Chicago: Chicago University Press, 1953.

Wu, John. *Lao Tzŭ/Tao Te Ching*. New York: St. John's University Press, 1961.

Xie Wu-liang, *Zhonguo zhexue shi*. Taibei, 1967.

Yabuuti, Kiyose, "Chinese astronomy: development and limiting factors", in *Chinese Science*. Edited by Sivin and Yoshida, 91–103.

Yang, C. K., *Religion in Chinese society*. (c) 1961 Regents of the University of California, (c) renewed 1989 C.K. Yang.

Yang Rong-guo, *Zhonguo gudai sixiang shi*. Beijing 1954. (originally published 1926).

Yoshida, Mitakuni, "The Chinese concept of nature", in *Chinese Science*. Edited by Sivin and Yoshida, 71–90.

Index